ECONOMIC DEVELOPMENT IN SOUTHEAST ASIA

ECONOMIC DEVELOPMENT IN SOUTHEAST ASIA

Edited by

BRAJENDRA KUMAR

AKANSHA PUBLISHING HOUSE
NEW DELHI - 110 002 (INDIA)

AKANSHA PUBLISHING HOUSE
R-37B, Vani Vihar, Uttam Nagar
New Delhi - 110 059
Email: ektabooks@yahoo.com

Showroom
4649/21B, Ansari Road,
Daryaganj, New Delhi-110 002
Phones: 23263193, 9811582579

Economic Development in Southeast Asia

First Edition 2007

ISBN 978-81-8370-109-9

[The responsibility for facts stated opinion expressed or conclusions reached and plagiarism if any in this volume is entirely that of the editor. The publisher bears no responsibility for them whatsoever.]

PRINTED IN INDIA

Published by Akansha Publishing House, New Delhi and Printed at Aryan Enterprises Offset Press, Delhi.

Preface

Not just trees but plants of many kinds still form the direct basis of daily life in Southeast Asia. Despite significant economic growth, burgeoning cities and a major shift away from agriculture as the predominant source of the region's income, the majority of people are still dependent upon agriculture. According to FAO estimates there were in 1997 more farmers and dependants than ever before—256 million of them, 51.3 per cent of the population, though a year later these values had dropped marginally. Farmers certainly do not produce anything like half of the region's income, though for lack of comprehensive data it is difficult to be sure just what proportion they do produce. Somewhere between a quarter and a fifth would probably be about right. The rest comes from the manufacture of goods and the provision of services, a very new situation.

The structural shift out of agriculture into manufacturing and services began at different countries at different times. The economies with significant manufacturing sectors are, of course, those longest integrated into the global capitalist system. There are still significant areas and numbers of people quite marginal to the global economy. But the structural shift is not a simple matter of rising shares of manufacturing and services in national economies. At the level of the region as a whole that is certainly happening whether measured by the share of primary industries in total production or by the proportion of workers in those industries. Through time the shift shows up first in production, later in the labour-force, for people usually need to move not merely from one economic sector to another but from one place to another, from country to towns and cities. This takes time. However, as these proportions have been falling, populations have still been growing, particularly in rural areas. Thus the number of people in the primary sector, especially in agriculture, has continued to grow even as the sector's share of production and in some countries of the workforce has fallen.

In much of the region, leaving aside the non-agricultural 'specialist countries', the agricultural workforce continued to expand into the early 1990s. Only in Malaysia was there earlier evidence of a fall in the actual number of agriculturalists. By the late 1990s Thailand also showed a fall, in part probably as a result of lower rural population growth rates as well as continued rural to urban migration. Indonesia, too, showed only a small growth in the agricultural labour-force. But while every country has lower rates of growth in its agricultural workforce, some clearly continue to show a piling up of people in this sector. Notable are Cambodia and Laos, followed by East Timor, Viet Nam and Myanmar, all of them still strongly agricultural and still significantly subsistence.

The economic crisis of the late 1990s may have influenced this picture, to some degree, by driving some marginal urban workers back to their villages of origin. But the consensus amongst experts is that a flow back to the land has not been significant. Any perceived economic improvement will see a shift of such workers back to manufacturing and services with a continued slowing, even reversal, of growth of the agricultural populations. This is confirmed by latest FAO data. These show just a slowing in growth of the agricultural population.

Another structural shift in the workforce has been in participation, though it is not possible to document this as closely as for changes in the agricultural sector. Overall it seems that a higher proportion of people are in employment. This stems from changes in age structure especially, though some of this change may merely reflect better enumeration. As populations age there is a reduction in the proportion of dependants under the age of 15. This frees women, especially, from household duties. So do later marriage and childbearing, while family-planning enables couples to reduce the period spent in childcare. These processes, when coupled with expanding employment opportunities, result in greater participation in the workforce both generally and specifically by women, except where religion or custom interfere. Clearly there is a great deal of variation in labour-force structure from country to country though some of this is probably the result of different views as to what constitutes participation. In fact overall participation rates lie between these extremes.

The relative shift out of agriculture has, of course, been paralleled by movement into manufacturing and services of various kinds. Here two broad processes may be distinguished. One is global. The move into services and out of manufacturing is characteristic of all developed economies. Singapore, notably, shares in this. The day when 30 per cent of its workers were in a manufacturing sector that owed its expansion to government intervention and initiatives in the face of 6 per cent unemployment has long gone. The manufacturing that remains is mostly 'hightech', because a rise in the cost of labour, brought about partly by the very success of those initiatives, has resulted in the disappearance of relatively low-skill labour-intensive industries such as clothing. Singapore is also rapidly reclaiming its traditional entrepot role as well as becoming the region's entrepreneur and provider of services, especially those in the financial sector.

The other shift, into manufacturing, is more local and characteristic of developing economies. In part this has come about as entrepreneurs in developed countries have sought to lower the costs of production by moving some or all of the manufacturing process offshore where wages are lower. This has been aided by lower costs of transportation—by container on land, sea and in the air—relative to the total costs of production. Structural change involves a good deal more than a simple shift from primary activities like farming, forestry and fisheries to secondary occupations, such as manufacturing and construction or to tertiary 'industries' such as trade, transportation, financial, business, community and personal services. Other sectors, such as mining (including petroleum extraction), transportation, electricity, gas and water production are relatively unimportant in terms of employment, but are economically crucial. Their shares tend not to change much through time.

On the other hand the share of other important sectors does change. Very generally manufacturing has expanded, for reasons just given and because the growth of population and increase in its purchasing power have made production for local markets more attractive. This expansion has been fairly steady, for time is needed to build factories, to equip them and to construct infrastructure to support them. Two levels of economic integration can be distinguished. First is integration between Southeast Asian countries with others outside the region. Second is integration amongst the countries within the region. Both reflect globalisation, for a significant flow of investment comes into the region from outside, especially to Singapore and Malaysia, yet both are also major investors, especially within the region as a whole.

This book examines the problems and prospects of economic development in Southeast Asia in a critical manner. This book will be of utmost use for the scholars, teachers, policy planners, economists and general readers.

—Editor

Contents

1

BUSINESS AND SUSTAINABLE DEVELOPMENT IN SOUTH EAST ASIA

—Simon S.C. Tay

CRISIS AND NEW CONTEXTS

Businesses face a new context in opportunities and regulations in South East Asia. Many indicators suggest that the crisis that affected many countries in the region since mid 1997 has bottomed out. Leaders of the Association of South East Asian Nations (ASEAN) at their 1999 Informal Summit, held in Manila, spoke confidently of a recovery.

There are good reasons to question whether sufficient reforms have been undertaken to prevent a recurrence of the crisis. Most, however, would tend to agree that the worst seems to be over. New opportunities arise in the wake of the crisis.

In many countries, more sectors have been opened to foreign investment. Many large local conglomerates, affected by the crisis, are rationalizing their operations and seek to sell parts of their holdings, either by shares, or in whole companies and plants. In some countries, liberalization is proceeding at the advice and behest of international agencies, such as the International Monetary Fund. In one or two others, such as Singapore, liberalization in the financial and other sectors (e.g., telecommunications) is proceeding as part of national strategies to meet the growing international competition.

Economic cooperation and promotion within ASEAN as a whole has been increased by the acceleration of the ASEAN Free Trade Area (AFTA) and ASEAN Investment Area (AIA). Throughout the crisis, government leaders have been prompt in declaring their abiding commitment to liberalization. Continued liberalization, together with AFTA and the AIA, promises to increase the ease of cross-border business, and hope to attract foreign businesses to think of investment in the ASEAN area more as a single entity, rather than as 10 different states.

Concurrent with these opportunities, there are new concerns and approaches in the region concerning regulation. In large part, this is a healthy response to the crisis. Liberalization without sufficient regulation in some sectors, especially in banking, contributed to the Asian crisis. There is now a search for good governance, in both corporate and public sectors, with an accompanying concern with the appropriate institutions, attitudes and instruments for such regulation. Despite the recovery in the major macro-economic indicators for most of the region, this search should continue. Reforms are required and may bring about substantial changes that will affect businesses.

What has happened in the ASEAN countries in the crisis? What further changes will come as part of that search for reform? There are good reasons to be cautious about analyses that generalize the causes of the crisis and the changes and policy responses that are arising in its wake. The specific financial and economic positions of the

ASEAN countries are quite different, both before, during and after the crisis. So too are their social and political systems.

Despite the contagion of the crisis, the ASEAN countries have quite greatly differed in their responses. This is, in some regards, a caution against much commentary about where the crisis will take the region. Change in political and economic systems is more complex and difficult to predict. This is especially so given that ASEAN has traditionally been seen as a way for member states to work together, despite considerable differences and diversity among themselves. There are, as such, good reasons to be sceptical about any analysis that suggests the different countries will all, and necessarily, evolve quickly and peaceably into free market democracies.

Similar cautions must be expressed about predicting the changes for business and for environmental governance, the focus of this essay. There is little prospect for a heightened and harmonized code concerning environmental standards in the region. Nor is there any strong indication that individual ASEAN states will take the same general approaches and directions. What can be seen with more certainty however, is that, just as new opportunities have arisen in the wake of the crisis, a new context for the environmental regulation of businesses is also emerging.

Concerns with the environment and sustainable development did not received much attention in the crisis or the preceding decades of growth. The implicit policy of governments in the region was, according to many analysts, "grow first, clean up later" (Bryant and Parnwell, 1996). During the extended period of growth in the East Asian "miracle", there were noticeable impacts on the environment (ESCAP, 1995; Hetttige and Wheeler, 1997). The crisis did nothing to alleviate this and, indeed, tended to worsen the situation (Tay, 1998a; World Bank, 1998).

In the post-crisis period, however, there are a number of reasons to argue that the environment will feature more highly on the agenda of many countries in the region. This is not so much because governments have changed their minds. Rather, it is the effect of actors within the state such as civil society and non-governmental organizations, as well as institutions and groups above the state. These forces, this essay argues, will likely press businesses to give more attention to sustainable development.

How they react to and interact with these new driving forces of course remains to be seen. Some may be defensive and continue with an attitude of "business as usual". They run the risk of failing to recognize the new driving forces and will face growing obstacles to their work and profitability. Others may be more proactive and responsive. They would seek to better understand, accommodate and even benefit from the changes. It is in this context that this essay will survey the changing dynamics of business and sustainable development in South East Asia.

There has been a growing amount of writing about the intersections between business and concerns with sustainable development. Many have been severely critical of the environmental and human impacts caused by international business, trade and investment, seen in the phenomena of globalization (Nader et al., 1993; Grieder, 1997). Some seem almost to regard businesses as an evil that the region would do better without. In some other writings, there is a recognition of the possibility that businesses can help promote sustainable development, with both economic growth and good standards in the protection of the environment. However, much of this has tended to assume that businesses will adopt the necessary habits and changes of mind to do so, or there is a certain tendency to preach, in moral terms, why they should do so.

This essay has different aims. By focusing on the driving forces that promote sustainable development, it sees the connections between businesses and sustainable development as a matter of policy and choice. Such choice, as with much of business, is driven by a mix of laws and regulations by the state, as well as by the businesses' own estimate of public opinion and profit concerns. In so doing, the essay hopes to contribute to the growing understanding of how private capital can make decisions that sufficiently take into account the public concerns over the environment and the promotion of public good.

The essay is structured in four parts. First, the pre-crisis approaches to sustainable development will be surveyed, together with the effects of the crisis on the environment. In the second part of this paper, we will give attention to the forces that bring greater attention to sustainable development, within the nation-states of South East Asia, and to the growth of civil society and non-governmental organizations (NGOs). In the third part, we shall survey the role of the broader, international community as driving forces for better environmental governance. Finally, the essay will consider different company choices in response to the changes and new driving forces.

PRE-CRISIS APPROACHES TO SUSTAINABLE DEVELOPMENT

The theoretical relationship between economic growth and the protection of the environment is both settled and yet controversial. It is settled in that the concept of sustainable development is well established in the aftermath of the Brundlandt Report and the UN Conference on Environment and Development (or Rio Summit). The promise of sustainable development is that we should decide and take action for our progress in such a way that we do not diminish the ability of future generations to pursue their development. The concept of sustainability reconciles the imperatives of both economic growth and environment protection.

But beyond this concept, the connections between economic growth and the environment remain controversial however in practice, in specific, concrete situations. Some feel that the concept of sustainable development has been misused to "skillfully disguise a step backwards" for environmental protection because it justifies the priority given to development (Pallamearts, 1993).

There continues to be concern among many environmentalists that economic growth and business activity worsen the environment. In the area of trade, some environmentalists believe that increased trade leads to the depletion of natural and environmental resources. As such, the wish to curb trade that harms the environment has led to many controversies, such as the Tuna-Dolphin case and Shrimp-Turtle cases in the WTO. Environmentalists are concerned that trade rules are being used. to strike down rules intended for better environmental protection. There also continues to be suspicion that trade and increased demand will, without such improved environmental protection, lead to further deterioration of nature and natural resources (Tay, 1997).

As regards investment, there have been concerns that the competition between countries to attract foreign direct investment will lead to a cut in environmental standards (and therefore costs) in a race to the bottom. South East Asia has not witnessed a single industrial accident of the scale of Bhopal in India, or of the Sandoz and Chernobyl incidents in Europe, but the role of foreign capital and transnational companies (TNCs) has nevertheless been suspect. Some studies point to examples in which TNCs extract natural resources in non-sustainable and callous ways.

One example of this is the role of Japanese TNCs in forest, wood pulp and other wood related products (Dauvergne, 1997). Another has been the exploitation of minerals, especially in the Philippines and Indonesia. There are also examples in the industrial sectors, where pollutants in production are difficult to monitor. In the Asian Rare Earth case, Malaysian authorities did not properly control the use and disposal of low level radioactive wastes by a company jointly owned by Malaysian and Japanese interests, with the result that pollution was suffered by the local and largely poor community (Harding, 1996). In many such cases, these TNCs have acted in concert with large companies controlled by elites or even governments. The environmental and health costs are then visited on local peoples who may have little power and voice to resist.

Worse, there are concerns that governments cannot respond with higher environmental standards without provoking TNCs and foreign capital to relocate to another country with lower standards. This fear of a race to the bottom continues to be raised despite the fact that empirical studies show mixed evidence of industrial migration in response to environmental standards (Esty, 1996; Revez, 1993).

On the other hand, some assert that economic growth is not harmful to the environment but actually creates the wherewithal to allow greater environmental protection. They believe that free and open market economies are the best basis for sustainable development and the environment. This belief, as regards free trade, can be seen in Principle 21 of the Rio Declaration.

Certainly, there is no clear evidence that closing the economy to foreign trade, investment and business is an alternative that benefits the environment. Indeed, closed economies have tended to be among the worst cases, as seen in Eastern Europe and South Africa, under apartheid.

In Asia, there is anecdotal evidence that foreign investment can also bring in higher standards of environmental protection as foreign multinationals in developing countries conform with their own standards and practices that are higher than those set by the host governments (Pangestu et al., 1996). Indeed, countries such as Singapore, that have experience in attracting foreign investment, the ability to monitor their activities and the administrative and legal capacities to enforce their laws, have shown that open economies and good environments can be reconciled (ESCAP, 1995).

A number of studies point to a conclusion somewhere in between the extremes that economic growth is wholly bad or wholly good for the environment. The experience of the OECD and East Asian NIEs has been that pollution is likely to first increase with economic growth, when starting up from low income levels, before then decreasing with further economic growth to higher levels of income. This is the observation of what is known as the inverted "U" or Kuznets curve of environmental quality. A recent study exemplifies this changing relationship between economic growth and environmental protection in the area of water pollution, finding considerable improvements as income levels reach US$6,000 per capita, and then remains stable thereafter (Hettige and Wheeler, 1997).

It is significant that, before the crisis, Japan and the NIEs had passed the US$6,000 per capita mark, whereas the second tier NIEs and others in Asia had not; second tier NIEs such as Thailand had per capita incomes in 1996 of less than US $4,000 and per capita incomes in China, Indo-China and most of South Asia were less than US$1,000 per capita.

Transposing these income levels onto the inverted "U" pattern of pollution, we might hypothesize that much of the region was going through the lower and more pollution intensive section of the development pattern. Some facts support this supposition.

Air pollution in Asian capitals, as measured in average levels of air particulate from 1991-95, were five times higher than those in the OECD and twice the world average. Water pollution, as measured in BOD levels and levels of suspended solids, were also substantially above world averages. The depletion of natural resources in water, arable land, timber and oil in Asia are also high, especially in SE Asia. For example, estimates are that the region will go from being a net exporter of oil, to becoming energy importers. For timber, deforestation and the end of the timber export industry in Indonesia and Malaysia are also envisaged in coming decades, just as Thailand and the Philippines have previously been commercially overlogged. With growing populations, some studies suggest increasing environmental and food insecurity in the region.

These environmental impacts of growth in Asia are not only in absolute terms, but also relative to GDP. Asia's energy demands only doubled every twelve years from the 1960s up to the crisis and, with an estimate at $1.40 output per kilogram of oil equivalent of energy, was much more energy-intensive and inefficient than corresponding figures for the USA (40%) and Japan (15%).

For most of the region, like many developing countries, while politicians spoke of sustainable development, there was a de facto policy of, "pollute first, clean up later" (Bryant and Parnwell, 1996). Much of Asia experienced rapid economic growth prior to the present crisis. But this "Miracle" exacted a high price on the region's environmental qualities and natural resources (ESCAP, 1995). The economic crisis that started in mid 1997 has also had impacts on the environment.

THE ENVIRONMENTAL IMPACTS OF CRISIS

There have as yet been few empirical studies to evaluate its precise environmental impacts. Trends however can be seen. There are three major reasons to believe that the environment in South East Asia has been worse off. These are: (1) decreased funds for environmental protection and infrastructure and weakened regulatory agencies and efforts to ensure compliance; (2) a resurgence of environmental problems associated with poverty; and (3) negative environment impacts from attempts to restart economic growth.

Decreased Funds and Weakened Regulation

Prior to the crisis, the newly industrialized economies (NIEs) of East and South East Asia strengthened their environmental laws and regulation, in response to growing public concern. In the decade before the crisis struck, Asia and especially the East Asian NIEs, made substantial investments to improve pollution control. Infrastructure investment in water supply and sanitation systems and, to a lesser extent, in mass transit systems had environmental benefits. Prior to the crisis, there were also some signs of improved and effective regulation over industrial activity; with a strong record in some countries, such as Singapore and improvements in some others, including Taiwan and Malaysia. The Asian Development Bank predicted that air and water quality would improve in the higher income countries of the region (Desai and Lohani, 1998).

The crisis has seen a slow down in the provision of such infrastructure. Investment in improved and less polluting technology has also been cut back generally.

There are concerns that environmental regulations and the regulatory agencies have been weakened. The Asian crisis was blamed, at least in part, on Asia's weakness in the governance of public sector, financial institutions and corporations. In many cases, environmental laws on the books were not enforced because of the lack of capacity or the prevalence of corruption. The crisis further weakened the regulatory reach of the public system on environmental compliance, worsening an already poor situation.

The Problems of Poverty

Second, the crisis has meant vastly reduced circumstances for many individuals and poverty for a considerable percentage. Alongside the profound human dimensions of the crisis are the environmental impacts that accompany poverty.

Even leading up to the crisis, the Asian Miracle displayed a number of negative social and human impacts in South East Asia. This included the increasing disparity in wealth distribution between elite and the masses, visible in the migration of people from rural areas to the cities, where they were very often confined to low-level employment or the informal sector, and lived in shanty-towns (Rigg, 1997).

The crisis has seen the return migration of urban poor to the countryside. While urban poverty has attendant problems, the reversal of this phenomena was no solution. The push factors that caused the initial migration still remain, especially landlessness. Consequently, many who returned to the countryside have sought new lands to cultivate.

Many helped themselves by clearing forest, belonging to the state or held in common, under traditional rights. Some take lands previously set aside for agro-industry or luxury elite uses, such as golf. Others turned to illegal hunting of endangered species of flora and fauna, or to illegal logging.

Such activities may be understandable where starvation is the alternative. The environmental impacts of such uncontrolled activities may however be considerable. This is especially where the landless turn to fire to clear land or drive out animals; a method that is polluting and often illegal, but always cheap and quick. The situation has been compounded when such land takings are unauthorized and give no secure title to its occupants. In such cases, the landless have the immediate imperatives to clear and use land, but not to maintain and sustain it over the longer term.

The industrial sector too has faced difficulties. The lower level jobs and informal sector in the region are most often associated with poor environmental and health standards. In many countries, there was a domestic sector of medium to smaller enterprises whose production was often low on technology and international competitiveness, and high on natural resources inputs and polluting by-products. Firms in these sectors have been unable to conform to higher environmental standards, especially as demanded by Western or international communities (Vossenaar and Jha, 1996). The crisis tended to make this worse as focus was on reducing cost and increasing market share, rather than sustainability.

Negative Environmental Impacts from Policy Responses

The third trend is that policy responses to the crisis may lead to negative environmental impacts. This may be intentional, if the environment is seen as a luxury concern that can no longer be afforded in the crisis. Or it may be unintentional, given that policy responses are driven by economic agencies, with little or no knowledge of environmental concerns and costs. While there has been difference and notable change in economic policies prescribed in the crisis, there have been three general edicts.

The first is the prescription for countries to export themselves out of the crisis. The second is to attract foreign direct investment. The third, and most general, is the aim to re-start the economy. Such prescriptions re-trigger the environmentalists' concern that Asia's growth, or in this case, its recovery will be at high environmental cost.

This is especially so in the case of trade. Many of the exports in the region (e.g., oil, timber, minerals) are extractive or otherwise high on natural resource input. Many are high also on polluting outputs, especially given lower standards in regulations and weak systems to enforce such regulations. The international trade system in the WTO does not assist in this regard. It has pointedly and repeatedly set aside environmental conditions imposed by importing countries, in favour of unfettered free trade. The regional trading systems such as APEC and AFTA have yet to conjoin their agendas for trade and investment with their environmental undertakings, and may not have the will to do so (Tay, 1996).

As for investment, there is no international system of supervision. As such, it is up to the national systems in the region to screen foreign investment for environmental impacts. Most countries in the region have laws or policies to do so and to undertake environmental impact assessments before deciding on foreign investment. But their track record has been mixed, and exceptions or absences are notable even before the crisis. What more now, when the hunger for FDI has increased and the competitiveness and stability of the region is in doubt.

In this context, it is of considerable concern that economists have tended to see the task in the aftermath of the crisis as being to "re-start" the stalled economies. For if the progress of the Asian Miracle consoled environmentalists it was that, with faith in the inverted U pattern of pollution, continued growth would drive the

Asian countries into that part of the curve in which the environment would come increasingly into the picture and with increasing resources to meet the environmental concerns.

As such, with the drop in the per capita income of most countries, it would seem that the region is being driven through another round of the lower end of that inverted "U", when growth coincides with pollution. The search for environmental protection and sustainable development seems like a game of snakes and ladders. And the crisis has brought the Asian economies back to the bottom of the inverted "U" shaped snake.

The three concerns for the environmental impacts of the crisis that have been discussed have been expressed in general terms. One example that may assist to focus the concerns is that of the South East Asian fires and the haze experienced in 1997 and 1998, coinciding with the economic crisis (Tay, 1999). This may be briefly considered to illustrate the environmental dimensions of the crisis.

These fires centred in Kalimantan and other parts of Borneo, and in Sumatra. Their effect was however both regional and global. The haze suffered by Singapore, Malaysia and parts of Thailand and the Philippines cost the region more than US$1.1 Billion in 1997, estimated in terms of lost tourism, and increased health costs alone. The global costs are almost immeasurable: climate change gases released in the months of the fires are estimated to equal those of industrial Western Europe, and the fires resulted in the loss of biodiversity rich areas of Kalimantan and the death of endangered species, such as the orang-utan. UN Environment chief, Dr Klaus Toepfer called the fires a global environmental disaster.

The cause of the fires was partly climatic: the El Nino weather pattern created dry conditions in the rainforests and other vegetation. However the primary and initial cause was manmade. The fires were started for land clearing operations, mostly by large scale, agro-industry companies in oil palm plantations and timber concessions. The use of fires, while illegal, could not be stopped by the regulatory system. This failure was because of corruption and cronyism, and also because even those agencies that had the will, lacked capacity.

The danger of fires in the region and the failure to avert or deal with the threat are systemic and persistent. Although the fires of 1997 and 1998 were the worst on record, large scale fires and haze also occurred in 1994, 1991 and further back into the 1980s. At root are not only climatic and geographical factors, but economic. The fires are used as the cheapest method for clearing land. The land clearing is central to the development of Indonesia's oil palm and timber industries. These industries reaped large profits, and continue to do so in the midst of the crisis. Those profits have accrued largely to elites associated with the ruling regime, and with some foreign investment and trade. The lands, moreover, are often appropriated from locals and become a focal point for resistance and contention (Barber, 1997).

In this situation, it is easy to see how the economic crisis might disable any real attempt to deal with future fires. The crisis focuses attention of limited resources on economic and political reforms, driving the environmental problems—even a global disaster such as the fires—to the bottom of the agenda.

Further, it is also possible that the remedies prescribed for the crisis will worsen matters. The call to increase exports as a means to increase revenues will, without sufficient regulation and effective implementation of regulations, tend to increase land clearing and the use of fires. The call for fresh capital in the form of FDI and for export credits is unlikely to give pause to whether the investments and exports are linked to fires or other environmental harms. The lack of jobs, social safety nets and other factors that drive people back to the countryside will increase competition for land, and may provoke locals to revenge by setting fire to estate lands. Without attention to the specific problems, the crisis both diminishes the capacity to respond to the environmental problems of the fires and may continue and strengthen the underlying factors that cause it.

Yet while these factors are of real concern for the environment and sustainable development in South East Asia, they are not the entire picture. In a number of cases, studies are beginning to suggest that the effects of the crisis on the environment and on the poor were not as severe as originally feared. Local communities and social forces may have been better able to cope than anticipated. There are also grounds for some optimism.

New driving forces are emerging that may promise a greater emphasis on the protection of the environment and the search for sustainable development. These forces will not of themselves determine the outcome. As noted earlier, interactions of political and economic systems in the ASEAN countries, both in and after the crisis, are diverse and complex. It can be seen, however, that these new driving forces do set a new context for environmental governance in the region and the regulations and regulatory processes that can potentially affect businesses. What are these new driving forces?

IMPROVING ENVIRONMENTAL GOVERNANCE: DRIVING FORCES IN THE REGION

The world movement for improved environmental protection has come from many different sources. The driving forces have included ethical and religious beliefs as well as the immediate and visceral reaction to large and well publicized environmental disasters that have killed or severely affected human and animal life. The environmental movement has been driven by a growing science that has begun to uncover the complex interdependence and possible fragilities of life on this shared planet. It has also been driven by the simple and basic need of many to obtain safe and sufficient access to the most fundamental resources of food and potable water. The drive for better environmental protection has also come through different players and institutions, such as the mass media, small groups of citizens and local communities, government leaders, non-governmental organizations, businesses, indigenous peoples, and international organizations.

These driving forces of environmental concern have not been completely absent in South East Asian countries. From a variety of reasons, Asia has witnessed the gradual emergence, since the 1980s, of an increasing environmental consciousness among the people of the region (Lee and So, 1999). In the pre-crisis days of rapid growth, however, they were often shut out and marginalized. National development plans were instead given priority.

The part played by civil society and NGOs has also been controversial and contested in much of the region. Governments in South East Asia have been among the most jealous in the international community of their monopoly in representing the state and reluctant to admit the legitimacy of such groups. Where they have relented, in the precrisis days, was where NGOs and civil society groups consciously dedicated themselves to supplementing the state and taking on a complementary role in promoting development (de Fonseka, 1997). This was the general nature of state-civil society relations in Asia up to the mid 1980s. The main tasks given to civil society in this minimal state conception were to promote production and market activities; deliver services to communities and groups beyond the reach of the state; and foster participation in the development process.

Only towards the start of the 1990s, did Asia experience a second and different wave of civil society. This conceived its role as being an autonomous and countervailing power to the state. This concept, drawing its roots from Western liberal thought, as well as events in Eastern Europe, witnessed non-governmental organizations and civil society more generally play a greater role in calling Asian governments to account for a wide range of issues, such as the environment, poverty alleviation, women's rights and human rights.

The second wave of civil society has, in some countries, fostered new arrangements and forms of political organization upon the existing political parties. This was often marked by cross-cuffing alliances among different sectors of civil society such as students, the media, the middle class and even business interests. A stark example of this was seen in events in Thailand following the aftermath of the May 1992 protests, and the push for democratic reforms. States have reacted to this trend by seeking to place legal controls on NGO activities and efforts to co-opt and demobilize civil society.

The third wave in Asia has been characterized as a reaction by governments to moderate the growing pressures from civil society groups and to incorporate them as an instrument of state. Observers have noted the trend for governments in Asia to place legal controls on NGO activities and efforts to co-opt civil society and demobilize the more political, policy advocacy groups (Riker, 1995). Other studies by country or by region also reconsider the balance between the state and civil society. This is often seen in the context of globalization, which poses a pressure on existing systems of governance. In general, country studies in South East Asia, and in Asia more broadly, perceive the growth of civil society and predict a change in the functions of government and civil society, and also for the private sector of business (Yamamoto, 1995).

The nature of the relationship between civil society and NGOs to government on one hand and to business on the other, varies from country to country. In many cases, it is changing and evolving in the context of the crisis and the response taken by governments. Broadly, speaking, however, we can see both differences and similarities in the second and third waves of civil society and what they mean for environmental governance.

The second wave seems more to correspond with the conception of a civil society opposed to the state. In the third wave, civil society cooperates with the state and is said by some to be compromised or co-opted in so doing. Yet they share a similarity in looking at state and civil society as being opposed to each other. The main difference between them is which of the opposing entities—state or civil society—is in the ascendant. There is, of course, a difference between opposing the state and of demanding that governments properly account to the people. However, in the minds of governments unaccustomed to being questioned, the difference is not felt. To those in power, strict and public accountability is often viewed as an erosion of their power, and a confrontation.

Present and unfolding developments since the advent of the economic crisis in 1997 have revitalized the interest in civil society. In the crisis, these actors have grown stronger, both generally and with particular regard to the environment.

Partly, this has been because of the emphasis on the need for systems of better governance and to root out cronyism, corruption and nepotism, or "KKN" as the Indonesian reformers call it. This general desire for good governance has particular importance for the environment. Accountability, greater and more widespread participation in decision making and aspects of democracy are all factors that potentially impact environmental protection.

In many cases, such as the Indonesian fires discussed briefly, environmental degradation in South East Asia has been linked to "KKN" practices. Elites collude with agencies of the state to monopolize access to natural resources such as forests and land. Together, these elites and businesses over exploit the country's natural resources for personal gain, without regard to longer term sustainability. The state's gain, moreover, in terms of taxes and payment for the use of the land, is relatively small. In some cases, there are even state incentives given to promote the unsustainable exploitation. In many cases, the over-exploitation leads directly to harms that are suffered by local populations. These harms include severe floods, or smoke haze, or soil erosion, or the expropriation of lands they have traditionally used (Tay, 1999). This has been strongly evident in the case of Indonesia. (Barber, 1997). It is also true of a web of legal and illegal logging that links the countries of Indo-China and Myanmar (Bry ant, 1997). Weak systems of governance and those that are closed to participation and opaque to inspection have tended to be mired in unsustainable practices that overexploit environmental resources.

This link brings the agenda of environmental protection closer to the agenda for good governance. Additionally, there is a stronger link between environmental protection and other aspects of sustainable development, such as the rights of participation. The link from environmental protection to human rights and other aspects of social responsibility is, in this regard, strengthened.

An important part in the push for better governance and an end to KKN has been played by civil society and by non-governmental organizations (NGOs). They have been active in supporting forces of change and have in some cases, such as Indonesia, become closely involved in the broader reform movement.

In South East Asia, the changes have been dramatic, especially in Thailand, Indonesia and Malaysia. Some observers see the final vindication of their thesis that democracy and civil society will come to the region. They see events in Thailand, the Philippines and, further afield, in South Korea as consolidating democracy. Others, to the contrary, are concerned with the failure of governance and a rising tide of anarchy, especially in Indonesia. They may also not be so sanguine about the strength and capacity of these democrats to govern effectively and therefore to deal with possible back-lash.

The longer term consequences of these trends has yet to become clear. What is clear however is that the crisis has provided a further opening for civil society actors and NGOs. In many South East Asian countries, civil society and NGOs seem now to be in the ascendant, or (at least) to be playing a bigger role than ever before. This is the situation in Thailand and Indonesia, clearly, as well as the Philippines, as the site of the original "people's revolution" that pushed former President Marcos from power. In many cases, the movement and actions of civil society actors and NGOs have been significantly amplified by a media that is increasingly independent and varied.

This growth in NGOs and civil society has included environmental groups. Indeed, in some cases, such as Thailand and Indonesia, environmental groups have been among the vanguard of civil society and NGOs. The crisis has created an opportunity for them.

In Indonesia, the growth of environmental civil society organizations and NGOs changed. In the pre-crisis days, they had tended to focus on around particular issues, such as opposition to dams, or for conservation. (Hirsch and Warren, 1998). In the crisis and immediately prior, local environmental struggles were often linked to broader politics and calls for political reform. This has led to a local challenge to the elite's monopoly over access and ownership to natural resources. Indonesian NGOs such as WALHI, the umbrella coalition for environmental NGOs, achieved considerable prominence in the crisis period as did the Indonesian chapter of the Worldwide Fund for Nature.

In such circumstances, the calls for political change and for greater environmental concern have tended to reinforce each other. This is particularly where, as in Thailand and Indonesia, a reformist or avowedly democratic government has come into power in the wake of the crisis.

Yet also in countries that have gone without such widespread reform, such as Malaysia and Singapore, there are also some signs of greater civil society and NGO movements, both generally and particularly for environmental concerns.

In Malaysia, NGOs that focused on environment and sustainable development witnessed considerable growth from the late 1970s. Examples of this are the Consumer Association of Penang and the Malaysian chapter of the Friends of the Earth. Another Malaysian NGO of note is the Third World Network, which has achieved some prominence internationally, especially in its work on the World Trade Organization and its relationship to sustainable development concerns of developing countries.

The growing strength of Malaysian NGOs is evidenced by their participation in several high profile cases that involved public protest or litigation in the courts against government agencies. An earlier example of this was the

Asian Rare Earth case in which NGOs supported a suit brought by local villagers against a company for health and other damage that arose from the improper storage and disposal of hazardous materials. The government agency that approved the company's activities was also implicated (Harding, 1996). A more recent highlight of the growing role of NGOs in Malaysia has been their participation in the controversy surrounding the building of the Bakun Dam in East Malaysia. The dam, which would impact traditional and indigenous lands, was approved by government authorities without an environmental impact assessment. On this basis, the court initially ordered that work be stopped and, although this has since been circumvented, the issue remains contested between government and NGOs.

In Singapore, the growth of NGOs has been less dramatic. In large part, this is because NGOs have eschewed public law suits. Using either private suasion or public petition, they have nevertheless been of increasing significance in the decision making process. A relatively early example of this was the role of Singapore NGOs and especially the Singapore Nature Society in the early 1990s in opposing the use of a nature reserve for a golf course.

More recently, NGOs, including the Singapore Environment Council, have sought to inform and involve NGOs about the Indonesian haze. Notwithstanding the political sensitivity between Indonesia and Singapore, the Council hosted an international dialogue on the issue in 1998. The dialogue included not only Singaporean activists but also regional and international NGOs, such as the WWF. This was followed by a presentation of the chairman's statement from the meeting to the ASEAN Senior Officials for the Environment, perhaps the first such presentation by an NGO (Tay, 1999).

These brief examples point a growth in the strength of NGOs and civil society actors during the crisis years. This drew from activities and progress made in the decades prior to the crisis. In many cases, however, their growth in the crisis years was exponential. This was a result not just of greater political space and change, but more fundamentally for some, it was a recognition of the connections between economics and environment, and the broader and more inclusive concerns of sustainable development.

Will these groups continue to be important in the post-crisis period? Their rapid growth and the underlying factors behind their growth suggest they may well endure and continue to grow. The actors in South East Asian countries have therefore increased, bringing new and locally, nationally and regionally sited forces for sustainable development.

Yet while these indigenous forces are of increasing importance, they are not the only driving factors in calling for improved environmental governance. There has been an increase in the international factors that push in this direction as well.

INTERNATIONAL DRIVING FORCES

Environmental concerns have risen steeply on the international agenda. From being a new and relatively obscure concern, interest peaked with the 1992 Rio or Earth Summit, which was attended by the highest number of leaders ever to converge on a single international meeting. Many governments, especially but not only the developed countries of the West, have subscribed to an increasing number of environmental declarations and treaties. There has also been a real growth in international NGOs that push for greater environmental protection.

Events in the late 1990s demonstrate the continuing and increasing strength of such non-state international actors. The case of the Brent Spar witnessed Greenpeace and other NGOs forcing Shell to change its plans for the disposal of this oil platform. The 1999 WTO Ministerial meeting in Seattle was disrupted by NGOs and other protesters, including those who felt that increased trade would harm the environment. Such headline cases demonstrate the increasing ability of NGOs and civil society actors to cajole large and powerful transnational companies and even block governments (Wapner, 1996).

The role of NGOs and civil society in the international community has also widened beyond environmental issues. Within the region but even more so in North America and Europe, sectors of society have voiced disquiet over the adverse costs of globalization. Many focused on the outflow of jobs, from their developed and more expensive economies to cheaper centers of production in Asia and elsewhere. Additionally, others voiced concern of the accompanying social and cultural costs in environmental pollution and degradation, or the lack of protection of human and labour rights, and the exploitation of vulnerable sectors of the populace, such as undocumented migrant workers, women and children. Globalization threatened, in this analysis, a "race to the bottom". In this debate, one focal point was the environment and its connection to international trade. The US sought to close its markets to goods that harmed species it wanted to protect, such as canned tuna that resulted in the accidental killing of dolphins, and shrimp imports that killed sea turtles. In human rights, the Asian values debate generated controversy, as did the use of Western sanctions against China and Myanmar.

There has been an increasing coalition of environmental groups with those concerned about other issues, such as labour and human rights, the social responsibility of transnational corporations and the effects of globalization generally. The coalition on these issues is strongly associated with non-governmental organizations (NGOs). In environmental protection, NGOs such as Greenpeace and the Worldwide Fund for Nature have become household names and, in human rights, so have Amnesty International and Human Rights Watch. NGOs have also organized around other specific areas that can be seen as relating to human rights or the environment, such as humanitarian emergencies, the women's movement, the anti-nuclear movement, and the campaign against land mines. Such NGO movements have become increasingly strong and acknowledged sources of influence in the international sphere, with established roles in fora such as the UN.

Yet while NGOs may be the core of non-state actors, a newer phenomenon seems to be emerging with globalization. This is the rise of an "international" or "world civil society". The idea of an international civil society is wider, including NGOs but also networks of scholars and individuals, trade unions, religious and other voluntary organizations, research institutes, media. This "society" is not confined to any state, but relies upon the global telecommunications of media and the internet as well as the supporting symbols and values of such systems. Some counterpose the concept of "globalization from above" that favoured the movement of capital and multinationals, with "globalization from below", by which networks of citizens organized themselves for common cause, across borders.

These tensions in institutions, policies and conceptions of international order ignited at the 1999 World Trade Organization (WTO) Ministerial Meeting, held in Seattle. The mass and partially violent demonstrations against the WTO meeting displayed a frustration with a globalization that the demonstrators perceived as undemocratic, bad for the environment, and bad for their individual economic prospects.

The emergence of civil society in Asia and the new approaches to governance it bodes is taking place in this context of globalization. This has two major implications for the role of civil society in environmental governance. First, it suggests that the evolution of environmental and social norms will be determined by both internal and external forces. Most analysts think of globalization primarily or even solely in economic terms: trade, investment, finance, corporations, technology, information—these are the bedrocks of globalization. However, with economic integration, as well as access to information technology and travel, NGOs are themselves becoming international. Even if they never leave their communities, they have access to international news on the Internet, they communicate regularly with people throughout the world, and of course, they feel the effects of economic globalization in their day to day work and social lives.

The growing international consciousness of NGOs helps to spur the globalization of norms, especially human right and environmental norms. In addition, coalitions between international and local NGOs create commonalities of language and philosophy. Interestingly, in Asia, the process of globalization of norms is generating a common critique of globalization primarily based on what the UNDP calls the "grotesque gap" between winners and losers (UNDP, 1999). In the future, civil society in Asia is likely not only to call for better environmental performance and protection of human rights but also for new economic and social policies which promote equity. There will be a struggle between forces seeking to withdraw from and those seeking to reform the processes of globalization.

It is also likely that trans-Pacific environmental partnerships and NGO coalitions will blossom in the next decade based not only on ethics but ecological self-interest. In March, 1999, a new report found that airborne chemicals from Asia—carbon monoxide, radon, aerosols, hydrocarbons, and other chemicals—were reaching the West Coast of the United States. Rising concern and activism in the U.S. is likely to give rise to both new governmental and civil society action.

The second implication of globalization for environmental governance civil in Asia is that local policymakers will feel a range of external pressures on policymaking. On the one hand, they will be pressed to not unilaterally raise industry standards for fear of loss of foreign investment. On the other hand, they will be pressed to accept standards set by the U.S. or Europe as conditions of market entry. Environmental issues will continue to be on the agenda for global and regional trade diplomacy—and NGOs will press to have their voices heard.

Yet while international factors have pushed for greater consciousness and attention to the environment, they are not the only determinants in how states actually behave. This is especially as international law and policy-making on the environment has often been characterized by a North-South divide. The South has, generally, been skeptical of the environmental agenda put forward by the international community. This is so even where they have recognized the relationship between environment and development, and increasingly participated in many environmental declarations and treaties In many cases, their environmental performance has lagged behind their statements.

In the North-South divide on the environment, the countries of South East Asia have almost always been on the side of the South. Either individually or collectively under the umbrella of ASEAN, they cast doubt over the appropriateness of environmental initiatives proposed by Western countries. Indeed, in the run up to the 1992 Earth Summit, countries such as Malaysia and Indonesia took a leading role to defend and justify their rights to continue logging trees as part of their national patrimony, and to limit the possibility of a world convention on forests. ASEAN too acted together to lobby to force Austria to back away from attempts that the latter had made to restrict the imports of tropical timber. The Malaysian prime minister, Dr. Mahathir Mohammed, was a leading spokesman against increased environmental protection, often denigrating them as "neo-imperialism" and ways of trying to stem the rise of developing countries by imposing new strictures on their growth.

This does not mean that Malaysia or other South East Asian countries can isolate themselves from globalization, and the increased transactions in trade, investment and between peoples, or that they wish to try to isolate themselves. However, many in the region have advocated globalization for economics, but regional or national particularities for culture and society. The Asian values debate that doubted human rights and "Western-style" democracy was emblematic of this. Asian spokesmen in this debate posited a world of convergence in economics but of essential (and essentialized) differences in social norms, culture and politics (Tay, 1996; Bauer and Bell, 1999).

By these means, many governments in the region have sought to partake of economic globalization through international trade and investment without agreeing to global standards and supervision in other areas, such as environmental protection and human rights. In contrast, international civil society have sought to meld the two together, and to otherwise reject the present models of globalization. Some governments from North America and Europe (but not all and not always), have tended to support this movement. They have generally sought to amend the WTO to allow for greater coherence with environmental protection, although the preferred means of doing so has been debated. They have also sought to foster greater adherence and compliance to international treaties and norms in the areas of environmental protection and human rights by pressing other states through international diplomacy or by measures relating to trade and aid.

There are other, additional means of pressure that are used to promote greater environmental protection and sustainable development. These are often the tools of NGOs and civil society groups, either directly or working through the governments of sympathetic, often Western states, and bear at least a brief mention.

One of these tools is the use of consumer boycotts, or the threat of such boycotts. In the field environmental protection, the Brent Spar case and the actions threatened against Shell is a prime example. In other areas of concern, companies that are thought to have invested in countries with poor human rights records or have overseas production facilities that fall short on labour rights are also targeted. The impact of potential consumer reaction on Nike operations in Asia is one example of this. One shortcoming of consumer boycotts, however, is that by their nature, they are only potent against recognizable consumer brands and companies.

A second and connected tool for NGOs and civil society in promoting environmental protection is the use of international standards, such as the ISO14000. This seeks to evaluate the product's content, production method and use for their impact on the environment and to guide management processes within the producer to minimize their impact. In a number of different product lines, ISO14000 has also sought to generate minimum standards. A similar attempt is seen in eco-labels. These have been adopted by many developed and developing countries to help consumers distinguish products that are relatively benign to the environment. Eco-labels however employ criteria that differ, one from another, rather than the internationally agreed approach of the ISO14000. Both ISO14000 and eco-labels depend on consumer preference to have an impact. They are also limited in that labeling that is compulsory or discriminatory may well be considered a violation of international trade rules under the GATT.

A third tool that is used is to seek control through the laws of the home country of transnational companies, where the laws of the host country provides no adequate remedy. For example, in the 1980s, litigation was brought against Union Carbide in the USA, its home country, for toxic pollution caused by a plant in India. Although this suit was ultimately unsuccessful, it demonstrated the real concern that transnational companies faced in accounting for their overseas operations. Other litigation has also been tried for environmental harms committed abroad, such as in the case of the exploitation of the Oriente in Ecuador by oil companies.

More recently, Unocal of the USA has been successfully sued in the USA for its continuing operations in Myanmar (Burma). The basis of the suit was that Unocal has collaborated with the Myanmar regime in human rights violations against the people of that country. The fact that the events happened in South East Asia and not on US soil was not an obstacle in view of the US Alien Torts Act, which allows for universal jurisdiction by American courts over human rights cases. While the Unocal case shows how such actions can be effective tools, there are several limitations, not least that the case concerned human rights, rather than environmental harm, which does not enjoy universal jurisdiction under US law. However, given the convergence between environmental harm and governance that this essay has pointed to earlier, there can be an increasing number of cases in which environmental harm and human rights violations may run together (Sachs, 1995).

Access to finance is a fourth important tool that can be used to try to affect the behaviour of developing countries and transnational companies in environmental protection and sustainable development. For countries, international finance by the World Bank and other inter governmental agencies now comes with conditions attached. These conditions go beyond economic terms, narrowly defined, to include environmental impact assessment and mitigation. Increasingly, social impacts and governance issues are also considered in loan approval. Private international finance is also taking similar approaches. Banks, insurance companies and accounting firms have also come to see how the lack of proper environmental protection has to be factored in as possible future liabilities. (French, 1998).

With these tools and the broader coalition between environmental and other interests, the driving forces at the international level that push for sustainable development have been growing stronger. Their strength, moreover, is not only in pressing at the international level against the states that they think are in default, but in their ability to pursue transnational companies that invest in such states through consumer action and in the courts of their home countries.

How have businesses reacted? What should they do in the changing context of South East Asia in the post-crisis years?

RESPONSES FOR BUSINESS

For many states in Asia, the first reaction to international civil society is to deny them. The reaction of businesses can be much the same, and some say has been so. Transnational companies may not move to a developing country to cynically exploit lower standards in environmental and other protections, or to benefit from lax enforcement. Many companies, however, may believe that their duty is met if they meet the laws of the land. If there are no laws, some feel they have no duty to meet. Increasingly, however, this has begun to change.

There is a sense that corporations face new rules on their conduct. After decades of highly publicized industrial disasters, management groups have begun to internalize environmental concerns. This is especially in Europe and America. Markers of this change in mindset include the spread of codes of conduct, such as the principles adopted by CERES (the Coalition of Environmental Responsible Economies) and the work of the Business Council for Sustainable Development. More than two-thirds of larger US corporations now have codes of business ethics, many of which include the environment. This is, in increasing cases, more than a matter of public relations (Wilson, 2000). Some commentators believe that concern with the environment and sustainability is a "megatrend" that companies must consider (Hanson, 1995). If not, they will fail themselves and humanity (Hawken, 1993).

Companies have responded better to market based instruments to regulate environmental performance (such as pollution trading permits), rather than the old command and control mode of supervision. Some have begun to look at longer term phenomena, such as global climate change, to see how they can anticipate and help take precautions to prevent the consequences (Wilson, 2000). In a number of instances, and particularly in Europe, companies in a particular industry have come to see the benefit of concluding voluntary and self-regulating environmental agreements (ELNI, 1998).

Increasingly, companies have also been able to reframe environmental concerns as questions of efficiency, leading to systemic efforts to reduce waste and resource use, while increasing productivity (Von Weizsacker, Lovins and Lovins, 1997; Romm, 1994). Some see that environmental management methods and technology alone cannot deliver sustainability; ethical and ecological concerns must instead be incorporated into strategic management (Welford, 1995; Crosbie and Knight, 1995). This shows a striking shift in corporate mindsets, from reactive thinking that sees environmental regulations only as an increased costs, to proactive thinking that sees them as challenges to innovation and reasons to improve productivity.

In this effort, companies have given much more attention to environmental monitoring as well as to audit and disclosure. Pioneering work in this respect was done by Shell in the summer of 1998, when it released its first environmental audit that was externally verified and covered its worldwide operations. Other companies too have improved their environmental reporting. There is a notable trend towards a more widespread practice, with greater standardization; mandatory requirements set by government or the industry itself; independent external verification and environmental benchmarking (Ellkington, 1998). This is an outgrowth of business ethics and the recognition of "reputational risk" that a company run in public opinion that will affect its standing, profitability and sustainability. The risk is not just moral, but also has legal and financial implications (Case, 1999; Speeding, 1996). This applies, additionally, to associated companies and firms that lend, ensure and service the corporation. This has led to greater recognition of environmental concerns among banks and accountants too (Elkington, 1998).

Such a view, with openness and transparency from greater accountability by companies to the community, strives to change the relationship of the company to the state and community. No longer is the company to be a closed entity, narrowly pursuing the narrow profit calculations of its shareholders and management.

Stakeholders in the community and the states that host these businesses are recognized.

After the calls of the 1980s for the minimalist state that would not interfere, many leading corporations have begun to redefine their relationship to the state. Rather than an absent state or an interfering one, the need is for the state to set the standards for environmental protection adequately and rationally, for which there are suitable and supportive ways of fostering compliance among companies. There is a similar need to engage develop partnership models between businesses and civil society.

The regulations, laws and social context for these movements have to date however largely been American or European (Speeding, 1996). There has also been some comparisons with Japan (Wallace, 1995). What is happening in the developing countries of Asia and more particularly South East Asia has been less closely studied. This is needed as, even in the developed economies, the responses of business corporations in responding to the challenges of environmental protection and sustainability are relatively new and still evolving. The observations of this article however point to a number of trends that will likely bring environmental concerns to Asia that ally with business concerns, especially for foreign investors.

The first factor is that, as surveyed, there is increasing knowledge of business practices and efficiencies, a body of business ethics and new ways of looking at business strategy to support this. Frameworks are changing in boardrooms worldwide, and especially in the USA and Europe. There are also clear wishes expressed by shareholders, consumers and civil society in their home countries. For these reasons, and even without the laws and regulations of their home governments or their Asian hosts, there is good and growing reason for companies to bring this mindset into South East Asia, apply their codes of conduct and principles on a worldwide basis.

The second factor is the trend in the region towards a stronger civil society and NGOs. Such a civil society and NGOs, that are better linked internationally and can act more surely locally, will drive towards better environmental practices in business. The more traditional way of doing this, especially for NGOs, is by using public protest and the media to make demands upon the state to better regulate such businesses. This is will continue and likely grow in the freer and more democratic South East Asian societies. Consumer boycotts and shareholder activism will also likely emerge in a recovering Asia that has learnt to be more concerned with private sector governance.

The third (and connected) factor is the drive to end corruption and collusion between business interests and the state. The reforming state in Asia is under pressure from both its citizens and the international community to address these issues in the wake of the crisis and to evolve better and more effective forms of governance. In this context, the callous exploitation of natural resources and uncontrolled pollution from industry can no longer be protected by vested interests. The state in Asia will seek to reassert its regulatory role.

In this, there is a danger that traditional views of command and control by the state will return. This should be avoided because of the higher cost and inefficiencies of such methods. Market based instruments and financing will need to be emphasized, with the requisite knowledge and capacity (Asian Development Bank, 1994). This would give a lighter touch to regulation and a helping hand in environmental protection that would assist both environmental performance and business performance.

Companies and investors in the region can help in this by responding not just to their bottom lines and government directives. They need to engage civil society at both the national and international levels, and the stakeholders in their host countries. This would include not just those in the capital cities, but also the local communities in their area of investment. Such engagement will need, of course, to go beyond an exercise in public relations. More effort is needed to shape strategy in relation to the concerns expressed. By such means, civil society and NGOs in Asia can interact with business in a "stakeholder" or partnership model.

If this can be done, the danger of protests, boycotts and "reputational risk" can be lowered for companies. For environmentalists, there would be the benefit of moving beyond sporadic protests over incidents of pollution, to help shape policies that can prevent such pollution in the first place. It is also a means to keep businesses in their communities on a sustainable basis, and to grow from such businesses.

The means and opportunities of doing so will necessarily differ from sector to sector and from business to business. The clean up of natural resource sector companies, such as those engaged in forestry and mineral exploitation, will clearly be different from the sustainable routes in the field of energy generation and use. Further, as South East Asia is a diverse region, there will be some variation between different countries as well.

The key strategic challenges for business, the environment and sustainable development in the region however are clear and universal. Companies will need to embrace the challenge of pursuing environmental protection, working at both the level of strategy and in the details of particular businesses (NCE, 1995). They must find ways to do so that will include reforming states or re-energized communities and citizens as partners and stakeholders, and not opponents, to recognize their common interests. They must seek paths and practices that will reconcile better environmental protection and profitability, working towards sustainable development.

REFERENCES

Asian Development Bank (1994). *Financing Environmentally Sound Development*, Manila; ADB.

Barber, Charles (1997). *Environmental Scarcities, State Capacity, Civil Violence: The Case of Indonesia*, American Academy of Arts and Sciences.

Bauer, Joanne R. and Daniel A Bell (1999) (editors). *The East Asian challenge for human rights*, Cambridge, UK; New York: Cambridge University Press, 1999.

Bryant, Raymond L. (1997). *The political ecology of forestry in Burma, 1824-1994*, London: Hurst & Co., 1997.

Bryant, Raymond L. and Michael Parnwell (1996). "Politics, Sustainable Development and Environmental Change in South East Asia," in: *Environmental Change in South-East Asia* (Parnwell and Bryant, eds.), New York, Routledge.

Bullard, Nicola et al. (1998). *Tigers in Trouble* (KS Jomo, editor), New York, Zed Books.

Case, Phil (1999). *Environmental Risk Management and Corporate Lending: A Global Perspective*, Woordhead Publishing, Cambridge, England.

Crosbie, Liz and Ken Knight (1995). *Strategy for Sustainable Business: Environmental Opportunity and Strategic Choice*, London; New York: McGraw Hill.

Dauvergne, Peter (1997). *Shadows in the forest: Japan and the politics of timber in Southeast Asia*, Cambridge, Mass.: MIT Press.

de Fonseka, Chandra (1995). "Challenges and Future Directions for Asian NGOs," in: *Government-NGO relations in Asia:*

prospects and challenges for people-centred development, Noeleen Heyzer, James V. Piker, Antonio B. Quizon (eds), *Kuala Lumpur: Asian and Pacific Development Centre*; Houndmills, Basingstoke, Hampshire: Macmillan Press; New York: St. Martin's Press.

Desai, Vishvanath V. and Bindhu Lohani (1998). "Asia's Environment: Challenges and Opportunities," in: *The future of Asia in the world economy*, edited by Colm Foy, Francis Harrigan and David O'Connor; Asian Development Bank; *Development Centre of the Organisation for Economic Co-operation and Development*, Paris, France: Organisation for Economic Co-operation and Development.

Eccleston, Bernard and David Potter (1996). "Environmental NGOs and Different Political Contexts in South-East Asia: Malaysia, Indonesia and Vietnam," in: *Environmental Change in South-East Asia* (Parnwell and Bryant, eds.), New York: Routledge.

Elkington, John (1998). "The 'triple bottom line' for twenty-first-century business," in: *Companies in a world of conflict: NGO's, sanctions and corporate responsibility* (John V. Mitchell, ed.) London: Earthscan, 1998.

ELNI (Environmental Law Network International) (1998). *Environmental Agreements: The Role and Effect of Environmental Agreements in Environmental Policies*, London: Cameron & May.

ESCAP (1995). *State of the Environment in Asia and the Pacific*, New York: UN.

Esty, Daniel (1996). "Environmental Regulation and Competitiveness," in: *Asian dragons and green trade: environment, economics and International* (Simon S.C. Tay and Daniel C. Esty, editors) Singapore: Times Academic Press.

French, Hilary (1998). *Investing in the Future: Harnessing Private Capital Flows for Environmentally Sustainable Development*, Worldwatch Paper 139, Washington, D.C.: Worldwatch Institute.

Greider, William (1997). *One world, ready or not: the manic logic of global capitalism*, New York: Simon & Schuster.

Hanson, Jon Lun (1995). *Invisible Patterns: Ecology and Wisdom in Business and Profit*, Westport, CT: Quorum Books.

Harding, Andrew (1996). "Practical Human Rights, NGOs and the Environment in Malaysia," in: *Human rights approaches to environmental protection* (Alan E. Boyle and Michael R. Anderson, eds) Oxford: Clarendon Press; New York: Oxford University Press.

Hawken, Paul (1993). *The Ecology of Commerce: A Declaration of Sustainability*, New York, NY: Harper-Business.

Hettige, Mani and David Wheeler (1997). *Industrial Pollution in Economic Development: Kuznets Revisited*, Washington DC: World Bank Development Research Group.

Hirsch, Philip and Carol Warren (1999) (editors). *The politics of environment in Southeast Asia: resources and resistance*, London; New York: Routledge, 1998.

Lee, Yok-shiu F. and Alvin Y. So (1999) (editors). *Asia's environmental movements: comparative perspectives*, Armonk, N.Y.: M.E. Sharpe, c1999.

Nader, Ralph et al. (1993). *The Case against "free trade": GATT, NAFTA, and the globalization of corporate power*, San Francisco, CA: Earth Island Press; Berkeley, CA: North Atlantic Books.

NCE (National Council on the Environment of Singapore, now Singapore Environment Council) (1995). *Greening the Bottom Line*, Singapore: NCE.

Pallamearts, Marc (1993). "International Environmental Law from Stockholm to Rio: Back to the Future," in: *Greening International Law* (Sands, ed.), London: Earthscan Publications.

Pangestu, Mari, and Kurnya Roesad (1996). "Experiences from Indonesia and Other ASEAN Countries," in: *Asian Dragons & Green Trade* (Tay & Esty, editors), Singapore: Times Academic Press.

Revez, Richard (1992). "Rehabilitating Interstate Competition: Rethinking the Race to the Bottom," *New York University Law Review*, 67: 1210.

Rigg, Jonathan (1997). *Southeast Asia: The Human Landscape of Modernization and Development*, London: Routledge.

Riker, James V. (1995), "From Cooptation to Cooperation and Collaboration in Government-NGO Relations: Toward an Enabling Policy Environment for People-Centred Development in Asia," in: *Government-NGO relations in Asia: prospects and challenges for people-centred development*, Noeleen Heyzer, James V. Riker, Antonio B. Quizon (eds), Kuala Lumpur: Asian and Pacific Development Centre; Houndmills, Basingstoke, Hampshire: Macmillan Press; New York: St. Martin's Press.

Romm, Joseph L. (1994). *Lean and Clean Management: How to Boost Profits and Productivity by Reducing Pollution*, New York: Kodanshu America.

Sachs, Aaron (1995). *Eco-justice: linking human rights and the environment*, Washington, DC: Worldwatch Institute.

Speeding, Linda (1996). *Environmental Management for Business*, New York: John Wiley & Sons.

Tay, Simon S.C. (1996). "The Way Ahead in Asia," in: *Asian Dragons & Green Trade* (Tay and Esty, editors), Singapore: Times Academic Press.

Tay, Simon S.C. (1997). "Trade and the Environment: Perspectives from the Asia-Pacific," *World Bulletin*, Vol. 13, No. 1-2 (Jan-Apr).

Tay, Simon S.C. (1998). "SE Asian Fires: A Haze over ASEAN and International Environmental Law," *Review of European Community and International Environmental Law*, Vol. 7 Issue 2.

Tay, Simon S.C. (1998a). "Asia's Economic Crisis: Impact and Opportunities for Sustainable Development," special report to the 4th Asia Pacific NGOs Environmental Conference, 26-27 Nov 1998, Proceedings, edited by Chou LM et al, and published by the Dept of Biological Sciences, National University of Singapore, Jan 1999.

Tay, Simon S.C. (1999). "SE Asian Fires: The Challenge to International Law and Sustainable Development,"

Georgetown International Environmental Law Review, Winter 1999.

UNDP (1999). *Human Development Report*, New York: Oxford U Press.

Von Weizsacker, Ernst, Lovins, Amory, and Lovins, Hunter (1997). *Factor Four: Doubling Wealth, Halving Resource Use*, London: Earthscan.

Vossenaar, Rene, and Veena Jha (1996). "Competitiveness: An Asian Perspective," in: *Asian Dragons & Green Trade* (Tay and Esty, editors), Singapore: Times Academic Press.

Wallace, David (1995). *Environmental Policy and Industrial Innovation: Strategies in Europe, the US and Japan*, London: Royal Institute of International Affairs and Earthscan.

Wapner, Paul Kevin (1996). *Environmental activism and world civic politics*, Albany: State University of New York Press, c1996.

Welford, Richard (1995). *Environmental Strategy and Sustainable Development*, London; New York: Routledge.

Wilson, Ian (2000). *The New Rules of Corporate Conduct: Rewriting the Social Charter*, Westport, Connecticut; London: Quorum Books.

World Bank (1993). *The East Asian Miracle: economic growth and public policy*, New York, N.Y.: Oxford University Press.

World Bank (1998). *East Asia: The Road to Recovery*; Washington, DC: World Bank.

Yamamoto, Tadadhi (1995) (editor). *Emerging civil society in the Asia Pacific community: nongovernmental underpinnings of the emerging Asia Pacific regional community*, Singapore: Institute of Southeast Asian Studies.

Zarsky, Lyuba and Simon S.C Tay (2000). "Civil Society and Environmental Governance in Asia," in: *Asia's Clean Revolution: Industry, Growth and the Environment* (David Angel and Michael T Rock, editors) Sheffield: Greenleaf Publishing, forthcoming.

2

REDEFINING THE VILLAGE AND RURAL LIFE: LESSONS FROM SOUTH EAST ASIA

—Jonathan Rigg

> How deprived had the generation before me been - a generation that had been satisfied with the accumulation of its own footsteps in the lanes of its villages.
>
> Pramoedya Ananta Toer, 1982

The 'Village'—as an idea, an organizing principle, and as a basis for life—remains very powerful, both in popular conception and in the work of many academics and field workers[1]. Villages are perceived to be units of society, production, identity and administration, and as such often form the structure on which analyses of rural life are based. Dasgupta in Village studies in the Third World, in which he talks of the 'historical continuity and stability of village' writes:

> The case for studying villages (as units of social science research) rests on its being close to the people, their life, livelihood and culture, and on its role as a

> focal point of reference for individual prestige and identification . . . villages have survived hundreds of years of wars, making and breaking up of empires, famines, floods and other natural disasters as the principal social and administrative unit.
>
> Dasgupta, 1978:1[2]

This conception of the village as an identifiable 'unit' is exemplified in Eric Wolf's designation of the village as a 'closed, corporate community' (1967) and in Marxist interpretations of the Asiatic Mode of Production where 'stagnant' rural society was governed by the communalistic nature of village life and a hydraulic system of wet rice production. Given the power of the village as an idea, it is imperative that we clarify our conception of what the village was, what it has become, and how processes of change have manifested themselves in the village.

This paper will bring together a body of recent (and some not so recent) research that has questioned the nature of the village—and in particular the nature of the 'traditional' village—in South East Asia.[3] A similar process of revisionism occurred rather earlier in work on South Asia where the view of the village as a 'little republic' has now been extensively challenged (see for e.g. Dumont, 1966; Dewey, 1972).[4] This effort is not just of theoretical and historical importance; it also has contemporary significance, for the simple reason that our views of the present are intimately tied to our conceptions of the past. It is also true that our understanding of the processes and effects of change (read: development) are closely linked to these images. It is argued here that most studies of rural development have at their heart an often unstated vision of the past, and this informs and colours the resulting assessment of the present, and also how the future should be, and is being, moulded. There are dangers here, and not just for the historian and historical geographer, for as the philosopher Bacon wrote: 'God forbid that we should give out a dream of our own imagination for a pattern of the world'.

The traditional village is often characterized as embodying five characteristics, each of which is usually deemed to be 'good'. The village is thought to be:

> egalitarian; corporate (community-oriented); peaceful; self-reliant (subsistence oriented); and in a sense, moral.

The modern village, by contrast, is thought to be characterized by:

> inequality; individualism; violence; dependency (commercialism); and again in a sense, immorality (see Table I).

The cause of the shift from 'traditional' to 'modern' is usually thought to be intimately linked to the processes of commercialization and commoditization—encapsulated in that much abused term, 'development'. Further, these notions of the past and present are deep-seated and persistent.

In the South East Asian context, the debate over the nature of the traditional village is exemplified in two important books published in the 1970s, of which the first has generally received the greater attention: James Scott's The moral economy of the peasant: rebellion and subsistence in South East Asia (1976) and Samuel Popkin's The rational peasant' the political economy of rural society in Vietnam (1979). Scott's book is the clearest enunciation of the view that villages were corporate, 'moral' economies, while Popkin's presents a contrasting interpretation. There is no need here to go into detail about these two well-known studies although because the two authors present, in terms of their own arguments, 'ideal types' of peasant mentalities, the debate is characterized by a rather polarized vision of rural life which is somewhat divorced from reality. A rural person is likely to act differently in different situations, and rural people are not likely to act the same way in similar situations. Variation and differentiation are likely to be common features in decision-making.[5] As Alexander and Alexander remark: 'Peasants, like capitalists, evidently take risks on some occasions and avoid them on others' (1982: 599). In essence, Popkin argues—and he wrote his book as a rejoinder to the work of the moral economists such as Eric Wolf and James Scott—that there has evolved a 'myth of the village', which has tended to romanticize traditional rural life:

> A way of life that may have existed only for lack of alternatives is extolled as a virtue. Peasants who had little or nothing to eat are assumed to have had a rich spiritual life. Sons who may have stayed with their fathers only in order to survive are credited with filial piety. What may have been the absence of incentives to change becomes a resistance to innovation and a defense of traditional ways. The rich who hid their wealth are perceived as having shown great modesty, and hostility among villages is converted to village solidarity. Somehow, what might only have been the necessities or oppressions of one era come to be interpreted as traditional values during the next.
>
> Popkin, 1979:3

Not only do Western academics address this issue of the 'roots' of the village. One of Thailand's most influential economists, Chattip Nartsupha, has written at length on the pre-capitalist village and, significantly, his ideas have been embraced by many NGO workers (see Chattip Nartsupha, 1986, 1991). To paraphrase his work, he believes the 'village-community' to be an 'ancient institution', 'naturally' set up by the people, based on 'subsistence production', 'self-sufficient', 'communal', 'self-sustaining', and 'relatively autonomous' (1986:157-59). This closely mirrors the characterization in Table I.

Although the Scott/Popkin debate is well known, a significant number of papers and books published since the late 1970s make it necessary to look again at the historical and cultural roots of the 'village'.

TABLE I
The image of the traditional and modern village

Traditional villages	Modern villages
egalitarian	unequal
corporate (community-orientated)	individualistic
peaceful/tranquil	violent/competitive
self-reliant	dependent
moral	immoral

Each element in this revisionist debate has tended to examine particular segments of village economy and society, often with reference to particular areas. The author will argue here that there is a pattern emerging in the literature which calls for a reappraisal of our understanding of the traditional village. This is important, because of its implications for our understanding of contemporary change, and the modern village. Further, the lessons are not just restricted to South East Asia; they strike a chord in other parts of the developed and developing worlds. If we are to assess development, it is necessary first to set down a marker from which change can be measured and upon which agents of change are operating. This 'marker' is the traditional village, and the 'agents' may be technology, commercialization (the market) or the state. As a caveat, it is accepted that the following discussion will suffer from a tendency towards reductionism and generalization in an attempt to tease out brooder issues. Finally in introduction, why is this of interest to geographers? In part because it is clearly interdisciplinary; but also because it touches on many issues that should concern geographers: history and space; the control of people and territory; development and change; and perceptions of the past and present. It is also true that geographers working in this area are thin on the ground (see the reference list) which seems a shame, as geographers should be better equipped than most to tackle an issue that spans time and space and crosses subject boundaries.

THE EGALITARIAN VILLAGE: A UNIFORMITY BORN OF POVERTY

That the traditional village was egalitarian—while the modern village is not—is widely accepted. In South East Asia this is most clearly linked to Clifford Geertz's influential book Agricultural involution: the processes of ecological change in Indonesia (1963) in which he coined the term 'shared poverty'. In essence, he saw an equality and uniformity in rural Java born out of a common experience of poverty, perpetuated by a process of 'agricultural involution'. He writes:

> Under the pressure of increasing numbers and limited resources, Javanese village society did not bifurcate as did that of so many other 'underdeveloped' nations, into a group of large landlords and a group of oppressed near-serfs. Rather it maintained a comparatively high degree of social and economic homogeneity by dividing the economic pie into a steadily increasing number of minute pieces . . . Rather than haves and have-nots, there were, in the delicately muted vernacular of peasant life, only

> tjujupans and kekurangans—'just enoughs' and 'not-quite enoughs'.
>
> Geertz, 1963:97

> In sharecropping and associated practices the ever-driven wet-rice village found the means by which to divide its growing economic pie into a greater number of traditionally fixed pieces and so to hold an enormous population on the land at a comparatively very homogeneous, if grim, level of living.
>
> Geertz, 1963:100

The process of involution ('the overdriving of an established form in such a way that it becomes rigid through an inward overelaboration of detail' [1963: 82]) and the outcome of shared poverty have become common academic currency across disciplines. Along with the elegance of his theory and of his writing, perhaps this is why—despite the many criticisms of Geertz's interpretation—his views still exert a powerful influence.[6]

The challenge to Geertz's view of history is based on painstaking work by such scholars as Breman (1980), Knight (1982), Hart (1986), Alexander and Alexander (1982), Husken (1981), Svensson (1991), White (1983) and Carey (1986). In summary, these scholars maintain that inequality has been built into Javanese village life for centuries; it may not have been based upon differences in income but upon variations in such things as power and prestige, patron-client ties, and access to land, but to say that there were not deep divisions within villages simply misrepresents the historical evidence. As Hart states: 'Within rural society, the pattern of access to land was highly differentiated . . . and a class of dependent landless households existed long before the full-scale colonial exploitation of Java' (1986: 20). Carey, likewise writes that 'it is dear that the structure of Javanese peasant society, at least until the first decades of the nineteenth century, gave important advantages to the group of 'landowning' peasants who could prosper independently by drawing on the labour services of a resident work-force of dependents and landless peasants (1986: 86). In short, Carey states that the village in early nineteenth-century Java 'contained very distinct social groups which enjoyed unequal access to the common village ricefields and the use of village labour . . .' (1986: 81). Boomgaard in his analysis of Java in the late eighteenth and nineteenth centuries believes that a 'model' Javanese village would consist of no less than nine strata (themselves differentiated): '. . . four strata of landowners (the village administration, the yeoman and gentry group, the modal virgate-owner, and the smallholder), three strata of landless families (cottar, Brinksitzer, Hausling), a group of resident servants, and two age groups: the elderly and the bachelors. There would also be a group of non-agriculturalists' (1989: 67; also see Elson, 1986: 68).

A similar re-assessment of egalitarianism versus stratification in rural populations has occurred in the work on Thailand. No longer is it assumed that a bounteous nature allowed all farmers to live happily and well, as encapsulated in Inscription No. 1 of King Ramkhamhaeng (1275-1317) of the Sukhothai period—a piece of ancient propaganda that every Thai schoolchild should be able to quote:

> In the time of King Ramkhamhaeng, this land of Sukhothai is thriving. In the water there is fish, in the fields there is rice.

Work by such scholars as Bowie and Koizumi (1992) indicates that rural people were differentiated, dynamic, and engaged in market exchange. Bowie writes in her discussion of textile production in Northern Siam,[7] that 'to suggest that the traditional nineteenth-century economy was a subsistence economy is to miss the significance of wealth in the context of poverty' (1992:815). This lies in stark contrast to the vision presented by writers such as Douglass who sees exchange relations—namely reciprocity and redistribution—preventing stratification arising by putting a limit on downward mobility among the poor, while constraining accumulation among the rich by placing on them a community-enforced redistributive ethic (1984: 4-5).

However, despite the weight of evidence that should urge us to take a more critical view of Geertz's vision (and of the many others who adopt such a perspective)[8], the notion of the traditional village as egalitarian is remarkably persistent. Perhaps this lies in the European (primarily English and German) ideal of the village which has its roots in the utopianists of the late nineteenth century (see Dewey, 1972: 300-16). Or perhaps it is merely the mirror image of the present—and all that is perceived to be unsavoury about current trends. As Peter Vandergeest in a recent paper on Thailand writes, 'we should be suspicious of theories based on contrasts between the past and the present, in which the past is constructed as that which the present is not' (1991: 423). Or possibly, and as Bowie remarks, this view of rural life has become accepted as self-evident by endless repetition (1992).

WE STAND AND FALL TOGETHER: THE CORPORATE VILLAGE

A second major thread that makes up the myth of the village is the notion of the corporate village, with its emphasis upon social redistribution and support networks. The very use of the terms 'village' and 'community' as synonymous indicates the extent to which people see place (locality, unit of space)—village (unit of administration)—and community (unity of society)—as interchangeable.

Douglass in his study of Thailand's integration into the world economy, for example, writes:

> As kingdoms (in pre-colonial South East Asia) rose and fell, the village had continued to act as a corporate entity—as the basic social, political and economic unit of the peasantry.
>
> Douglass, 1984: 2

and

> Villages were inward looking and, in most ways, were self-reliant, providing an encompassing cultural, economic and political life.
>
> Douglass, 1984:28

Douglass concludes in his assessment of traditional rural relations: 'The apex of social relations of the peasantry in Thailand was neither the clan, caste or class but the corporate village' (1984: 33).

Yet, across South East Asia, if one scratches the surface of the 'moral' economy, the extent to which self-interest and individualism is the driving force becomes clear. In many instances, what may appear to be an example of redistribution from the better-off to the worse-off, on closer analysis, is nothing of the sort. The general point is that traditional villages were not made up of farmers working for the betterment of the community as a whole; they were made up of households and families working for their own ends first and foremost, ends which in some cases overlapped with those of the wider community. Kemp argues that in the case of Thailand, cooperative action is either short-term and informal (e.g. reciprocal labour exchange or long khaek), or more accurately described as part of a wider system of patron-client relationships (1991: 320).

The debate over the corporate village is best exemplified in the bawon system of rice harvesting in Java, noted by Raffles in his *History of Java* (1817) and since much debated. Under this system, every member of a village had the right to help in the harvest of any piece of land, and up to 500 harvesters have been recorded working on fields as small as 0.25 hectares.[9] The rice was harvested with a finger knife or ani ani, panicles being cut one by one. For their work the harvesters would receive a share—or bawon—of the rice they had harvested, usually between one-seventh and one-ninth, depending on their relationship to the land owner.[10] The rice would be measured out in bundles for division between the harvester and the landowner, and the payment to the former rounded up to the appropriate fraction.[11]

The bawon system has been portrayed as a classic example of how the corporate village works, redistributing wealth from those with land, and, therefore, with rice, to those without, or at least with less. As Alexander and Alexander explain, it appears on first glance almost as if culture has gained hegemony over economics (1982). Much of the debate has focused on the switch from the bawon to the tebasan system where the standing crop is sold to a middleman (or penebas), thus circumventing the community obligations inherent in the bawon system—and turning the tables to allow economics ascendancy over culture. This is seen as a striking metaphor for all the changes that are buffering Javanese village life. But here the author is more concerned with whether the bawon system was ever an example of corporate village behaviour akin to James Scott's 'moral economy'.

In her book Land, labour and livelihood in a West Java village, Joan Hardjono argues that the bawon system evolved as a production management system in a context where labour was short and land was relatively abundant, and where rice had to be harvested over a relatively short period to prevent the crop from spoiling as it stood in the field. It was designed to ensure adequate labour could be enticed into harvesting a crop at short notice. Today, in most areas of Java, villages have moved from labour shortage to labour surplus and so farmers have adapted the bawon system to take account of this shift in relative resource abundance/scarcity. In particular, the bawon system has changed complexion and moved from being an 'open', to a closed system of harvesting. As Hardjono describes, farmers try all manner of ploys to ensure that only they, close relatives and friends engage in the harvest: they keep the date secret; they start the harvest at the crack of dawn (custom dictates that new harvesters cannot join after harvesting has begun); they harvest only one field at a time; they harvest only a portion of the field claiming they are preparing a nursery bed for the next crop; or they only begin harvesting when another larger landowner has begun their own harvest, thereby drawing people away from the potential labour pool. This brief discussion of the bawon system illustrates the key point that relations of mutual help and assistance are not necessarily indicative of a moral economy. Indeed, and as Vandergeest argues, they may merely be mystifications of exploitation (1991: 441).

THE AUTONOMOUS, SUBSISTENCE-ORIENTED VILLAGE

A third major thread that makes up the image of the traditional village is autonomy and self-reliance. This vision is linked to the ideas enshrined in the Asiatic Mode of Production, which in turn built upon European images of the village and village life (see Dumont, 1966). In this vision, the village is seen to be have been composed of a collection of families isolated from the state and from the wider national economy, focused inwards, a self-reliant and self-contained community—the archetypal 'little republic'. In Thailand, this is evident in the work, for example of

Hirsch (1989), Turton (1976 and 1984), Douglass (1984) and in the author's own work (Rigg, 1991), as well as in the work of those who adhere to what has been termed the Community Development Perspective or CDP. Seri Phongphit, a leading light of the CDP writes, in general terms: 'In community, members were interrelated. They were self-reliant, because the community was self-reliant . . . Modern society makes people less and less self-reliant' (1986: 15). At a wider level, Hirsch observes that '...distinct loci of village and state are a feature of pre-colonial South East Asian society, in which the close village and associated institutional mechanisms were within the territorial boundaries claimed by the state but largely outside the institutional boundaries of the central regime' (1989: 35). Douglass concurs, stating:

> Prior to the subordination of their economies to the imperatives of economic exchange . . . southeast Asian villages had been left with substantial autonomy over their own internal affairs . . . (Leaders were) rarely...either interested in or capable of intruding directly into village life.
>
> Douglass, 1984: 2

Civilized space may have been limited in pre-colonial South East Asia, but settlements were generally in communication with one another and with a central power, however tenuously. Vandergeest writes that 'nineteenth-century rural settlements (in Siam/Thailand) were part of the overall political system, not only through patron-client relationships or ritual enactments, but through relations of exploitation constituted through serfdom and slavery' (1991: 440). Likewise, Terwiel (1989) and Bowie (1992) both show the remarkable extent to which 'central' powers in Siam controlled the lives of villagers in the nineteenth century, and earlier. Terweil concludes that 'one of the rather unexpected findings (of his study) has been the discovery of the size and efficacy of the nineteenth-century government apparatus . . . it would seem that the population registered for corvee did indeed have to perform duties, or pay to be exempted, and that living at some distance from Bangkok did not place a person beyond the reach of government officials' (1989:251).[12] Focusing upon Java, Elson makes the same point, clearly stating that 'the village was no isolated and independent entity but was tightly bound to a larger world outside' (1986: 65). This encompassed extensive trading links, leading Elson to write that '(early nineteenth-century Java) was thoroughly enmeshed in and was an integral part of the wider money economy'. In political terms, he comes to the same conclusion, arguing that villages and villagers were no more self-sufficient and autonomous in politics than they were in commerce.

Historical studies also seem to indicate that commercialization of village life occurred far earlier than usually assumed. Koizumi's analysis of the payment of suai (head tax) in north-eastern Siam appears to show that a commercial economy existed in this remote region a century and a half ago. The conclusion is based on the evidence that suai payments in money had replaced payment in kind by the middle of the nineteenth century. Similarly, Bowie concludes in her study of textile production in nineteenth-century Northern Siam that 'this examination...reveals a society with a complex division of labor, serious class stratification, dire poverty, a wide-ranging trade network, and an unanticipated dynamism' (1992: 819). Lefferts agrees with this characterization, and makes the point that village-produced textiles have always been seen by their producers village women—as commodities for sale (1993).

Likewise, in Java and Sumatra, the image of a stagnant, subsistence-oriented village economy is difficult to sustain even before the intensification of the colonial presence at the beginning of the nineteenth century. As Boomgaard remarks, 'if there is any constant element in the history of Java, it is its well-attested function as a large-scale rice exporter perhaps as early as 900 [AD] . . . (peasants) were producing rice far in excess of their own requirements for a considerable time' (1991: 16). In the same volume of papers, White—examining secondary material on Java—notes that the level of 'proletarianisation' was high in agriculture in the first decade of the twentieth century (1991: 46). The degree of monetization of the Javanese rural economy is attested by the fact that cash-wage labouring was widespread on the island in the early nineteenth-century. By the middle of the century, Knight highlights a series of features which are indicative, in his view, of a fairly well-developed capitalist rural economy: the concentration of power and wealth among a small section of the rural population; the renting and sale of land; wage labouring; and commodity food production (1982:138-41). For Sumatra the evidence for commoditization at an early date is rather thinner. Nonetheless, Sherman and Sherman believe that the Batak living in the vicinity of Lake Toba, a backwater even by South East Asian standards at that time, were well-integrated into a trading and money economy. The ability of the Dutch to give a guilder price for many agricultural and other products at the beginning of the twentieth century is indicative, in his view, of a pre-existing market economy (Sherman and Sherman, 1990: 45-6).

COLONIAL ORIGINS OF THE 'VILLAGE'

A further area that needs to be considered is whether the 'village' as a discrete, identifiable entity ever really existed in South East Asia. It is often assumed that the village pre-dated the colonial period and pre-dated 'development'. Seri Phongphit in a book he edited with the main title Back to the roots, writes with respect to Thailand that 'Village was an institution. It was the basis of (the) community' (1986: 15). However, this entrenched idea that the village existed as a physical, social and economic entity before development and the state 'imposed' themselves on rural South East Asia is open to question. There is considerable evidence to indicate that villages were creations of the colonial period, designed to facilitate administration and control. Whether the units of social relations and geographical space in the period prior to these nineteenth and twentieth-century administrative reforms in Siam/Thailand, Malaysia, Indonesia and elsewhere corresponded with villages as they exist today, is doubtful. In Siam, Prince Damrong reformed village administration in the early 1890s. Bunnag describes how implementation of the plan was achieved near Bang Pa-In in the province of Ayutthaya, north of Bangkok:

> . . . Luang Thesachitwichan asked the heads of ten households, whose houses were situated near one another, to elect a village eider (phu yai ban). He then asked the elected eiders of villages, the number of which was governed by the natural features of the locality, to choose one of themselves as commune (tambon) eider (kamnan) . . . Phraya Sisuriyaratchawaranuwat . . . began to persuade the heads of five to twenty households to elect a village elder . . . (and) then asked approximately ten village elders to choose a commune elder.
>
> Bunnag, 1977: 110

Such was the manner in which Siam became a kingdom of villagers.

Historians of the region have been at pains to point out that in pre-colonial South East Asia, land was an abundant resource; it was people who were scarce.[13] Thus rulers and states were concerned to control people, not land 'as it was in followers that power and wealth were primarily expressed' (Reid, 1988:120). La Loubere's seventeenth-century account of his visit to Siam describes a system of warfare whose guiding principle was to capture people as booty so that they could be settled on land under the control of the ruler in question:

> They busie themselves only in making slaves. If the Peguins [Burmese], for example, do on one side invade the lands of Siam, the Siameses will at another place enter on the lands of Pegu, and both parties will carry away whole villages into captivity.
>
> La Loubere 1969: 90

When King Rama III of Siam took Vientiane, on the banks of the Mekong River, and captured King Anu in 1828-1829, he devastated the city and resettled all the population in the Siamese provinces of Lopburi, Suphanburi and Nakhon Chaisi. Over the following years, he undertook a programme of massive resettlement of Lao people on the Khorat Plateau (the Northeastern region) from lands formerly part of the Lao kingdom. As Wyatt notes, 'over 40 new muang (districts) were created some formed by the immigration of a whole community, with its chao muang and his family from across the river (Mekong)' (1982: 172). Grabowsky in a recent paper even goes so far as to argue that 'Forced resettlement campaigns . . . (were) an important aspect or even the main rationale of wars in traditional Thailand and Laos . . .' (1993: 2). He quotes the old Northern Thai (Yuan) proverb kep phak sai sa kep kha sai muang—'put vegetables into baskets, put people into towns'. So, even at this early date, the rural populations of South East Asia found themselves under the sway of rulers whether local lords or kings—and sometimes found themselves physically uprooted and resettled in a manner not dissimilar from today's state-directed resettlement schemes such as the transmigration programme in Indonesia and Malaysia's FELDA scheme. At the end of the nineteenth century, the wars between Burma and Siam had led to the almost utter depopulation of Chiang Mai, a city of considerable size and grandeur. A Northern Thai chronicle recorded that Chiang Mai '...had become a jungle overgrown by climbing plants, it turned into a place where rhinoceroses, elephants, tigers and bears were living' (quoted in Grabowsky, 1993: 9). The underlying assumption in many studies is that because the population of South East Asia was comparatively small, then this population would have been thinly distributed and, by implication, isolated from central powers, such as they were. More likely, however, is that people were concentrated in discrete geographical areas where environmental conditions were most conducive to human settlement, taking added reassurance from their proximity to one another. Much of the region would simply have been unpopulated by sedentary cultivators.

The most detailed investigation into the very existence of the 'village' prior to the nineteenth century has been undertaken by Kemp with respect to Thailand (see Kemp 1988, 1989, 1991). In a series of articles, and to the apparent horror of some scholars,[14] he has questioned whether there was any such thing as the 'village', let alone the 'community':

> We are . . . at the 'roots', not of the village community as a historical phenomenon but of its theoretical invention arising out of early colonial writings on India and their incorporation into both Marxist and non-Marxist social theory.
>
> Kemp, 1991: 325

> The term muu baan, variously translated as 'village', 'administrative village' or 'administrative hamlet', refers to a formal administrative division which in at least some areas was arbitrarily imposed on the

> landscape in a way which either combined or divided existing communities however defined, or provided a wider social framework where none had hitherto existed.
>
> Kemp, 1988: 8

Hart, writing on Java, paints a similar picture. She states that 'contrary to the stereotypical view of the traditional Javanese village as a closed "little republic" extending from time immemorial, villages only became administrative and territorial units in the early nineteenth century at the instigation of the colonial state' (Hart, 1986: 20). The colonial state found that it was necessary spatially and administratively to define villages in order to control the population and then be in a position to extract surplus from them. And to assist in this process of extraction, it was also necessary to formalize the role of the village head. Breman talks of the desa (village) as a 'harnessed construction'; a 'construction' insofar as it was an administrative unit imposed on people and on space, 'harnessed' in that it allowed the colonial state to have greater control over the two sources of wealth in any colony—people and land (Breman, 1980).

Even on Bali, often regarded as the finest example of a society structured in the interests of production, the Dutch manipulated, reformed and spatially reorganized people and space. In the early part of the twentieth century, the Dutch superimposed the desa perbekelan—the administrative village—onto the existing desa adat, or customary village. Only rarely did the two coincide in spatial and population terms (Warren, 1991: 216). As Adrian Vickers writes in his book Bali: a paradise created:

> Even on the village level, the level which the Dutch were supposedly preserving, there was massive change. The banjar . . . were made into wards of the

> village, whereas previously some banjar had in fact included householders outside the area of a village, and village and banjar identity were quite separate. This rationalised the size of villages... People found themselves in new villages to which they had previously never had any connection. Thus were the old 'village republics' restored.
>
> Vickers, 1989: 133-4

In this way, in Bali, the desa or village became an ambiguous term, and may always have been such. People were organized—or organized themselves—in different ways, according to the task at hand; the spatial configuration was rarely consistent so that sometimes the banjar or hamlet was a sub-village (sub-desa) grouping, while on other occasions it crossed between villages. In the case of the subak irrigation associations, these usually grouped people between villages in accordance with the requirements of irrigation (usually people depending on water from the same source). It has even been suggested that village membership corresponds with where people are buried; those who make offerings at the same temple, are buried in the same graveyard and thus belong to the same desa irrespective of whether their dwellings are grouped together or dispersed (see Warren, 1991: 221).

A similar story involving the bureaucratization of space to assist in the control of people and resources is evident in Malaysia. Shamsul writes that the Malaysian village was:

> created, recreated, sub-divided, rejoined and sometimes imagined to exist, in the name of development. The 'village' has become the 'contested terrain' simultaneously proliferating 'terrains of meaning' regarding what a 'village' is. But one thing remains clear—the 'village' is the most powerful

> instrument through which administrative, political and social control has been effected in rural Malaysia.
>
> Shamsul, 1989: 20

As in Bali and Thailand, the 'village' in Malaysia in this case the kampong—is an ambiguous term; it can refer to the 'village' or to a single dwelling, or indeed to a wider geographical area encompassing more than a single 'village' is. Evers believes that the European tendency to equate the control of people and of space as almost one and the same has led us to assume that the territorial designation of the kampong is consistent with a corresponding social designation (Evers, 1977: 208; see also Scott's discussion of what constitutes the kampong in his study of Sedaka 1985:86-90 and de Koninck, 1992). As in Bali and the close relationship of temple and village membership, so Evers notes how 'those taking part in the election of the mosque committee belong to one kampong, irrespective of where they actually live' (1977: 208). To support the view that this 'problem' of village designation is not just restricted to Thailand and Malaysia but to the South East Asian region as a whole, Kemp quotes work on hamlets in Vietnam, barrios in the Philippines and phum in Cambodia, all showing how the idea of village and community is flawed.

An important issue which Kemp does not address in detail is the extent to which governments have attempted to forge a village identity which accords with the artificially-imposed spatial and administrative divisions. In Malaysia, with the introduction of rural development programmes after World War II, the state has manipulated rural populations to create a sense of 'Kampung-ness' (village-ness) by conscripting people to work on common projects masquerading as gotong-royong (traditional self-help) schemes (Shamsul, 1989: 10). In Thailand, scholars such as Tapp (1988) and Chaianan Samudavanija (1985) have similarly noted how participatory development efforts are better described as forms of 'mass mobilization' or 'forced labour'. Across South East Asia, the state has not only created the 'village', but it has introduced policies to ferment and then cement a sense of village identity. In Thailand, there are village development committees, village heads, cooperatives and farmers' associations, women's groups and many other klum (groups) which draw their membership, in nearly all cases, from the designated administrative village. The continuous manipulation and organization of people in the context of the village—whether or not that bears any relation in social, historical or economic terms with what existed previously—must be creating a new sense of village identity. To an extent, then, image has become—or is becoming—reality.

IMPLICATIONS FOR DEVELOPMENT

If the above is correct, then it has important implications for how 'development', and all that it entails, is operating. Development has not intruded into egalitarian, homogenous, corporate and self-reliant villages, but into 'communities' where inequality and individualism were already in evidence. With reference to the current situation in Java, Hart writes:

> The key to understanding the distinctive features of agrarian differentiation in Java lies in recognising that the rural elite is not simply a capitalist class that has emerged in response to technologically determined commercialisation. They are in essence a class of favoured clients of the state whose opportunities to accumulate hinge in critically important ways on their links with the state apparatus.
>
> Hart, 1986: 199

These class structures would have placed certain members of the village population in a superior position to exploit the expanding opportunities for accumulation that accelerated commercialization provided. It was not a case of new technologies operating on a tabula rasa and creating class structures; but rather of 'capitalism' building upon structures that already existed. Thus, the assumption—for example—that reversing or halting the introduction of the technology of the Green Revolution would somehow throw the process of differentiation into reverse, is highly unlikely. Indeed, there are those who argue that the Green Revolution is becoming increasingly 'small-holder friendly' and thereby affords the wong cilik—the little people—the chance to escape from their entrenched (pre-commoditization) positions (e.g. Lipton and Longhurst, 1989; Hayami, 1981, 1984; Rigg, 1989).

Not only is an understanding of the village in history important from the point of view of interpreting the effects of development programmes and technological packages on rural areas, but also in conceptualizing new ways of 'doing' development. As the author has recently written regarding the CDP in Thailand:

> In the CDP's case, the problems that farmers face are seen to be linked—primarily—to the operation of the market and of the 'state', which has led to the commoditization of village life; in turn, the solution to these problems involves a degree of delinking from the national and world economies, the promotion of self-reliance, the resuscitation of 'tradition', the development of a community culture, and a move into integrated fanning based on traditional technologies and methods.
>
> Rigg, 1993: 1712

In this example, the view of the past, the interpretation of change and the prescriptions for the future are all linked to the 'image' of the village discussed above. One of the difficulties that the author has with the CDP and perspectives of its ilk—which are becoming increasingly influential in the developing world—is what he feels is a critical misinterpretation of history. They pedal a powerful vision of traditional village life and use this, in part, to set the contemporary development agenda. An indication of the wish-fulfillment that seems to be part and parcel of this, and other perspectives is provided by a poem written by Thai development worker and CDP activist Apichart Thongyu and entitled 'Reflections of a village development worker'. Significantly, it was translated from the Thai and reproduced in an academic volume on community management (Apichart Thongyou, 1987). Quoting only three verses of the 24-verse poem gives an indication of the views that the development worker in the title of the piece holds dear:

> No noisy sounds of confusion, no loud sounds of people-crowds, no heaps of noise from engines, no sound of search for freedom, no sound of calls for honour and rank; only quietude, life, and love.
>
> One hundred sixty years of this village, no introduction to Dharma, no ethical theories, no economic plan, no articles of government, no philosophical theory. Only the life of people, propogated in tranquil bliss.

The poem ends:

> Turning back to look once again, to be sure. Water in the stream is clear and clean, Mother with a new silk skirt, Father with a checkered sarong, People with Virtue, life with simplicity. Questions are not exhausted, even at parting: Undeveloped, really? Backward, really? In the time that has passed, only one type of development was seen: that of myself!

The discussion in an earlier section of this paper regarding the degree to which villages in South East Asia were commoditized and tied into wider regional and/or national (and international) economies, also has implications for recent work on the rural-urban divide. Drawing on research in Java, Terry McGee has argued that Asia has a geographical characteristic which sets it apart from other parts of the world. That is, the presence of high-density agricultural regions based on the intensive cultivation of wet rice where so-called Extended Metropolitan Regions (EMRs) have developed. In short, McGee maintains that Asia exhibits region-based urbanization, not city-based urbanization, in which formerly agricultural populations have been drawn into the processes of urbanization and industrialization, in situ (see McGee, 1991; McGee and Greenberg, 1992). This raises the question of whether these EMRs are rural or urban in character. Indeed, McGee has coined a term to reflect this spatial identity crisis: kotadesa—a combination of two Indonesian words, kota (town) and desa (village). Kotadesasi (the suffix si to indicate that this is a process as well as a form) is a: 'process involving the growth of distinct regions of agricultural and non-agricultural activity characterized by intense interaction of commodities and people' (quoted in Ginsburg, 1991: 38).

McGee clearly has his mind set on contemporary developments. But the roots of the kotadesa often lie in pre-colonial spatial and economic forms where villages were already tied into wider trading networks and where the notion of 'rural' and 'urban' worlds distinct and discrete—was already difficult to sustain in an absolute sense. Today, such is the level of interaction between urban/industrial and rural/agricultural, that these two (imaginary) worlds have become part of a single operating unit and, to use Bruce Koppel's phrase, the division, ersatz (Koppel, 1991: 48). He writes: 'There are good reasons now to argue for the middle ground, for the reality of rural-urban linkages not as derivations or reflections, but as representative and indicative of independent social facts . . .' (1991: 48).

An important issue which has not yet been addressed is that of 'morality'. Table I lists 'morality' and 'immorality' as characteristics of traditional and modern villages respectively. These are powerful terms, but they do underlie much of the debate over what is being 'done' to villages. There is an influential ideology of development which tends to glorify the past and denigrate the present. As this ideology—with its ideologically-loaded terminology of self-reliance, participation, community culture and self-reliance—has managed to take the moral high ground, debate is often restricted (see Midgley, 1986; Burgess, 1993; Friedmann, 1992). Burgess also notes in a recent paper the extent to which 'radical/popular' writers now dominate the media interpretations of development (1993: 22-23). The author is not against this: it says a lot about the accessibility of their work, and by implication the inaccessibility of much academic work; an issue which, to coin a phrase, the closed, corporate academic world should heed. However, and academic deficiencies aside, it does worry the author that the 'morality' of the traditional village may well be founded on a series of false premises about the 'village'. The 'roots' of the village, so often held up for all to admire, may be fiction.

Vandergeest goes so far as to argue in the Thai context that villages are more autonomous and community-oriented today than they have ever been. He writes that the struggle for autonomy is 'on-going, as villages continue to reject development as a gift, and redefine it as their right' (1991: 434). There is, indeed, a body of thought which maintains that the potential for and necessity of participation increases with development, so that rather than undermining formerly participatory societies, modernization does quite the reverse. This view is founded on the belief that economic growth leads to greater differentiation and specialization, and, therefore, increased dependency, and thus the requirement that people cooperate and participate to a greater degree.

Arguably, the above discussion leads to the conclusion that the 'village' does not exist. Or at least that it does not exist in terms of those popularly-defined notions that are reputed to be characteristic of traditional village life. There is also a case to be made that just as participation may increase with development and economic differentiation, so it may be that village 'coherence' does too. Now that villagers are being born with the help of village health workers, being sent to 'village' schools, being counted, recorded and administered as part of a village, and in multifarious ways being accorded the status of belonging to village 'x', then it is not too much to state that the 'village' has been created.

REFERENCES

Alexander, Jennifer and Alexander, Paul 1982. *Shared poverty as ideology: agrarian relationships in colonial Java*. Man 17(4): 597-619.

Apichart Thongyou, 1987. *Reflections of a village development worker*. In Korten, David C, (ed.) *Community management: Asian experience and perspectives*. West Hartford, Connecticut: Kumarian Press: 40-45.

Boomgaard, Peter 1989. *Children of the colonial state: population growth and economic development in Java, 1795-1880*. CASA Monographs no. 1. Amsterdam: Free University Press.

——, 1991. *The non-agricultural side of an agricultural economy, Java 1500-1900*. In Alexander, P., Boomgaard, P. and White, B. (eds) *In the shadow of agriculture: non-farm activities in the Javanese economy, past and present*. Amsterdam: Royal Tropical Institute: 14-40.

Bowie, Katherine A. 1992. *Unraveling the myth of the subsistence economy: textile production in nineteenth century Northern Thailand*. J. Asian Stud. 51(4): 797-823.

Breman, Jan 1980. *The village on Java and the early-colonial state*, Comparative Asian Studies Programme (CASP). Rotterdam: Erasmus University.

Bunnag, Tej 1977. *The provincial administration of Siam 1892-1915*. The Ministry of the Interior under Prince Damrong Rajanubhab. Kuala Lumpur: Oxford University Press.

Burgess, Michael 1993. *Aid and Third World development: a critique of dependency theory and the role of non-governmental organisations*. Current Affairs Bull. 69(12): 21-7.

Carey, Peter 1986. *Waiting for the 'Just King': the agrarian world of south-central Java from Giyanti (1755) to the Java War (1825-1830)*. Modern Asian Stud, 20(1): 59-137.

Chaianan Samudavanija, 1985. *Village bureaucracy and development*. Bangkok: The Public Affairs Group and Friedrich Ebert Stiftung.

Chattip Nartsupha, 1986. *The village economy in pre-capitalist Thailand*. In Seri Phongphit (ed.) *Back to the roots: village and self-reliance in a Thai context*. Bangkok: Rural Development Documentation Centre: 155-65.

——, 1991. *The 'community culture' school of thought*. In Chitakasem, M, and Turton, A. (eds) *Thai constructions of knowledge*. London: S.O.A.S: 118-41.

Collier, W.L., Gunawan Wiradi and Soentoro 1973. *Recent changes in rice harvesting methods: some serious social implications*. Bull. Indonesian Econ. Stud. 9(2): 36-45.

Collier, W.L., Gunawan Wiradi and Makali 1974. *Agricultural technology and institutional change in Java*. Food Res. Inst. Stud. 13(2): 169-94.

Dasgupta, Biplab 1978. *Introduction*. In Dasgupta, B. (ed.) *Village studies in the Third World*. Delhi: Hindustan Publishing Corporation: 1-12.

Dewey, Clive 1972. *Images of the village community: a study in Anglo-Indian ideology*. Modern Asian Stud. 6(3): 291-328.

Douglass, M. 1984. *Regional integration on the capitalist periphery: the Central Plains of Thailand*. Research report series no. 15. The Hague: Institute of Social Studies.

Dumont, Louis 1966. *The 'village community' from Munro to Maine.* Contributions to Indian Sociology 9 (December): 67-89.

Elson, R.E. 1986. *Aspects of peasant life in early 19th century Java.* In Chandler, D. and Ricklefs, M.C. (eds) *Nineteenth and twentieth century, Indonesia.* Clayton, Victoria: Centre for South East Asian Studies: 57-81.

Evers, Hans-Dieter 1977. *The culture of Malaysian urbanization: Malay and Chinese conceptions of space.* Urban Anthrop. 6(3): 205-16.

Friedmann, John 1992. *'Empowerment,' the politics of alternative development.* Oxford: Basil Blackwell.

Geertz, Clifford 1963. *Agricultural involution: the process of ecological change in Indonesia.* Berkeley: University of California Press.

Ginsburg, Norton 1991. *Extended metropolitan regions in Asia: a new spatial paradigm.* In Ginsburg, Norton, Koppel, Bruce and McGee, T.G. (eds) *The extended metropolis: settlement transition in Asia*, Honolulu: University of Hawaii Press: 27-46.

Gordon, Alec 1992. *The poverty of involution: a critique of Geertz' pseudo-history.* J Contemporary Asia 22(4): 490-513.

Grabowsky, Volker 1993. *Forced resettlement campaigns in Northern Thailand during the early Bangkok period.* Paper presented at the 5th International Conference on Thai Studies, School of Oriental and African Studies, London, July.

Hardjono, Joan 1987. *Land, labour and livelihood in a West java village.* Yogyakarta: Gadjah Mada University Press.

Hart, Gillian P. 1986. *Power, labor and livelihood: processes of change in rural Java.* Berkeley: University of California Press.

Hayami, Y. 1981. *Induced innovation, green revolution and income distribution: comment.* Economic Development and Cultural Change 30: 169-76.

——, 1984. *Assessment of the Green Revolution.* In Eicher, C.K. and Staatz, J.M. (eds) *Agricultural development in the Third World.* Baltimore: The Johns Hopkins Press: 389-96.

Hayami, Y, and Hafid, A. 1979. *Rice harvesting and welfare in rural Java*. Bull. Indonesian Econ. Stud. 15(2): 94-112.

Hirsch, Philip 1989. *The state in the village: interpreting rural development in Thailand*. Development and Change 20(1): 35-56.

Hobsbawm, Eric and Ranger, Terence (eds) 1983. *The invention of tradition*. Cambridge: C.U.P.

Husken, Frans 1981. *Regional diversity in Javanese agrarian development: variations in the pattern of involution*. Working paper no. 10, Sociology of Development Research Centre, University of Bielefeld, Germany.

Kemp, Jeremy 1988. *Seductive mirage: the search for the village community in Southeast Asia*. Dordrecht: Foris.

——, 1989. *Peasants and cities: the cultural and social image of the Thai peasant community*. Sojourn 4(1): 6-19.

——, 1991. *The dialectics of village and state in modern Thailand*. J. Southeast Asian Stud. 92(2): 312-26.

Knight, G.R. 1982. *Capitalism and commodity production in Java*, In Alavi Hamza, Burns, P.L., Knight, G.R., Mayer. P.B. and McEachern, Doug (eds) *Capitalism and colonial production*. London: Croom Helm: 119-58.

Koppel, Bruce 1991. *The rural-urban dichotomy reexamined: beyond the ersatz debate?* In Ginsburg, N., Koppel, B. and McGee T.G. (eds) *The extended metropolis: settlement transition in Asia*. Honolulu: University of Hawaii Press: 47-70.

Koizumi, Junko 1992. *The commutation of Suai from Northeast Siam in the middle of the nineteenth century*, J. Southeast Asian Stud. 23(2): 276-307.

Koninck, Rudolphe de 1992. *Malay peasants coping with the world: breaking the community circle?* Singapore: Institute of Southeast Asian Studies.

La Loubere, Simon de 1969. *The kingdom of Siam*. Oxford in Asia Historical Reprints. Kuala Lumpur: Oxford University Press. First published in 1691.

Lipton, Michael and Longhurst, Richard 1989. *New seeds and poor people*. London: Unwin Hyman.

Lefferts, H. Leedom Jr. 1993. *Continuity and change in Tai textile development*. Paper presented at the 5th International Conference on Thai Studies, School of Oriental and African Studies, London, July.

McGee, T.G. 1991. *The emergence of desakota regions in Asia: expanding a hypothesis*. In Ginsburg, N., Koppel, B. and McGee, T.G. (eds) *The extended metropolis: settlement transition in Asia*. Honolulu: University of Hawaii Press: 3-25.

McGee, T.G. and Greenberg, Charles 1992. *The emergence of extended metropolitan regions in ASEAN*, ASEAN Econ. Bull. 9(1): 22-44.

Midgley, James 1986. *Community participation: history, concepts and controversies*. In Midgley, James (ed.) *Community participation, social development and the state*. London: Methuen: 13-44.

Popkin, Samuel L. 1979. *The rational peasant: the political economy of rural society in Vietnam*. Berkeley: University of California Press.

Raffles, Stamford 1817. *The history of Java*. London: John Murray.

Reid, Anthony 1988. *Southeast Asia in the age of commerce 14501680: the lands below the winds*. New Haven: Yale University Press.

Rhum, Michael R. 1993. *Reply to Katherine Bowie*. J. Asian Stud. 52(3): 673-5.

Rigg, Jonathan 1989. *The new rice technology and agrarian change: guilt by association?* Progr. Hum. Geogr. 13(3): 374-99.

——, 1991. *Southeast Asia: a region in transition*. London: Unwin Hyman.

——, 1993. *A reply to Kevin Hewison*. World Devel. 21(10): 1709-13.

Schweizer, Thomas 1987. *Agrarian transformation? Rice production in a Javanese village*. Bull. Indonesian Econ. Stud. 23(2): 38-70.

Scott, James C. 1976. *The moral economy of the peasant: rebellion and subsistence in Southeast Asia*, New Haven: Yale University Press.

——, 1985. *Weapons of the weak: everyday firms of peasant resistance*. New Haven: Yale University Press.

Seri Phongphit 1986. *Introduction*. In Seri Phongphit (ed.) *Back to the roots: village and self-reliance in a Thai context*, Bangkok: Rural Development Documentation Centre (RUDOC): 13-21.

Shamsul, A.B. 1989. *'Village,' the imposed social construct in Malaysia's developmental initiatives*. Working paper no. 115, Sociology of Development Research Centre, University of Bielefeld, Germany.

Sherman, D. George and Sherman, Bruyns, Hedy 1990. *Rice, rupees and ritual: economy and society among the Samosir Batak of Sumatra*. Stanford, California: Stanford University Press.

Stoler, Ann L. 1988. *Rice harvesting in Kali Loro: a study of class and labour relations in rural Java*. In Taylor, John G. and Turton, Andrew (eds) *Sociology of 'developing societies'*; Southeast Asia. Basingstoke: Macmillan: 111-22.

Svensson, Thommy 1991. *Contractions and expansions: agrarian change in Java since 1830*. In Morner, Magnus and Svensson, Thommy (eds) *The transformation of rural society in the Third World*. London: Routledge: 145-85.

Tapp, Nicholas 1988. *Squatters or refugees: development and the Hmong*. Paper presented at the symposium on the peripheral areas and minority groups of South-East Asia, Centre of South-East Asian Studies, University of Hull.

Terwiel, B.J. 1989. *Through travellers' eyes: an approach to early nineteenth-century Thai history*. Bangkok: Duang Kamol.

Toer, Pramoedya A. 1982. *Awakenings*. Melbourne, Australia: Penguin Books.

Turton, Andrew 1976. *Northern Thai peasant society: twentieth century transformations in political and jural structures*. 5. Peasant Stud. 3: 267-98.

——, 1984. *Limits ideological domination and the formation of social consciousness.* In Turton, Andrew and Tanabe S. (eds) *History and peasant consciousness in South East Asia.* Senri Ethnological Studies No. 13, National Museum of Ethnology, Osaka: 19-73.

Utong Prasasvinitchai, 1993. *Crop selection in context: rethinking farmers as decision makers.* Paper presented at the 5th International Conference on Thai Studies, School of Oriental and African Studies, London, July.

Utrecht, Ernst 1973. *American sociologists in Indonesia.* J. Contemporary Asia 3(1): 39-45.

Vandergeest, Peter 1991. *Gifts and rights: cautionary notes on community self-help in Thailand.* Development and Change 22: 421-43.

Vickers, Adrian 1989. *Bali: a paradise created.* Berkeley: Periplus.

Warren, Carol 1991. *Adat and dinas: village and state in contemporary Bali.* In Geertz, Hildred (ed.) State and society in Bali. Leiden: KITLV Press: 213-49.

White, Ben 1983. *'Agricultural involution' and its critics: twenty years on.* Bull. Concerned Asian Scholars 15(2): 18-31.

——, 1991. *Economic diversification and agrarian change in rural Java, 1900-1990.* In Alexander, P., Boomgaard, P. and White, B. (eds) *In the shadow of agriculture: non-farm activities in the Javanese economy, past and present.* Amsterdam: Royal Tropical Institute: 41-69.

Wolf, Eric R. 1967. *Closed corporate peasant communities in Mesoamerica and Central Java.* In Potter, J.M., Diaz, M.N. and Foster, G.M. (eds) *Peasant society: a reader.* Boston: Little, Brown and Company: 230-46, (first published 1957 in South Western Journal of Anthropology 13(1): 1-18.

Wyatt, David 1982. *Thailand: a short history.* New Haven: Yale University Press.

NOTES

1. The author also places himself in the category of academics who, in Jeremy Kemp's phrase have been 'seduced' by the

'mirage' of the village (Kemp, 1988). The author would also admit that he is still tempted to glorify the village—something that says a great deal about the power and pervasiveness of the ideology of the village in the West.

2. However, Dasgupta does not characterize the village as a closed, autonomous society, accepting a degree of interaction with the wider economy.

3. 'Tradition' is an elusive thing and in this context it is used in only the loosest, popular, sense. See Hobsbawm and Ranger's *The invention of tradition*, 1983.

4. Dewey writes: 'Around the patriotic image of the village community countess administrative utopias were woven; each constructed on exaggerated notions of the village's community and each foundering on the villages' fissiparous tendencies' (1972: 327-8).

5. Utong Prasasvinitchai, in a fascinating recent paper on crop selection strategy in Thailand, talks of decision-making being a multifarious adaptation to changing personal and wider contexts in which bundles of inter-related factors are brought to bear in a continually changing, dynamic environment (1993). The room for generalization—except in terms of emphasizing complexity—is highly restricted.

6. For critiques of Geertz, and in particular of his notion of agricultural involution in Javanese rice cultivation, see White, 1983; Gordon, 1992; Utrecht, 1973.

7. Before 1939, when Prime Minister Phibun Songkhram changed the country's name to Thailand, the Kingdom was known as Siam.

8. See Bowie, 1992: 797-805 for a summary in the case of Thailand.

9. In some areas it seems that anyone had the right to engage in the harvest; large numbers of itinerant harvesters—usually landless labourers—would travel from village to village searching for work.

10. Although Stoler records a highest bawon of one half and a smallest of one twenty-fifth of the harvest for close relatives and orang lain (other people—harvesters from

outside the village) respectively (1988:117 - 1 18). She also notes that poor close relations may be awarded all the crop they have harvested.

11. For background to rice harvesting systems in Java see Hayami and Hafid, 1979; Collier et al. 1973 and 1974; Hart, 1986 and Schweizer, 1987. It should be noted that these accounts show how marked are the differences between harvesting systems across Java; to generalize about how 'development' is causing them to adapt or to be replaced ignores these very' important local and regional variations.

12. In an otherwise rather sceptical reply to Bowie's paper (1992), Michael Rhum nonetheless feels compelled to agree that: 'It is not simply that villages (in Northern Thailand) were forced by economic necessity to engage in trade and therefore were implicated in a larger world, but rather that they were both constituted by and constitutive of that world' (1993: 674).

13. Although population estimates must be regarded as gross approximations, Reid calculates that in 1600 South East Asia had a total population of 22.4 million, increasing to 32.4 million by 1800 (Reid, 1988: 14). By comparison, today the region (the six countries of ASEAN plus Vietnam, Laos, Cambodia and Burma [Myanmar]) supports a population of about 450 million.

14. Referring specifically to Kemp, Seri Phongphit writes: 'It seems to us that we are "talking different languages". It is not true that there is a common 'scientific language' . . . A village community is not a 'unit-like' matter or a 'thing'. It is not like a motor vehicle that can be divided into its component parts and analysed, one piece after another. A village community is a living structure . . .' (1989: 3).

15. In Thailand, the commonly used words for house, household and village—ban—are also one and the same (officially, a village is a muban, although most people talk of Ban (Village) Nong Si for example).

3

AGRICULTURAL EXPANSION AS A TOOL OF POPULATION REDISTRIBUTION IN SOUTHEAST ASIA

—Rodolphe de Koninck, Steve Dery

Agricultural expansion has been closely linked to the history of mankind or, more specifically, to the history of agriculture. In fact the latter's basic itinerary has been one of nearly constant spatial spread, the rhythm of this expansion depending on climatic, cultural, political and overall historical conditions. But, whatever those conditions, feeding and clothing the growing number of humans and providing for their rising needs and expectations have always implied some form or other of agricultural encroachment on forests and grasslands. Of course, with the improvement of agricultural technology, intensification has also contributed to the increase in production, particularly since the middle of the twentieth century. In Southeast Asia, this intensification, the so-called Green Revolution, has in some specific areas, Java for example,[1] played an even more important role than land expansion or extensification.

But, even with the success of that Green Revolution in increasing tremendously both land and labour productivity, even with the reduction in land devoted to agriculture in most of the industrial countries, global expansion of agricultural land continues and is likely to do so for at least a few more decades.[2] More importantly, the dynamics of agricultural expansion have been and remain inherently linked to those of economic and political development, not the least of which is State territorial formation. These linkages may take several forms, including the following.

First, land colonization, whether planned or not, whether or not it involves spontaneous or monitored land opening, often acts as a safety valve against agrarian problems linked to inadequate or inequitable land distribution; it may even be used as a proxy for land reform or redistribution, or in conjunction with the latter. Second, the territorial spread of agriculture, particularly in contemporary Southeast Asia, often comes as a direct or indirect response to internal or external demand for agricultural produce, basically cash crops, in which case the demand emanates mostly from the industrial countries. This has been particularly obvious, from the late 1950s onwards, in Malaysia with the Federal Land Development Authority (FELDA) rubber and oil palm schemes,[3] and is even more apparent today with the New Economic Zones (N.E.Z.) developed in the Central Highlands of Vietnam for the cultivation of coffee, tea, mulberry, cashew nuts, etc.

Third, the expansion of land devoted to agriculture may also result from, or lead to a geopolitical strategy, in the fundamental sense of the word geopolitical. In fact, it would seem that: "Throughout history, in just about every major region of the world, the very formation of numerous States, the gathering of the pieces that comprise them and the colonization of their borderlands have relied at least partially on the peasantry, or on a process of peasantization.

By "planting" or "sowing" peasants, and then "protecting" them, many States have secured their territory. By establishing its control, whether or not as a result of a planned process, over agriculturalists located on the frontiers of a coveted domain, as well as in the heart of the country, a State consolidates its very base."[4] This seems to be the case in several countries of Southeast Asia, notably in contemporary Indonesia and Vietnam.[5]

Fourth, in contributing to what is nowadays called regional development, the agricultural colonization of areas located on the margins of a country often entails a "taming" of nature and of people, a process linked to the above mentioned geopolitical strategy. Thus, in Southeast Asia, the establishment of pioneers—most from the dominant ethnic groups occupying the more densely settled lowland areas—in peripheral and generally mountainous regions, is done at the expense of forests and of forest people, both of which are thus "domesticated" and brought into the national mainstream.[6]

Finally, the development of the frontier also brings about a massive redistribution of population and may actually contribute to overall national population growth, as suggested recently by Charles Hirschman.[7] While the four above mentioned processes and linkages are not always evident or even operational, population redistribution is more visible. It is also the central process, to which all the others are articulated. Migrations of people, whether planned or not, whether controlled fully or only partially—at least at their outset—by the State or by State builders, represent a key feature of the history of Southeast Asia, including its contemporary one. It has been the object of valuable research,[8] but much more remains to be done before a full picture of the contribution of migration to the ongoing making of Southeast Asia emerges. Our intention with this paper is not, of course, to fill this gap entirely, but to underline some of the key features. With this in mind, we intend, first, to examine and to illustrate statistically and cartographically four country cases of population redistribution through agricultural expansion, and, second, to underline the role of the State in these matters while pointing out the advantages it may thus gain in terms of territorial formation and consolidation. In this last regard, it will be asked whether the experiences of Southeast Asian States can in some ways be compared to those of European ones where agricultural expansion played a key role in State formation.[9] We will thus be attempting to pursue Hirschman's query concerning the specificity of demographic changes in twentieth-century Southeast Asia.[10]

These population displacements occurred during the twentieth century and were all planned, at least partially. The ones examined here concern the Philippines, Indonesia, Vietnam and Thailand.

AGRICULTURAL EXPANSION AND POPULATION REDISTRIBUTION

The Philippines: The Southern Conquest

Although very limited until the turn of the nineteenth century, agricultural colonization in the Philippines was accelerated "after about 1820 when the port of Manila was opened to foreign ships of any flag, demand for export crops set off migration of peasants from the old seacoast and river towns into the interiors and caused vast areas of forest and grassland to be converted to farm within a couple of generations".[11] After the country fell under American administration at the turn of the twentieth century, the rhythm of expansion was further accelerated, with a definite emphasis on southward migrations. The island of Mindanao, almost as large as Luzon and never wholly controlled by the Spaniards, was to become the major frontier in the Philippines. Although spontaneous migrations of settlers had begun earlier, colonization of Mindanao was made an official goal of the central government which established, between 1913 and 1917, six agricultural colonies in the archipelago's southernmost large island. Involving Christian settlers from Luzon and even more from the Visayas,—where it was officially meant to relieve population and agrarian pressure—and with Tagalog and Cebuano people being the most numerous, this expansion was initially focused on the western flank of the island, where the "population consisted primarily of various indigenous Moslem groups",[12] the so-called Moros. Here was a classical case of a concerted strategy of cultural dilution.

As generally occurs with pioneer fronts, particularly in the Tropics,[13] most of the small settlers subsequently met with considerable difficulties, many of them being forced off the land by large scale owners, including ranchers, who then employed them as labourers.[14] But whatever the problems faced by the pioneering peasants, additional colonization programmes were launched, including by the National Land Settlement Administration, starting in 1939. After the Second World War, these programmes were expanded, several agencies being involved, in a context where the counterinsurgency function of land pioneering was emphasized.[15] Later on, starting in the sixties, agricultural expansion was even advocated as an essential element in the agrarian reform programme.[16] While in 1940, just over five million hectares or 17 per cent of the country's total land area was devoted to agriculture, by 1980, it had reached nine million hectares or about 30 per cent of the national territory.[17] By this time, 34 per cent of the island of Mindanao was devoted to agriculture, versus 25 per cent for Luzon.[18]

The impact of this agricultural expansion and of the migrations—still partly spontaneous—that fueled it has been substantial on the distribution of population. The relative weight of Mindanao in demographic terms has more than tripled between 1903 and 1990 (from less than seven to 22 per cent of the national total), the population increase having been more substantial during the second half of the century. Most of the southward redistribution has occurred at the expense of the Visayas. That the latter as well as Luzon are still much more densily populated than Mindanao[19] should riot distract from the fact that, had the redistribution of population "in favor" of Mindanao not occurred, average densities would be even higher in Luzon and in the Visayas than they are today. Luzon has maintained its demographic preeminence, its relative weight being slightly superior to 50 per cent. In fact, while prior to the Second World War, Luzon's relative demographic weight had declined for several decades, since then it has been on the rise. This is exclusively linked to the growth of the Manila metropolitan region, the national capital taking, as in all countries of Southeast Asia, more than its share of the increase in the urban population.

Nevertheless, notwithstanding this metropolization and the overall urbanization process, the actual redistribution of population that has occurred over the century, largely through agricultural expansion, has resulted in a relatively better spread of population densities at the national scale.[20] Some regions have clearly seen their share of the national population decrease: this is the case, on Luzon, with the Ilocano region on the northwest coast, or with several provinces in the Visayas, notably on the islands of Mindoro, Panay, Negros, Bohol, Leyte and Samar. Other regions have seen their share increase: this is quite evident first with Luzon's central plain and particularly among the provinces forming as well as surrounding the Manila metropolitan region; second with the island of Palawan; and third with Mindanao, most of its twenty-odd provinces being concerned.

Indonesia: Relieving the Core and Integrating the Periphery

The agricultural colonization programmes of Indonesia, another large archipelago country, are perhaps better known,[21] if only because they are still very active, involve a larger number of people, and cover a much greater area. Here also the planned displacement of people from the very densely populated core of the country, in this case primarily the island of Java and to a lesser extent that of Bali, was initiated by the colonial authorities. The Dutch administration's so-called Kolonisatie programme was officially launched in 1905. As in the Philippines, the motives behind it were not confined to simple attempts to decongest the core of the country. They were also associated with the Dutch's ambition to develop commercial agriculture in the outer islands, particularly in Sumatra, and to augment the supply of rice to Java. The programme was only relatively successful for, by the time of the Japanese invasion in 1942, only some 200,000 settlers had been "implanted" in the outer islands, in fact most of them just across the Strait of Java, in the province of Lampung in southern Sumatra.

But a start had been made and, after the war of independence (1945-49), the programme was reactivated by the authorities of the new Republic of Indonesia. Given the name of transmigrasi, it became increasingly important in the context of a country trying to pull itself together after years of turmoil. Thus, in the early 1950s, some of the demobilized soldiers of the republican army were given land to cultivate in the province of Lampung, at that time still the major pioneering area of Indonesia.[22] The practice of distributing land to demobilized soldiers, generally in frontier regions, is as old as the history of demobilization itself. It was applied by the Romans in Gaul[23] and by the Chinese on the margins of theft Middle Kingdom.[24] In fact, according to Berque, the utilization of soldier-settlers for strategic purposes is an "Oriental" invention, having first been employed by the Chinese at the time of the Han dynasty.[25] The Japanese resorted to it as recently as during the late nineteenth century in Hokkaido.[26] It also occurred along both of Indonesia's international borders; first along the Kalimantan border with the newly formed federation of Malaysia, during the Confrontation of 1963-65,[27] and then during the 1980s along Irian Jaya's border with Papua New Guinca (but apparently not along the border with East Timor, prior to its occupation which began in 1975), in a context where goals of cultural dilution and strategic control were quite evident.[28]

Massive transfers of population, mostly from Java, were subsequently accelerated, particularly with the 1969-74 development plan. But even with the growing involvement of the State in the transmigration programme, the flow of independent settlers has remained considerable. Between 1950 and 1992, more than half of the estimated 2.5 million transmigrant families (involving some ten million people) were spontaneous settlers.[29] Most of these so-called "spontan" were still heading for Sumatra. While the latter has remained the major destination for all transmigrants, Kalimantan, Sulawesi and Irian Jaya have been receiving an increasing proportion of the number of new settlers.

The outmigration of landless peasants or of agricultural workers from Java is not the only important migratory movement in Indonesia. The flow of people to Java, including that of dissatisfied transmigrants returning to their home island—partly to the cities, thus joining internal Javanese rural-urban migrations—contributes to the migratory balance; but the latter remains in favour of the outer islands.[30] The development of pioneer fronts in these islands has been associated with large scale agricultural expansion, which has been particularly intensive since the 1950s. Between 1960 and 1990, for the whole of Indonesia, cultivated land grew from twelve million to about twenty million hectares.[31] However, much of the accompanying increase in actual production, particularly that of rice and principally on Java, has been due to the rapid adoption of double cropping and the reliance on high yielding varieties, combined with the use of fertilizers and other chemical inputs.[32] In fact, while closely linked to massive investments in irrigation infrastructure, these types of development have been the major cause behind the country's attainment of self sufficiency in rice production. But, notwithstanding the achievements of the Indonesian Green Revolution, the spread of sedentary agriculture in the outer islands,[33] including the expansion of cash crops and of private plantation agriculture, has been a major factor behind the growth of the country's agricultural production. And it has also contributed to a relatively better balanced distribution of population.

Between 1905 and 1990, the share of Java's population in the archipelago decreased from nearly 80 per cent to 60 per cent, while that of Sumatra has nearly doubled from 11 to 20 per cent. The relative weight of just about all the outer islands, particularly Sulawesi, increased substantially between 1905 and 1930. However, since the latter date, only Sumatra and, to a lesser degree, Kalimantan have seen their relative weight continue to grow significantly, while for all others it stabilized.[34] Furthermore, some of the apparent evolution in the relative distribution of population among the various islands of the archipelago might be due to underenumeration which, for the earlier census, particularly the one taken in 1905, probably occurred in the more remote islands and areas.[35] Whatever the case, population redistribution occurred primarily in the direction of Sumatra as, in fact, it still does.[36] Finally, some migratory movements contribute more to urban and industrial population growth, as in Irian Jaya, than to agricultural development. Nevertheless, as in the Philippines, over and beyond the remaining exceptional demographic weight of the command island, in this case

Java, population redistribution through agricultural expansion has contributed both to a reduction in that relative weight and to a greater integration of some of the peripheral areas,[37] one of which, southern Sumatra, is now definitely part of the country's "centre".

Vietnam: After the Southward Drive, the Westward Expansion

The history of Vietnam is closely linked to the southward expansion of the Viet people. Originally from Southern China, the Viet became established in the Red River delta during the initial centuries of the first millenium, and finally and "officially" wrested their independence from the Middle Kingdom in the year 939. During the next eight centuries, the Viet continued their southward migrations, gradually settling the narrow coastal plains of Annam (Trung Bo), all the way to the southernmost regions of the Mekong delta. The Nam Tien, the drive to the south, was spearheaded essentially by agriculturalists, often peasant-soldiers. The pre-established lowland people, particularly the Chum and the Khmer, were either assimilated or pushed aside, peacefully or manu militari. Of course, the history of Vietnam from the tenth to the eighteenth century involves much more than the southward drive. It was also fiddled by numerous conflicts, involving recurrent struggles against the Chinese and, perhaps even more significant, internal divisions and civil wars.[38] Nevertheless, during that period, the domain of the Viet nation was delineated by its own wet rice cultivators in the alluvial, coastal and deltaic plains which, except for the Mekong delta, are backed by the Annam Ridge (Truong Son).

By the time the French began to carve out their colonial domain in the region, during the second half of the nineteenth century, a geographical cum ethnic division was fairly clearly established on the eastern flank of the Truong

Son. The vast majority of the representatives of the other ethnic groups—apart from the Chum and the Khmer—were confined to the highlands, while the vast majority of the much more numerous Viet (along with the Hoa) remained in the lowlands. During the first decades of the twentieth century, the French administration did attempt, mostly through the development of plantation agriculture, to encourage the settlement of Viet people in the Central Highland (Tay Nguyen) provinces and to "sedentarise" the minorities practising itinerant agriculture.[39] But this policy met with limited success and the earlier pattern of spatial and ethnic division was still prevalent after the departure of the colonial authorities.[40] The French were more successful however with the development of plantation crops in provinces located closer to Saigon and in promoting rice production in Cochinchina and particularly in the Mekong delta.[41] Agricultural expansion was facilitated by improved drainage and transport infrastructure as well as by population growth, itself fueled by internal migrations. Thus was established yet another export oriented rice bowl in continental Southeast Asia, rivalling those of Burma and Thailand.

In the Tay Nguyen, the spatial and ethnic division began to evolve more noticeably after 1954. In South Vietnam, the Diem administration established "land development centers" where several tens of thousands of lowlanders, mostly refugees from the North, were resettled.[42] Following frequent clashes between the Kinh settlers and representatives of various minority groups, the resettlement programme was interrupted in the early 1960s. But, after the 1975-76 reunification of North and South Vietnam, land pioneering by lowlanders was renewed with the establishment of the New Economic Zones (N.E.Z.). Such N.E.Z. had already been developed between 1961 and 1966 in North Vietnam itself. From the Red River delta provinces, some one million people had been resettled "in sparsely populated upland areas of Bac Thai, Son La and

Lai Chau provinces",[43] to relieve demographic pressure in the delta and to intensify the settlement of peripheral provinces. After reunification, this reliance on New Economic Zones to decongest more heavily populated regions, notably the Red River delta, and to integrate peripheral and less densely populated ones, particularly the Tay Nguyen, was clearly associated with agricultural expansion. The latter even involved further colonization of those areas of the Mekong delta which were still not totally saturated, including, for strategic reasons, provinces bordering with Khmer Rouge administered Cambodia. Between 1975 and 1990, the amount of land devoted to agriculture throughout the country grew by about 60 per cent (from 4.3 to 6.9 million hectares).[44] This marked rate of increase, which is apparently being maintained, concerned not only rice land—also the object of successful intensification policies—rice having in the process become a major export crop—but, even more, land devoted to exclusively export oriented cash crops (such as coffee), cultivated mostly in the N.E.Z of the Tay Nguyen.

The various figures available concerning the number of people that did move to the N.E.Z. between 1976 and the late 1980s vary considerably: from one and a half to five million. This is due to a number of reasons, including: (1) the turmoil under which these population migrations and transfers occurred, particularly during the few years that followed reunification; (2) the fact that, for a number of reasons, a substantial but undetermined number of settlers did not remain in their N.E.Z. and returned to their region of origin; (3) the notorious and often deliberate unreliability of official Vietnamese statistics; (4) the political sensitivity of the issue of population transfers, particularly those which involve ethnic contacts and sometimes conflicts.

One thing is certain: the combined effect of population migrations—whether or not related to armed conflicts—and of planned massive population transfers, those of the

French colonial authorities and, even more, of the post 1975 reunification communist authorities, has been a spectacular redistribution of population. The magnitude of the transformation of the relative demographic weight of the various regions of the country probably has no equivalent in the region.[45] For example, between 1926 and 1991, the share of the national population living in the Red River delta provinces dropped from nearly 34 per cent to about 20 per cent; another noticeable drop in this relative weight concerns the provinces of what was formerly Annam (today's regions III and IV), whose share of the total population of Vietnam evolved from more than 30 per cent to less than 24. The major gains, in terms of relative proportions, concern the crescent-shaped group of essentially mountainous provinces surrounding the Red River delta (from 9 to 17 per cent), the Mekong river delta and the northern portion of former Cochinchina (in short, the whole of the Nam Bo) and, to a lesser extent, the Tay Nguyen (region V).[46]

As implied above, the demographic filling in of the Tay Nguyen is a relatively recent phenomenon as it was only intensified after the 1975 reunification. It is probably responsible for at least two-thirds of the increase of nearly two and a half million people that occurred in the region's population between 1926 and 1991. And, although the resulting densities are still relatively low, particularly by Vietnamese standards,[47] the current expansion of the N.E.Z. is focused on the Central Highlands,[48] with the consequence that the former predominance of ethnic minorities groups is gradually being diluted.[49] Whatever the case, as in the Philippines and in Indonesia, redistribution is a predominant pattern in the twentieth-century evolution of the population of Vietnam. And in a context where the Nam Tien, or southward drive, seems to be giving way to a Tay Tien or westward drive, the Viet people are increasingly pushing their way out of their traditional lowland domain.

Thailand: A Unique Case?

Although the size of its territory is equivalent to 27 per cent of Indonesia's, the extent of Thailand's agricultural land is greater: according to the FAO, about 23 versus 20 million hectares in 1991.[50] This means that nearly 45 per cent of the country's territory is devoted to agriculture, an exceptional proportion, unrivalled in Southeast as well as East Asia, and only surpassed by Bangladesh and a few European countries such as Denmark and Hungary.[51]

Associated with its overall economic expansion, Thailand's centrally planned agricultural expansion began during the reign of King Chulalongkorn (1868-1910),[52] and has continued unabated throughout the twentieth century, the rate of growth having even increased since the 1940s. Between 1910 and 1940, the amount of land devoted to agriculture was multiplied by two; between 1940 and 1970, it was further multiplied by a factor of three and between then and 1991, it has at least doubled again.[53] Overall, during that 80 odd year period (1910-91), the expanse of agricultural land has increased elevenfold. Over the same period, population grew from about eight or nine million to just over 55 million, a sixfold to sevenfold increase. Few if any other countries in Asia have managed to maintain for so long a pace of agricultural expansion that surpasses of their population growth to such an extent.

At least two other characteristics distinguish Thailand's agricultural growth within Southeast Asia. First, contrary to what has occurred in countries such as Indonesia and Vietnam, Thailand has relied on territorial expansion of agriculture and very little on intensification. For example, while in Indonesia and Vietnam, average rice yields have increased by 34 and 50 per cent respectively, between 1980 and 1991, in Thailand the growth rate has been limited to five per cent.[54] In fact the country's rice yields remain among the lowest in the region. The national average for the years 1990 to 1992, which was even inferior to that of Laos, stood at about 60 per cent of the Vietnamese average or at 45 per cent of Indonesia's admittedly exceptional achievements. In addition, improved irrigation infrastructure and the practice of double cropping remain much less developed than in most other countries of the region.[55]

Second, this phenomenal increase in the amount of land devoted to agriculture has not been accompanied by massive migrations or population transfers. Although the settlement of Thai peasants in some of the peripheral regions, particularly in or near predominantly tribal areas, such as in the North or along the Burmese border, has been encouraged,[56] no major frontier development programme, comparable to those of the Philippines, Indonesia, Vietnam or even Malaysia, has been engineered by the Thai State. Thailand did encourage the spread of agriculture, in part by establishing colonization perimeters and thereby increased steadily its agricultural production and export base, while relieving agrarian pressure in the central plain; but this sponsored colonization has remained much less important than spontaneous land opening by individual agriculturalists.[57] In other words, agricultural expansion has not been linked to any plan to move large numbers of people from densely populated parts of the country to less densely populated ones. Nevertheless, such movement has occurred not only in the Central plain but also in almost all the peripheral regions, and has been instrumental in maintaining a relative equilibrium in the country's population distribution.

For example, although the Northeast has been the object of even more exceptional agricultural expansion, particularly since the early 1960s,[58] its share of the nation's total population has hardly varied. In fact, since the beginning of the century, it has remained at about one-third of the national total (Table I). The same can be said of the Central region itself, whose own percentage share has only increased from 31 to 33. Some contraction in the distribution of the nation's population is noticeable, but it has remained quite limited, only the North and the South having seen their relative share decrease, respectively by two and a half and less than one per cent. Overall, the evolution in the relative demographic weight of the various provinces and regions has been even more balanced than in the Philippines.

TABLE I
THAILAND: EVOLUTION OF POPULATION BY MAJOR REGION, 1919-90

Administrative Region	*Percentage of National Population* 1919	1947	1960	1990
Central	30.9	31.1	31.5	32.9
Bangkok	5.2	6.8	8.1	10.8
Southeast	5.4	5.3	5.4	5.9
North-East	33.6	35.6	34.2	34.9
North	21.9	20.9	21.8	19.4
South	13.6	12.4	12.5	12.8
TOTAL (%)	100.0	100.0	100.0	100.0
Total population ('000)	9,207	17,443	26,258	54,532

Sources: For 1919, 1947 and 1960: Constance M. Wilson, *Thailand: A Handbook of Historical Statistics* (Boston: G. K. Hall, 1983); for 1990; 1990 Population and Housing Census (Bangkok, 1992).

Within each major administrative region, some redistribution has occurred, some of it obviously fed by migrations from without, for example, in the Central plain, in favor of a few of the provinces in its upper part (particularly the Sukhotai basin) and of the Bangkok metropolitan region, in the lower part. In fact, the only significant increase in the relative demographic weight of a given region has been that of the so-called BMA (Bangkok Metropolitan Area): from just over five per cent of the national population total in 1919 to nearly eleven per cent in 1990.[59] Other forms of redistribution within the regions are noticeable, such as in the Northeast with a decrease in the relative demographic weight of the easternmost province, Ubon Ratchatani and its neighbour, Yasothon, balanced by an increase for a few of the provinces located further north, such as Udon Thani and Nong Khai, facing the Laotian capital of Vientiane across the Mekong river.

In itself, the expansion of Thailand's agriculture is characterized by several other features, some of which are unique within the region. First, as implied above, it has been achieved much more by a gradual, proximate expansion of existing agricultural land, rather than by the opening up of new lands to be found in peripheral and sparsely populated areas. Both Harald Uhlig and Philip Hirsh captured that specificity when they compared Thailand's agricultural expansion during the early twentieth century to that of the first phase of European agricultural expansion during the Middle Ages.[60]

Second, as pointed out by Uhlig,[61] spontaneous land expansion has played a key role. Usually carried out without the direct support of State planning by individual agriculturalists or by small communities, it has, however, been frequently sponsored, even financed by various interest groups—such as agricultural or forest product merchants—intent on obtaining additional supplies of marketable wood or cash crops.[62]

Third, the central State has nevertheless played a crucial if at times indirect role in supporting spontaneous agricultural expansion, by its massive investments in infrastructure. These include drainage and irrigation works but also, and even more important, a road and railway construction programme of a magnitude unrivalled among

Southeast Asian countries. As pointed out by David Feeny, these investments in transport infrastructure, sometimes at the expense of irrigation works, were essential to consolidate precarious, peripheral or marginal settlements, and at times even resulted from strategic considerations.[63]

Fourth, while remaining a world leader in terms of rice exports, Thailand has managed to diversify what was a nearly monocultural production base. In 1920, rice was planted on 98 per cent of all cultivated land; since then that share has decreased gradually and irrevocably to less than 50 per cent nowadays. Although, between 1920 and 1986, this has taken place in a context where the amount of land devoted to the cultivation of rice has been multiplied by four, that rate of expansion has been largely surpassed by other crops, among which are rubber, cotton, tobacco, soya beans, corn, cassava and sugar cane. In the Northeast alone, in 1940, some one hundred thousand hectares were devoted to the cultivation of the latter three crops; by the late 1980s, the figure was nearly five million hectares.[64]

Thailand's nationwide and century long agricultural expansion is certainly one of the important factors behind another essential feature of the country's geography: a relatively well-balanced population distribution. For, notwithstanding the highly exceptional share of the nation's urban population that is concentrated in the Bangkok Metropolitan Area, the territory of Thailand is more thoroughly occupied and its population more evenly distributed than is the case for most other countries in Southeast Asia. This can be assessed from two different angles. First, in some countries, such as Laos, the occupation and therefore the mastery of much of the national territory remains tenuous if only because of very low average population densities. Second, even if the average population density of Thailand (just over one hundred persons per square kilometre) is less than half of that of Vietnam or the Philippines, regional population distribution is better balanced. In nearly all of the other countries of the regions—with the notable exception of the city-state of Singapore—there exist huge contrasts between regions of high density and others that are very sparsely populated. Even in Laos, such contrasts occur between the ribbon-like valley of the Mekong river, particularly as it follows the Thai border, and the highlands.[65] In fact most countries, with the exception of Thailand and to some extent Vietnam and the Philippines—and once again Singapore—contain some nearly empty regions. In Thailand, only provinces bordering with Burma still have areas with relatively sparse populations, somewhat like Palawan in the Philippines or some of the northernmost and Central Highlands provinces of Vietnam.

ON THE ORIGINALITY AND DYNAMISM OF STATE FORMATION IN SOUTHEAST ASIA

In each of the four countries examined, as suggested in the introduction, and as illustrated throughout the text, agricultural expansion has: (1) been instrumental in relieving agrarian pressure in the more densely populated core areas; (2) served to feed a growing demand for agricultural exports; (3) helped to consolidate central State control over peripheral and border areas; (4) along with this geopolitical process, contributed to the integration or even assimilation of minority peoples; (5) resulted in a redistribution of population throughout the national territory. All of these interrelated processes have been at play in the Philippines, Indonesia, Vietnam and Thailand, albeit at different times and with varying intensities. Probably the most intense and uniformly significant one has been population redistribution.

As also pointed out above, agricultural expansion as a tool of population redistribution and of State territorial formation is not unique to Southeast Asia. Several examples exist elsewhere in Asia and in Europe.[66] But, in Southeast

Asia, it does seem to play a central role about which the following points and propositions should be made or emphasized.

Agricultural expansion appears as an exceptionally crucial feature in the historical and contemporary construction and consolidation of most of the territorial states that make up the region. It can be estimated that, since the early 1950s, in the Philippines, Indonesia, Vietnam and Thailand alone, between 25 to 30 million people migrated to pioneer areas. Furthermore, within the region, this expansion has not been unique to these four countries. For example, although covering smaller areas and involving smaller numbers of people, Malaysia's land development programmes have in relative terms been just as spectacular. Financed by massive State investments, they have played a key role in national agrarian and agricultural development policies and have been associated with the consolidation of Central State control over previously sparsely populated areas, particularly in the internal regions of Peninsular Malaysia.[67] As for contemporary Cambodia, its case is rather unique in that, during the bloody reign of the Khmer Rouge (1975-89), forced migrations, coupled with agricultural expansion, were employed in an attempt to consolidate State territorial control.[68]

Agricultural expansion may in some cases make up for slowness in agricultural intensification, as in Thailand, while in others, as in Indonesia, the two may be combined. For the motives behind agricultural expansion are not uniform through time and space. Important differences exist between different historical periods and different forms of agricultural expansion, whether spontaneous, State sponsored, gradual or massive. The same caveat applies to different forms of intensification, such as, on the one hand, those that occurred in the late nineteenth and early twentieth centuries in the three great rice bowls of continental Southeast Asia, when they were in fact combined with expansion and, on the other, those that are associated with the contemporary Green Revolution. But whatever the combination of motives behind agricultural expansion, and the tools relied on to pursue it, one of its basic consequences appears to be population redistribution or, at least, as the case of Thailand suggests, regional demographic consolidation.

Whether or not the actual expansion and the actual migrations are initiated by the State, the latter must eventually intervene, if only to ensure, consolidate and at the same time legitimate its control and its administration of the territory and its inhabitants. Of all the propositions made here, this one is particularly crucial. In the Southeast Asia cases examined, to which the Malaysian one could surely be added, the consolidation of the State and its strengthening have relied on and in turn allowed for agricultural expansion. As with the development of irrigated agriculture, which is closely related to the development of a strong state, a point repeatedly made by Pierre Gourou in several of his works,[69] agricultural expansion needs, or eventually calls for, and contributes to a strong State. Another of Gourou's major points,[70] often reemphasized by various authors, who do not always recognize Gourou's contribution and seem to attribute it to Clifford Geertz,[71] is that there exists a close relationship between high population densities and irrigated rice cultivation, the latter requiring more labour than other food crops and at the same time generating more food per unit of cultivated land. The same argument can be made, although with less force, about the development of the frontier. In Southeast Asia, the latter generally involves the expansion of forms of agriculture—wet rice cultivation and cash crops—which are generally labour intensive and thus contribute to strong population growth within the colonization areas themselves and to overall national population growth.[72]

This points to a fundamental question, raised by Hirschman,[73] concerning the reasons behind the maintenance of high national fertility rates throughout most of Southeast Asia until the 1960s. According to Hirschman, this fertility, which has been a major cause behind the regions' continuing strong population growth, should have begun to slow down earlier than it has.[74] We suggest that this might be due, at least in part, to the relatively important role played, in overall national population growth, by higher natural population growth rates in frontier areas. While further research, well beyond the scope of this paper, would be needed to demonstrate this, there is some evidence that fertility rates are much higher in the agricultural expansion areas than in the core areas.[75]

The efficiency of the territorial consolidation of the State is usually closely related to the degree to which it is accompanied by the creation or the development of a landed peasantry, such peasantry being not only more tied to the land but also to the State, which finds an interest in guaranteeing its status. Agricultural expansion generally provides an ideal scenario for the increase in the number and proportion of land-tied peasant households.

Of course, among the motives behind agricultural expansion, population redistribution or territorial consolidation may not even be the most dominant. Economic and commercial considerations may, at times, be even more crucial: for agricultural expansion and economic growth are inherently linked, notably when frontier agriculture generates an exportable surplus. Nor must population redistribution policies depend only on agricultural ones: industrial and urban policies also have a determinant impact on migrations.

By its very nature, agricultural expansion has a tremendous impact on the land: it modifies its use, particularly in that it generally takes the place, precisely, of the forest. As it turns out, throughout Southeast Asia, the retreat of the forest has been massive over the last decades.[76] While this retreat is linked to a number of complex factors, these appear closely articulated, and agricultural expansion is often the central factor. If, in some contexts, such as in Kalimantan, the main cause of deforestation seems to be logging, in Sumatra it is clearly agricultural expansion.[77] The two are often interactive, as in the Philippines or in Malaysia.[78] As for the hardy but erroneous belief that minority peoples, through their traditional practice of swidden agriculture, are a major cause of deforestation, evidence keeps accumulating as to the actual preeminence of land expansion as the real cause behind the increase of either "amateur" swiddening by land pioneers, and related fuel wood consumption, or of slash and burn practices by tribal peoples in ecologically fragile environments.[79]

In causing the retreat of the forest, agricultural expansion eventually and inevitably brings about the stabilization or even "sedentarisation" of the "nomads" of the forest. That process seems to meet with the needs of modern State formation, which includes, as mentioned earlier, a territorially legitimizing alliance with a landed peasantry. As J.E. Spencer pointed out clearly in 1966, with reference to shifting cultivators in Southeastern Asia, settled agriculturalists are easier to tax.[80] And as Roger Brunet so aptly added: "The State is panoptic: it likes to see those that it likes, and even more those that dislike it."[81]

Finally, while very few, if any, of the above-mentioned processes are unique to Southeast Asia or to the four countries on which this study has been focused, their articulation as well as their outcome do appear unique. More than in Europe, more than in other regions of Southern or even of Eastern Asia, agricultural expansion seems to have played and to continue to play a key role in

State formation.[82] A current trend in most countries of the industrial world and even of the Third World, particularly in Africa, is for the growth of population to be associated with an increasing contraction of the national ecumene, a densification of the centres and a desertion of the margins. In Southeast Asia, the opposite is occurring in a context where the rhythm of agricultural expansion—often along with agricultural intensification—and production is in fact surpassing that of population increase. And that, ultimately, is one of the essential components behind the current and original dynamism of State formation and overall economic development in the Southeast Asian region.

NOTES

1. Jean-Luc Maurer, *Modernisation agricole, developpement economique et changement social*. Le riz, la terre et l'homme a Java (Paris: Presses Universitaires de France, 1986); Anne Booth, *Agricultural Development in Indonesia* (Sydney: Allen and Unwin, 1988), pp. 100-138.
2. Nicos Alexandratos (ed.), *World Agriculture Toward 2000, an FAO Study* (New York: New York University Press, 1988), chapter 4.
3. R. Wikkramatileke, "Federal Land Development Authority in West Malaysia 1957-1971", *Pacific Viewpoint* 13, 1 (1972): 62-86; Shamsul Bahrin and Lee Boon Thong, FELDA. *Three Decades of Evolution* (Kuala Lumpur: FELDA, 1988).
4. Rodolphe De Koninck, "The Peasantry as the Territorial Spearhead of the State in Southeast Asia: The Case of Vietnam", Sojourn. *Social Issues in Southeast Asia* 11, 2 (1996): 231-58.
5. *Ibid.* and "La paysannerie et l'Etat en Asie du Sud-Est: une affaire de compromis ... a suivre", *Espaces Temps* 53 (1993): 130-44.
6. Rodolphe De Koninck, "Forest Policies in Southeast Asia: Taming Nature or Taming People?", in *Le defi forestier en Asie du Sud-Est / The Challenge of the Forest in Southeast*

Asia, ed. Rodolphe De Koninck (Quebec: Universite Laval, Documents du GERAC, 7, 1994), pp. 33-48.

7. Charles Hirschman, "Population and Society in Twentieth-Century Southeast Asia", *Journal of Southeast Asian Studies* 25, 2 (1994): 381-416 (397 and 398).

8. See, for example, Robin J. Pryor, ed., *Migration and Development in Southeast Asia* (Kuala Lumpur: Oxford University Press, 1979); G. W. Jones and H. V. Richter (ed.), *Population Resettlement Programs in Southeast Asia* (Canberra: Australian National University, Development Studies Centre, Monograph no. 30, 1982); A. Pagonini (ed.), *Migration from the Philippines* (Quezon City: Scalabrinians, 1984); Walther Manshard and William B. Morgan (eds.), *Agricultural Expansion and Pioneer Settlements in the Humid Tropics* (Tokyo: The United Nations University, 1988); Robert R. Reed, *Patterns of Migration in Southeast Asia* (Berkeley: Center for South and South East Asian Studies, University of California, 1990); Jan Bremen, *Labor Migration and Rural Transformation in Colonial Asia* (Amsterdam: Free University Press for Center for Asian Studies); Chang Kok Eng, "International Migration in a Rapidly Developing Country: The Case of Peninsular Malaysia", *Malaysian Journal of Tropical Geography* 25, 2 (1994): 69-78; Charles Hirschman, "Population and Society in Twentieth-Century Southeast Asia".

9. See, for example, Charles Tilly, "Reflections on the History of European State Making", in *The Formation of National States in Western Europe*, ed. Charles Tilly (Princeton: Princeton University Press, 1975), pp. 3-83.

10. Charles Hirschman, "Population and Society in Twentieth-Century Southeast Asia", p. 413.

11. Brian Fegan, "The Philippines: Agrarian Stagnation Under a Decaying Regime", in *Agrarian Transformations. Local Processes and the State in Southeast Asia*, ed. Gillian Hart, Andrew Turton and Benjamin White (Berkeley: University of California Press, 1989), p. 127.

12. Karl J. Pelzer, *Pioneer Settlement in the Asiatic Tropics* (New York: American Geographical Society, 1945), p. 129.

13. Pierre Gourou, *Les pays tropicaux*, 4th ed. (Paris: Presses Universitaires de France, 1966), p. 122 sq.

14. Pelzer, *Pioneer Settlements*, p. 134.

15. Benedict J. Kerkvliet, *The Huk Rebellion. A Study of Peasant Revolt in The Philippines* (Berkeley: University of California Press, 1977), p. 239.

16. Shamsul Bahrin, "Rural Resettlement Programmes in the Asean Region", in *Beyond Settlement: A Comparative Study of the Impact of Resettlement Programmes in Southeast Asia*, ed. Shamsul Bahrin (Singapore: Institute of Southeast Asian Studies, 1988), pp. 1-28 (3).

17. Charles A. Fisher, *South-East Asia. A Social, Economic and Political Geography* (London: Methuen, second edition, 1966), p. 711; National Economic and Development Authority, Philippine Statistical Yearbook 1986 (Manila, 1987), p. 278.

18. *Philippines Statistical Yearbook* 1986, pp. 278-80.

19. In 1990, average population densities, in persons per square kilometre, were as follows: Philippines: 202; Luzon, 286; Cebu, 520; Negros, Leyte and Bohol all above 225; Mindanao, 136; cf. Rodolphe De Koninck, L'Asie du Sud-Est (Paris: Masson, 1994), p. 103.

20. To facilitate the comparison between the two dates, the base maps have been standardized, that is aligned on the provincial divisions as they stood in 1990. Recent editions of the Philippines Statistical Yearbook do in fact provide figures on the basis of that contemporary provincial breakdown.

21. See, for example, Pelzer, *Pioneer Settlements*; Joan Hardjono, *Transmigration in Indonesia* (Jakarta: Oxford University Press, 1977) and "The Indonesian Transmigration Programme in Historical Perspective", *International Migration* 26, 4 (1988): 427-38; Daniel Benoit, P. Levang, M. Pain and O. Sevin, *Transmigration and Spontaneous Migrations in Indonesia* (Paris and Jakarta: ORSTOM, Departemen Transmigrasi, 1989); Muriel Charras and Marc Pain, M. (eds.), *Spontaneous Settlements*

in Indonesia: Agricultural Pioneers in Southern Sumatra (Paris and Jakarta: ORSTOM, CNRS and Departemen Transmigrasi, 1993).

22. Benoit et al., *Transmigration*, p. 106.

23. Marcel Le Glay, "La Gaule romanisee", in *Histoire de la France rurale*, ed. Georges Duby et al. (Paris: Seuil, vol. 1, 1975), pp. 195-285 (239).

24. Owen Lattimore, *Inner Asian Frontiers of China* (London: Oxford University Press, 1940); Studies in Frontier History. Collected Papers 1928-1958 (London: Oxford University Press, 1962).

25. Augustin Berque, *La riziere et la banquise*. Colonisation et changement culturel a Hokkaido (Paris: Publications Orientalistes de France, 1980), p. 64.

26. *Ibid.*, p. 65.

27. Karl Fassbender and Susanne Erbe, *Towards a New Home: Indonesia's Managed Mass Migration*. Transmigration between Poverty, Economics and Ecology (Hamburg: Verlag Weltarchiv GmbH, 1990), p. 30.

28. Marcus Colchester, "The Struggle for Land. Tribal Peoples in the Face of the Transmigration Programme", *The Ecologist* 16, 2-3 (1986): 99-110.

29. World Bank, *Indonesia Transmigration Sector Review* (Washington, D.C., 1990); see also Spontaneous Settlements in *Indonesia*, ed. Muriel Charras and Marc Pain.

30. Muriel Charras, "L'Indonesie: le premier archipel du monde", in *Asie du Sud-Est, Oceanie*, ed. Benoit Antheaume et al. (Paris: Belin, 1995), pp. 42-76 (51 and 67); Graeme J. Hugo, Terence H. Hull, Valerie J. Hull and Gavin W. Jones, *The Demographic Dimension in Indonesian Development* (Singapore: Oxford University Press, 1987), p. 196.

31. De Koninck, *L'Asie du Sud-Est*, p. 134. This refers to actual land devoted to agriculture and does not take into account the increase in cropped land, resulting essentially from the increase in the practice of annual double cropping of rice.

32. Booth, *Agricultural Development*, p. 41.

33. *Ibid.*, pp. 43-44.

34. These statements concern the large islands and groups of islands and not necessarily all components of the latter. Some islands (such as Bali), provinces (such as Southeast Sulawesi) or kabupaten (such as Jayapura in Irian Jaya), have been the object of specific and different forms of demographic evolution.

35. Fisher, *South-East Asia*, p. 290; Widjojo Nitisastro, *Population Trends in Indonesia* (Ithaca: Cornell University Press, 1970), p. 62.

36. Daniel Benoit and Olivier Sevin, "L'emigration javanaise: mythes et realites", *Annales de geographie* 571 (1993): 255-76.

37. Hugo et al., *The Demographic Dimension*, p. 106.

38. Le Thanh Khoi, *Histoire du Viet Nam des origines a 1858* (Paris: Sudestasie, 1981).

39. Gerald C. Hickey, *Sons of the Mountains: Ethnohistory of the Vietnamese Central Highlands to 1954* (New Haven: Yale University Press, 1982), p. 309 sq.; Ron Hill "Primitives to Peasants?: The Sedentarisation of the Nomads in Vietnam", *Pacific Viewpoint* 26, 2 (1985): 449-57.

40. See, for example, the map entitled "Ethnolinguistic Groups of Mainland Southeast Asia", in Frank M. LeBar, Gerald C. Hickey, John K. Musgrave and Robert Lee Williams, *Ethnic Groups of Mainland Southeast Asia* (New Haven: Yale University Press, 1964). A simplified version can be found in De Koninck, "The Peasantry as the Territorial Spearhead".

41. Pierre Gourou, *L'Asie* (Paris: Hachette, fourth edition, 1964), p. 330.

42. Gerald Cannon Hickey, *Free in the Forest: Ethnohistory of the Vietnamese Central Highlands 1954-1975* (New Haven: Yale University Press, 1982), p. 6.

43. Gavin W. Jones and Stewart E. Fraser, "Population Resettlement Policies in Vietnam", in *Population Resettlement Programs in Southeast Asia*, ed. G.W. Jones and H.V. Richter (Canberra: Australian National University, Development Studies Centre, Monograph 30, 1982), p. 115.

44. *The Far East and Australasia* 1993 (London: Europa Publications, 1993), p. 956.

45. The 1926 figures and the location of the 1926 provincial boundaries relied on from J. Bouault, Geographie de l'Indochine (Hanoi: Imprimerie d'Extreme-Orient, 1930). In Bouault's book, no single map represents the provincial divisions for the whole of what corresponds to contemporary Vietnam. Rather, different maps provide the information separately, for portions of what was then Tonkin, Annam and Cochinchina; furthermore these maps are drawn at different scales varying between 1:3,300,300 and 1: 5,000,000. However, Bouault's maps seem to have been carefully drawn and although it is obvious that, in adapting them, we had to resort to some amount of approximation, we are confident that the final result is reasonably reliable. It should also be noted that, to facilitate the comparison between the 1926 and 1991 maps, the international boundaries of Vietnam were standardized, for the two maps, on the basis of the 1991 one. The regrouping of the 1926 provinces along the lines of the seven contemporary regions also entailed a number of small adjustments.

46. Region V includes four provinces: Kon Turn, Gia Lai, Dac Lac and Lam Dong; it corresponds, roughly, to the area which, in 1926, encompassed the three provinces of Kon Turn (since divided into Kon Turn and Gia Lai), Darlac (today's Dac Lac) and Haut Donnai, the sizes and boundaries of all these provinces having been modified since.

47. In 1991, population densities, as measured in persons per square kilometer, varied between 72 (Lam Dong) and 24 (Kon Tum), with a regional average of 50, versus 207 for the country as a whole.

48. Although Vietnamese Government officials remain vague

about future expansion prospects, evidence from the ground, as seen by the first author on the occasion of field visits to several N.E.Z. during April and May 1995, seems to indicate that such prospects are substantial.

49. Grant Evans, "Internal Colonialism in the Central Highlands of Vietnam", Sojourn. *Journal of Social Issues in Southeast Asia* 9, 1 (1992): 274-304; Rodolphe De Koninck, Tran Dac Dan, Yann Roche and Olivier Lundquist, "Les fronts pionniers du Centre du Vietnam: evolution demographique et empreinte toponymique", *Annales de geographie* 105, 590 (1996): 395-412; De Koninck, "The Peasantry as the Territorial Spearhead".

50. *FAO Production Yearbook* 1992.

51. Rodolphe De Koninck, *Le monde a la carte* (Quebec: Fischer Presses, volume II, third edition, 1995).

52. Leslie E. Small, "Historical Development of the Greater Chao Phrya Water Control Project: an Economic Appraisal", *Journal of the Siam Society* 61, 1 (1973): 1-24; David B. Johnston, "Opening a Frontier. The Expansion of Rice Cultivation in Central Thailand in the 1890's", *Contributions to Asian Studies* 9 (1976): 27-44; David Feeny, *The Political Economy of Productivity: Thai Agricultural Development, 1880-1975* (Vancouver: University of British Columbia Press, 1982).

53. Some official sources are even more "generous" concerning Thailand's agricultural land. According to the FAO, in 1991 total agricultural area stood at slightly over 23 million hectares (or 45.1 per cent of the country's total land area); however, according to the Thai Forestry Sector Master Plan (Bangkok: Royal Forestry Department, 1993), it had reached more than twenty-nine million hectares (or 57 per cent of the country's total land area). Drawn from satellite imagery, the latter figures probably include fallow land. Not infrequently, data compiled from satellite imagery and aerial photography tend to overestimate the amount of land devoted to agriculture. "Because cloud cover is at its minimum in the dry season, aerial photography and satellite image surveys are generally conducted in that season. Given that much of the cropping in Thailand is

rain fed, it is difficult in the dry season to distinguish between areas that were cropped in the previous wet season and areas that were fallow; thus the tendency for these surveys to overestimate the area under cultivation": see David Feeny, "Agricultural Expansion and Forest Depletion in Thailand. 1900-1975", in *World Deforestation in the Twentieth Century*, ed. J. F. Richards and R. P. Tucker (Durham, NC: Duke University Press, 1988), p. 282.

54. *FAO Production Yearbook* 1993; De Koninck, L'Asie du Sud-Est, p. 293.

55. Randolph Barker, Robert W. Herdt and Beth Rose, *The Rice Economy of Asia* (Washington, D.C.: Resources for the Future, 1985), p. 98; World Bank, *World Development Report* 1994. Infrastructure for Development (Oxford: Oxford University Press, 1994).

56. Robert J. Muscat, *The Fifth Tiger. A Study of Thai Development Policy* (New York: M.E. Sharpe, 1994), p. 233.

57. Harald Uhlig, "Spontaneous and Planned Settlement in South-East Asia", in *Agricultural Expansion and Pioneer Settlements in the Humid Tropics*, ed. Walther Manshard and William B. Morgan (Tokyo: The United Nations University, 1988), p. 13.

58. Detailed and reliable figures per province and region are hard to come by. It is at least possible to calculate that, between 1939 and 1985, the Northeast's share of the nation's rice land has increased from 31 to 50 per cent. See Robert L. Pendleton, "Land Use in Northeastern Thailand", *Geographical Review* 33, 1 (1943): 15-41 and Statistical Yearbook 1987-88 Thailand (Bangkok: National Statistical Office, 1988).

59. Constance Wilson, *Thailand. A Handbook of Historical Statistics* (Boston: G. K. Hall, 1983), pp. 32-34 and 1990 Population and Housing Census (Bangkok: National Statistical Office, 1992).

60. Harald Uhlig, "Spontaneous and Planned Settlement in South-East Asia", 1984, p. 14; Philip Hirsch, "Spontaneous Land Settlement and Deforestation in Thailand", in *Changing Tropical Forests: Historical Perspectives on*

Today's Challenges in Asia, ed. J. Dargavel et al. (Canberra: Centre for Resource and Environmental Studies, 1988), pp. 359-76 (360). On Europe, see Georges Duby, Guerriers et paysans, [VII.sup.e]-[XII.sup.e] s. Premier essor de l'economie europeenne (Paris: Gallimard, 1973); L'economie rurale et la vie des campagnes dans l'Occident medieval (Paris: Flammarion, 2 vol., 1977).

61. Uhlig, "Spontaneous and Planned Settlement in South-East Asia", p. 14.

62. Larry Lohman, "Land, Power and Forest Colonization in Thailand", in *The Struggle for Land and the Fate of the Forest*, ed. Marcus Colchester and Larry Lohman (London: Zed Books, 1993), pp. 198-227 (207).

63. David Feeny, *The Political Economy*, p. 80 sq; see also Fisher, *South-East Asia*, p. 490; Philip Hirsch, "Deforestation and Development in Thailand", *Singapore Journal of Tropical Geography* 8, 2 (1987): 129-38 (137) and "Spontaneous Land Settlement", p. 366.

64. Raymond Blanadet, *L'Asie du Sud-Est. Nouvelle puissance economique* (Nancy: Presses Universitaires de Nancy, 1992), p. 262.

65. These contrasts are not evident because of the scale and of the population density categories used. But they definitely are when population distribution is represented with more precision. See, for example, W. G. East, O. H. K. Spate and Charles A. Fisher, *The Changing Map of Asia*, 5th ed. (London: Methuen, 1971), p. 246 and Warwick Neville, "The Distribution of Population in Southeast Asia", *New Zealand Journal of Geography* (Oct. 1990): 2-7.

66. See, for example, as already mentioned, Augustin Berque, *La riziere et la banquise. Colonisation et changement culturel a Hokkaido*, p. 64 and Charles Tilly, "Reflections on the History of European State Making", pp. 3-83.

67. Rodolphe De Koninck, "Enjeux et strategies spatiales de l'Etat en Malaysia", *Herodote* 21 (1981): 84-115; "Les politiques du developpement agricole en Malaysia ou l'impatience de l'Etat tutelaire", *Archipel* 31 (1986): 131-53.

68. See, for example, M. A. Martin, *Le mal cambodgien* (Paris: Hachette, 1989).

69. See, for example, *Les paysans du delta tonkinois* (Paris: Ecole Francaise d'Extreme-Orient, 1936); La terre et l'homme en Extreme-Orient (Paris: Colin, 1940); Riz et civilisation (Paris: Fayard, 1984).

70. Repeatedly made in the above-mentioned works as well as in L'utilisation du sol en Indochine Francaise (Paris: Centre de politique etrangere, 1940), Les pays tropicaux (Paris: Presses Universitaires de France, 1947) and L'Asie (Paris: Hachette, 1953).

71. See, for example, Hirschman, "Population and Society in Twentieth-Century Southeast Asia", p. 397, referring to Clifford Geertz's *Agricultural Involution: The Processes of Agricultural Change in Indonesia* (Berkeley: University of California Press, 1963).

72. Charles Hirschman emphasizes this point in his "Population and Society in Twentieth-Century Southeast Asia", pp. 398, 399 and 408.

73. *Ibid.*, p. 414.

74. *Ibid.*, p. 407 sq.

75. See, for example, David S. Gibbons, Rodolphe De Koninck and Ibrahim Hasan, *Agricultural Modernization, Poverty and Inequality* (Farnborough: Saxon House, 1980), p. 15; Charras and Pain (eds.), *Spontaneous Settlements in Indonesia*, p. 74.

76. See, for example, De Koninck (ed.), *The Challenge of the Forest in Southeast Asia*; or Stephane Bernard and Rodolphe De Koninck, "The Retreat of the Forest in Southeast Asia: A Cartographic Assessment", *Singapore Journal of Tropical Geography* 17, 1 (1996): 1-14.

77. Frederic Durand, *Les forets en Asie du Sud-Est. Recul et exploitation: le cas de l'Indonesie* (Paris: L'Harmattan, 1994).

78. David Kummer, *Deforestation in the Postwar Philippines* (Chicago: Chicago University Press, 1992); Wilfrido D. Cruz

and Maria C. Cruz, "Population Pressure and Deforestation in the Philippines", *ASEAN Economic Bulletin* 7, 2 (1990): 200-212; Stephane Bernard, "Le defi forestier dans la peninsule malaise" (M.A. diss., Universite Laval, Quebec, 1995).

79. See, for example, Jean Boulbet, Paysans de la foret (Paris: Ecole Francaise d'Extreme-Orient, 1975); Michael Dove, "Theories of Swidden Agriculture and the Political Economy of Ignorance", *Agroforestry Systems* 1 (1983): 85-99. Hirsch, *Deforestation and Development*, p. 6; Thai Forestry Sector Master Plan. Subsectorial Plan for People and Forestry Environment (Bangkok: Royal Forestry Department, 1993), p. 17; Feeny, *Agricultural Expansion and Forest Depletion*, p. 121; Orawan Kooachoraen and Darunee Paisarnpanichul, "Promotion of Commercial Crop Cultivation", in *The Future of People and Forests in Thailand after the Logging Ban*, ed. Pinkaew Leungaramsri and Noel Rajesh (Bangkok: Project for Ecological Recovery, 1992), pp. 88 and 94; Do Dinh San, *Shifting Cultivation in Vietnam: Its Social, Economic and Environmental Values Relative to Alternative Land Use* (London: International Institute for Environment and Development, 1992), p. 37.

80. J.E. Spencer, *Shifting Cultivation in Southeastern Asia* (Berkeley: University of California Press, 1966), p. 3. Concerning the advantages for the State to "widen access to land", to sedentarize the nomads, to "extend the tax base" and to control migration for those very purposes, see Bremen, *Labour Migration*, pp. 4, 5 and 72.

81. Roger Brunet and Olivier Dollfus, *Mondes nouveaux* (Paris: Hachette, 1990), p. 63. In French, the statement reads as follows: "L'Etat est panoptique: il aime voir ceux qu'il aime et surtout ceux quine l'aiment pas". This need for the modem State to territorialize its control was emphasized several times by Rodolphe De Koninck. See for example "Enjeux et strategies spatiales de l'Etat en Malaysia"; "Pourquoi les paysans? Interrogations sur la territorialite de l'agriculture familiale", *Cahiers de geographie du Quebec* 29, 73-74 (1984): 261-74; "La paysannerie comme fer de lance territorial de l'Etat: le cas de la Malaysia", *Cahiers des sciences humaines* (ORSTOM) 22, 3-4 (1986): 355-70;

"Qui a peur de la foret? Les veritables enjeux de la foret tropicale", *Cahiers de geographie du Quebec* 36, 99 (1992): 503-514. With specific reference to the forest realm, see Nancy Lee Peluso, Peter Vandergeest and Lesley Potter, "Social Aspects of Forestry in Southeast Asia: A Review of Postwar Trends in the Scholarly Literature", *Journal of Southeast Asian Studies* 26, 1 (1995): 196-218.

82. On this issue of the relationship between agricultural expansion and State formation, see Steve Dery, "Expansion agricole et deforestation: le modele sud-est asiatique", *Cahiers de geographie du Quebec* 30, 109 (1996): 29-48.

4

PUBLIC LAND FOR THE PEOPLE: THE INSTITUTIONAL BASIS OF COMMUNITY FORESTRY IN THAILAND

—Jin Sato

Thailand is one of the few countries where communal rights to productive forests have no formal recognition. This does not mean that they are non-existent, however; in reality, we see many examples of communal forest use throughout the country, especially in the northern region.[1] This paradox, and the newly proposed Community Forestry Bill which is supposed to fill in the gap, are the subjects of this article.

The specific issue addressed here is the institutional basis of community forestry in Thailand with a focus on 'public land', which local people can access collectively to support their livelihood. With a majority of people living in the countryside, policies related to land use certainly have a significant impact on quality of life. Yet because state intervention regarding land use has been carried out by various government agencies without much coordination among them, repeated confusion and conflicts have occurred, not only between farmers and the state but also among the agencies themselves. The key agencies include the Royal Forest Department (RFD) and Agricultural Land Reform Office (ALRO) in the Ministry of Agriculture and Cooperatives and the Department of Lands under the Ministry of Interior.[2]

It is an interesting coincidence that the promulgation of the new constitution in September 1997, known as the 'democratic constitution', came right after a major economic crisis in July the same year. Popular participation in resource use and management, once considered merely as an instrument for rural development, is now viewed as a central force to help overcome the economic crisis. However, the official recognition of the people's right to participate does not necessarily correspond with the actual practice of resource control. In fact, the new constitution may have increased incidents of land conflict now that people stand a better chance of gaining at least something; the number of reported disputes over land control is increasing, notably with the massive and sustained protests in front of the Parliament by the 'Assembly of the Poor', formed in December 1995. In March 1997, an NGO supporting this demonstration identified 121 sites in the country where potentially violent conflicts between government and farmers were taking place. Among those sites, about 75 per cent involved the use and ownership of land and forests and 12 per cent were related to dam construction.[3]

Many observers of resource developments have come to realise that forest and land issues do not relate merely to the physical environment but are essentially social and political problems. Socio-political problems require socio-political solutions; top-down technical treatment such as reforestation or zoning has so far proven ineffective. Forest plantations, for example, have made little progress and domestic timber is constantly in short supply. (Oddly enough, in 1985 the amount of illegally logged timber confiscated by the court exceeded that of the legally produced product.)[4] The alternative bottom-up approach of strengthening the community's organisational capacity, on the other hand, may also fall short in the face of state power where the competition for land-based resources is concerned. In Phattalung province, for example, villagers intimidated by the extractive activities of outsiders attempted to call the RFD for help, only to find out later that their local forest had been declared a national park. Ironically, the villagers who wanted to protect the forest were the first to be expelled.[5] It is futile to debate whether villagers have the capacity to manage or conserve a forest once they have been deprived of their incentive to do so.

In light of these considerations, it is not enough to seek sustainable forest use with an exclusive focus on the village-level mechanics of collective action, as has been effectively demonstrated by Elinor Ostrom and others. As will be discussed below, all forests are by definition legally under the ownership of the state; the relationship between resources and people must therefore be properly examined in the context of a broader political economy.[6] A much-debated political solution to resource problems, especially since the 1990s, has been the transfer of resource management responsibilities from the state to the hands of local communities. In Thailand, the enactment of a 'Community Forestry Bill' is considered as one such solution to the problems of deforestation and social justice.[7]

Of course, it would be naive to expect that another new piece of legislation will result in a radical shift in power relations, particularly between the people and the state. However, since the Community Forestry Bill can potentially help thousands of people living in and around the forests, the current debate and the history behind it deserve closer attention. This article will discuss the development of the concept of 'public land' and its implementation to serve the people living near state-owned resources. Community forests can be seen as one example of a struggle for resources taking place on public land. To fully grasp the implications of the Bill, it is necessary to understand the history and the place of these forests within the broader context of public land.

The discussion will first summarise the recent debate over the Community Forestry Bill, and then trace the history of competition over land and forests with a focus on policies that have affected public and communal lands. The final section examines the institutional foundation and the prospects for the development of community forestry in Thailand.

DEBATES OVER THE COMMUNITY FORESTRY BILL

The opinions of scholars, activists and those involved with the formulation and implementation of policy in Thailand regarding the link between forests and local people appear to be divided into two groups. The first views local people as a threat to forests and gives overall priority to ecological preservation in the interest of the state as a whole. Thus, from this perspective, forests should be 'protected' from local people. The second view emphasises the rights of local people to stay where they are and attempts to find a balance between meeting local needs and achieving conservation objectives. These two opposing points of view even create divisions among various government agencies and NGOs. This contrast became more salient in the long process of drafting the Community Forestry Bill, which has yet to be enacted. Since the completion of a first draft by the RFD in 1992 and the subsequent counter-proposal of a 'People's Version' by a coalition of activists and NGOs in the following year, there have been six versions all together.[8]

TABLE 1
Modification of the House version by the Senate

Contentious Articles in the Draft CF Bill	*House Version*
Article 18 Who can apply for a community forest?	50 people over 18 years old
Establishment of community forest in protected forests	Eligible communities must consist of indigenous people who have been protecting the forest for at least five years before filing an application
Article 29 Expansion of community forest area	Each community forest board may allow expansion of community forest area if the need can be demonstrated
Article 31 Gathering of trees and wild products in the community forests	Not restricted, nor subject to existing forestry-related laws
Contentious Articles in the Draft CF Bill	*Panel Version Proposed to the Senate*
Article 18 Who can apply for a community forest?	100 people over 18 years old
Establishment of community forest in protected forests	Eligible communities must be indigenous people who have been protecting the forest for at least five years before the bill takes effect
Article 29 Expansion of community forest area	Expansion of community forest is prohibited
Article 31 Gathering of trees and wild products in the community forests	Restricted under existing forestry-related laws (permission needed from RFD)

Source: Secretariat of the Senate, Raingan.

The Bill contains rules and regulations regarding the use of state-owned forests by local community members, and it is the first piece of legislation to be proposed by a petition of more than 50,000 voter signatures as allowed by the most recent Thai constitution. Under this bill, local communities interested in establishing community forests are required to organise a committee which will be responsible for overseeing forest-related activities for the purpose of conservation and sustainable utilisation in a participatory fashion.

In October 2001, the Lower House passed the Bill, including the controversial Article 18 allowing the establishment of community forestry inside protected forest areas, thus incorporating the spirit of the 'People's Version'. It is likely to face further modification, but it may still be helpful to highlight the major points of dispute by looking at the recent revision process of the Senate.[9]

On 15 March 2002, the Senate made a vote to approve the panel version with an additional crucial clause to the modification on Article 18, stipulating that 'community forests should not be allowed inside the protected forests'.[10] From the perspective of those who supported the Lower House version, this was a disappointing result, even worse than the stricter modification made by the Panel for the Senate. The bill has now been returned to the House to be considered again. If the House changes its resolution and supports the Senate's version, the bill will be promulgated; if not, a joint Senate-House panel must be set up to reconsider the bill.

Critiques of the Senate version highlight four problems with regard to Article 18: (1) small communities having less than 100 adult members would be excluded from the application; (2) a significant number of community forests are operating mainly inside the protected areas and excluding them would take the teeth out of the bill; (3)

TABLE 2
Number of farmers cultivating and residing inside and around wildlife sanctuaries (as of 1998)

Region	*Number of protected areas*	*Both residence and farmland inside the protected area*		
		No. of households	*Population*	*Area* *
Central	9	2,832	10,313	94,029
North	16	8,352	42,300	103,930
South	13	2,368	21,181	157,359
Northeast	—	1,359	5,851	49,223
Total	38	14,911	79,645	404,545

Region	*Residence outside but farmland inside*		
	No. of households	*Population*	*Area**
Central	1,163	4,483	39,686
North	538	1,754	11,845
South	7,503	28,366	113,835
Northeast	3,180	15,156	95,564
Total	17,109	78,902	295,340

* Area given in rai (1 rai = 0.16 ha)

Source: Kaisarung Phunphon, Kanbukruk phua khrong phuenthi khong ratsadon nai khet raksaphan satpa(Bangkok: RFD Report, 2542/1999), p. 40.

new groups who wish to apply after the promulgation of the bill, no matter how capable and suitable, would automatically be disqualified to establish community forests; and (4) restricting people's rights goes directly against the spirit of the new constitution, especially Article 46, which explicitly encourages the participation of indigenous people for natural resource management. Moreover, the reality is that there are still thousands of people living inside the protected areas, as can be seen from Table 2.

Given the Senate's refusal to allow the establishment of community forest inside protected areas, the definition of such an area is particularly important. If 'protected area' only refers to national parks and wildlife sanctuaries, this will amount to approximately 15 per cent of the country. On the other hand, if it includes 'conservation zones' as defined by the Cabinet resolution, the total figure is 27 per cent, which would affect a far larger number of people than those represented in Table 2.

The Panel version proposed to the Senate included the definition of protected areas as: national parks, wildlife sanctuaries, non-hunting areas and other lands suitable for protection such as watersheds and places with environmental value stipulated by the Ministry regulations.[11]

The words 'suitable for protection' were added to the Lower House version, implying the possibility of future expansion of the term 'potential area' and thus limiting the area available for community forests given the stipulations in the approved version.

Defining 'protected area' is as important as allowing the establishment of community forests inside it. To understand what is worth 'protecting' from the view of the state is to understand the state's view of what is worth leaving aside for the ordinary people. In reality, the 'state' is composed of various agencies with different mandates and objectives. In order to understand the context behind the emergence of such often conflicting policies, let us move on to examine the evolution of their programmes.

HISTORY OF STATE CONTROL OF 'PUBLIC LAND'

Thailand has increased its agricultural production through territorial expansion with very little reliance on intensification.[12] The land area allocated for agriculture doubled between 1910-40 and tripled again between 1940-70. Reduction of forest areas has been clearly detected by satellite images, particularly since the 1970s. Official statistics reveal that the 38 per cent forest cover in 1970 had shrunk to 25 per cent by 1998. Even the often underestimated official figures show that Thailand has lost 50 per cent of its forest in the past 30 years.[13]

Scarcity of land has introduced changes in tenure patterns in Thailand. In most places the traditional right to land was limited to usufruct: rights were given to the current user of the land, and the concept of ownership in a modern sense was absent. Locally known as 'squatter's rights', this system continued to be practised in many places until a clear private ownership system was introduced. Even today, many of the cultivators possess no legal documents of ownership despite their de facto private use.[14] This ambiguity of ownership in rural society, particularly in collective lands such as communal forests, religious forests, and fallow farmland, has made it possible for the government to confiscate these lands as state territory with ease.

During the rapid privatisation of agricultural lands, the Thai government paid little attention to unoccupied areas except for those that contained valuable resources such as teak. Management of public land became an issue only when there were conflicts between illegal encroachers and the regional forestry officials trying to maintain the boundaries of forest reserves.[15] This tended to evolve into a political agenda, particularly when the government became more sensitive about farmers' occupation of its land. Conflicts between farmers and officials have stimulated successive governments to strengthen their protection measures, and areas with valuable natural resources have been the first places to be 'protected' in this way.

The purpose of the 1964 National Forest Reserve Act was to legalise 'permanent forests' mapped on paper and to accelerate demarcation by the state. This law allowed forests to be designated as 'reserves' without a royal decree. The latest statistics show that forest reserves (45 per cent of total land) represent almost twice the area covered by actual forest, making it clear that the word 'reserves' is void of meaning.[16] Particularly since 1989, when the government declared a ban on commercial logging, rights to areas formerly designated for concessions have become ambiguous; this development has encouraged widespread encroachment on those lands by landless farmers. The government is now confronted with the critical task of curtailing further 'environmental refugees' from moving into the protected forests or settling in urban slums.

Diminishing forest resources and the expansion of protected areas have altered the nature of forest administration in Thailand. Forest reserves in the traditional sense were patches of forest waiting to be harvested. The mandate of the RFD was therefore to manage these reserves in an economically profitable way by allocating concession rights and receiving royalties. However, the depletion of forest lands and the banning of commercial logging in 1989 created both a financial and an identity crisis for the Department, as it was forced to transform its mandate from one of production to one of protection.[17]

It is interesting to observe, however, that the RFD has been able to increase its budget and staff dramatically, particularly since the ban in 1989. For example, its total budget more than doubled between 1990 and 1994. The rapid expansion of protected areas has been crucial for the

TABLE 3
List of permits for the use of land inside the forest reserves

Objectives	*No. of Cases*	*Rai*
Blasting and crushing of rocks	305	2,908
Mining	1,839	303,939
Road construction	963	297,537
Electricity generation	376	81,253
Irrigation	1,662	841,486
Educational projects	1,167	91,625
Religious facilities	698	29,517
Agriculture and recreational areas(1)	1,408	2,187,181
Government facilities	430	215,418
Research	59	69,128
Trespassing, grazing, watering	97	1,085
Conservation of forest reserves	70	85,609
Tree plantations	340	265,011
Others (e.g., waste disposal)	921	951,235
Total	10,335	5,422,938

(1) This does not include land reform areas.

Source: Data provided by the RFD Permit Division, August 2002.

Department's sustainability as a bureaucratic institution; scattered around the country, these areas are virtually its regional colonies.[18] With exclusive autonomy inside the protected forests and backed by the power of the law, chief officials in these areas often obtain enough power to profit on the side, as seen in the notorious illegal logging case in Salween National Park in Mae Hong Son province. In these areas, an increase in budget was justifiably requested to supply and strengthen local forest guards and to enhance monitoring capabilities. Protection of forests was advocated not only on the basis of environmental objectives, but also as a way to attract foreign assistance. An increase in the availability of economic assistance and the expected income from tourism have been some of the basic motivations behind the expansion of protected areas.[19]

As long as control over land rests with the RFD, another increasingly significant source of income has been the process of granting land use permits. Since 45 per cent of Thailand's total landmass is classified as reserves, companies and state agencies cannot initiate any project without seeking RFD permission. Table 3 shows the distribution of permissions given to various projects inside the forest reserves.[20]

Competition for land has intensified due not only to population increase but also to large-scale projects by state and private agencies. This explains why the RFD has not lost its standing despite the rapid decrease of forest cover, and has even expanded its budget and manpower after the logging ban. Understanding how the Department sustains itself provides important insight into its opposition to handing over the control of land to local people.

DEGRADED FORESTS FOR THE PEOPLE: LAND REFORM AND FOREST CONSERVATION

As struggles for control of land intensified, land ownership became highly competitive among the different departments in the government, particularly where property demarcation was still vague. These areas, typically called degraded forest, were formerly covered with forest but have now been transformed into agricultural land. Most of this land is legally owned by the state and has been designated by the RFD for future plantation sites or handed over to the Agricultural Land Reform Office to be distributed to the landless poor. The status of this land is therefore ambiguous and controversial in many ways. The precise number of farmers actually living on these lands is uncertain, and estimates vary between 1.5 and 8 million (from about 2 to 13 per cent of the total population respectively).[21]

There are numerous examples of acute conflicts between farmers and the government over these degraded forests, the most publicised being the land allotment project for poor farmers living in forest reserves under the Kho. Cho. Kho (National Rural Development Committee) scheme in 1991. This project, carried out by the military, aimed to evict farmers from forest reserves by compensating them with a small piece of land elsewhere. According to the original plan, more than 250,000 households—about 1 million people—were to be relocated by the end of 1996. However, strong protests by the farmers at the early stage of the plan forced the government to cancel it. The end of Thailand's Communist insurgency and the lure of potential profits from eucalyptus plantations led the RFD to align itself with paper pulp companies supported by the military, and many farmers were displaced from their dwellings to make way for eucalyptus trees. These developments are said to have helped the military to reclaim its presence after the fading of the Communist threat in the 1980s.[22]

In an attempt to protect the remaining forest area from further encroachment, the government implemented certain 'participatory' projects that gave various degrees of land rights to farmers illegally residing on state-owned land. Projects that took place in the forest reserves were implemented by the following governmental agencies without much coordination among each other: (1) plantation and forest village projects by the RFD; (2) plantation programmes by the Forest Industry Organisation (FIO); (3) the land reform programme by the Agricultural Land Reform Office (ALRO); (4) self-help settlement projects by the Department of Public Welfare (DPW); (5) and cooperative land allotment projects by the Department of Cooperative Promotion (DCP).[23]

Among the projects that took place in the forest reserves, the most significant is the land reform programme implemented by the ALRO, a scheme whereby the government obtains unused land from landlords or state-owned areas and distributes it to landless farmers.[24] In addition, the ALRO will support the development of infrastructure (e.g., pond digging, road construction) along with the provision of land certificates. The land to be obtained was originally sought from large-scale landlords. However, it soon became apparent that obtaining land from powerful landlords would be politically difficult, and even if it were possible, this group could not supply as much land as was needed. Since the mid-1980s, the government has shifted its attention to forest reserves as a potential source of land to be given to the landless. This move has naturally motivated some capital investors to encroach further onto forest land; as a result, the attempted 'reform' has in some cases intensified the concentration of land in the hands of the elite.[25]

Most of the other projects mentioned above are no longer being funded, even those by the RFD. The cabinet resolution of 4 May 1993 ordered the ALRO to be primarily responsible for land allocation projects related to forest reserves. Because these are state-owned lands, the RFD projects inside the reserves could only give farmers usufruct rights and not full ownership title. Land reform, on the other hand, allowed farmers to obtain their own land with certain restrictions; in other words, it was a mechanism for farmers to reclaim rights over ambiguous public lands. Table 4 shows the increase in the number of landless farmers in Thailand. With the decline in economic growth from the late 1990s, and the increasing difficulty of finding jobs in the cities, the problem of rural landlessness is re-emerging as one of the key items on the development agenda.

TABLE 4
The number and proportion of landless farmers in Thailand (1987-91)

Holdings	*1987*	*1991*
Landless (0 rai)	463,635 (8.2%)	500,398 (7.8%)
Nearly landless (less than 5 rai)	576,019 (10.1%)	828,265 (13.1%)
Smallholdings (5-10 rai)	670,015 (11.8%)	818,194 (12.8%)
More than 10 rai	3,982,197 (70%)	4,246,212 (66.4%)
Total	5,691,866 (100%)	6,393,069 (100%)

Note: 1 rai=0.16 ha

Source: S. Chirapanda, The Thai land reform programme (Bangkok: ALRO, 1996).

The connections between forest conservation policies and land reform merit a closer look. Strengthening conservation (to cover up to 25 per cent of the total land) and accelerating land reform have been central objectives of the government for the past several decades. To reconcile these possibly conflicting objectives, the RFD has conducted a detailed zoning operation inside the forest reserve areas since the late 1980s. The zones are classified into three categories: (1) conservation (C) zones for protection; (2) economic (E) zones for plantation and utilisation; and (3) agricultural (A) zones to be transferred to the ALRO for distribution (see Table 5). The results of this zoning exercise were used as a guideline to be followed in the Seventh National Social and Economic Development Plan (1992-6) in which a specific target of 25 per cent was given for conservation zones.

TABLE 5
Zoning by the RFD

Categories	*Conservation (C) Zone*	*Economic (E) Zone*
Criteria	The land in this zone is covered with forest trees that are healthy and suitable for preservation. If RFD follows its customary practice, these areas will be listed as appropriate for designation as national parks or wildlife sanctuaries.	The forests on land in these zones have been degraded, but the soil's capability assessment indicates that these areas are not suitable for cultivation of rice or upland crops. The areas are suitable for the cultivation of tree crops, particularly forest tree plantation crops.
Categories	*Land Reform (A) Zone*	
Criteria	The lands in this zone have been deforested and are occupied by permanent settlers. The communities are permanent and people are cultivating a combination of rice, upland cash crops and permanent tree crops. These areas have been designated to be degazetted following normal procedures and will be taken out of the forestry sector.	

Source: MIDAS Agronomics, Study of conservation forest area demarcation, jprotection, and occupancy in Thailand (Bangkok: prepared for the World Bank, 1991), Vol I, Appendix II, p. 1.

These tables clearly show the problems that arise from this zoning method. The most important issue is what will happen to farmers living inside C and E zones. The growing political power of NGOs working against forced relocation together with the basic lack of land where these people could relocate have created certain tensions over state-owned forest land. As a result of protests by farmers and NGOs, the government did issue a Cabinet resolution in May 1993 which basically allowed those farmers who could prove that they had been living in protected areas prior to demarcation to remain. This resolution was revoked a few years later, however, when there were changes in political circumstances. The basic underlying fact is that there is no land available for those who have been evicted. The government is now forced to recognise the presence of 'illegal encroachers' on state land by issuing them land certificates to curtail further encroachment—though it has taken a long time to reach that point.

The May 1993 resolution transferred jurisdiction over land amounting to 44 million rai (about 30 per cent of total forest reserves) from the RFD to the ALRO in order to accelerate the land reform programme. The potential for these degraded forests to become plantation sites and land to be given to landless farmers naturally created tension between two offices. The conflict became clear when an agreement was made in August 1995 which explicitly stipulated that areas defined as forest would now have to be returned to RFD control.[26] Previously there had only been an informal agreement which instructed the ALRO to maintain roughly 20 per cent of the land under forest cover either by planting or by conserving existing forests that remained inside the land reform area. (This 20 per cent was never demarcated on the map, as will be explained below.) The ALRO had no obligation to return those forest lands to the RFD. Based on this agreement, however, approximately 10,000 million rai are now being surveyed.[27]

The fact that the RFD was forced to give away 30 per cent of its territory to the ALRO clearly demonstrates the consequences of forest mismanagement by the state. Demarcation that reflects the politics of departmental interests instead of those of local villagers is bound to fail. Technical solutions unable to address the inherently political nature of the problem have led to further deterioration of the forests. It is in this context that one must understand the nature and significance of the Community Forestry Bill under discussion.

PUBLIC LAND FOR THE PEOPLE

The government's effort to artificially demarcate state forests and private farmlands has proven unrealistic since many of the rural people, especially the poor, rely on forest resources on a daily basis. According to the present system, the richer the forest, the more difficult it is for local people to utilise it. The new regulations imposed by the RFD would be stricter in forests that are rich enough to attract local people for their daily use. If this is the case, one might ask where within the present administrative boundaries a forest can be found that might provide enough incentive for local people to enforce and coordinate resource management at the village level. From a legal perspective, the only law that defines collective space for the people is the Civil and Commercial Code of 1932; Article 1304 refers to land that is a 'public asset of the nation'. There are three categories mentioned: (1) degraded vacant land; (2) assets to be used collectively by the citizens; and (3) assets exclusively for the national interest, namely facilities for military purposes. The first category can be privatised if one follows the appropriate legal procedures, while the second can be protected from privatisation. However, examples given in the code refer only to roads, lakes and coastlines, not to forests. Also, it is important to note that common lands in the past were designated not to protect the communal or collective rights of villagers but to secure the openness of the resources to prevent them from falling into private hands.[28]

The official origin of the community forest concept in Thailand appears to support the above mentality. As early as the 1950s, there was an explicit reference to the importance of communal forests: in 1956, as an appendix to the 1954 land code, the Ministry of the Interior issued an informal agreement among the land-related departments regarding the procedures that all land allotment projects should follow. The agreement made explicit that when the government redistributed part of the state land to the people, approximately 20 per cent of the land should be kept as forest to be used by the local people. 'Forests' in the agreement included trees along the roads, those serving as a windbreak, and those located near residential areas to be used for construction and firewood. Although this guideline was never strictly implemented, this recognition in an official document of the need for community forests deserves attention.[29]

One might ask why the government promoted this kind of arrangement, given the fact that in the 1950s there must have been an abundance of forest surrounding farmland. A plausible explanation was provided by a retired Director-General of the Department of Land in an interview with the author. According to him, the creation of a communal woodlot inside the newly established village boundaries was encouraged because most land allotment projects took place close to forest reserves where one could find vacant state-owned land for resettlement. This conservation-oriented policy with the apparent intention to help local people had another side, however. According to the retired official, the intention of the government at that time was to attract local people to the newly created community woodlot so that they would not go into reserved forests in search of wood or land. It is quite possible that it was the uneven distribution of rich forests, rather than a complete lack of them, that motivated the government to promote communal forests. Furthermore, this 20 per cent principle was seldom referred to or implemented until the mid-1990s, when the RFD began to reclaim its jurisdiction over the forests that existed inside land reform areas.

At present, the community forests that the RFD officially provides for the people can be found only inside the E zones, and they emphasize plantation rather than local use. Access to forests in C zones is not permitted under the current legal system, although it is sometimes granted on an unofficial basis. If healthy forests are first to be protected by the RFD, it is generally the degraded areas that would be left for people to use. An official document produced by the RFD confirms this conventional view: 'Community forests are those under the Forestry Act and Forest Reserve Act that do not exist inside national parks, wildlife sanctuaries, non-hunting areas or watersheds which are protected by government regulations. In addition, they cannot be on those lands to which the government prohibits access in the national interest.'[30] Such a statement suggests that the RFD has little incentive to hand over economically productive forests to local villagers.

Other than the plantation-oriented activities preferred by the RFD, three options for local access to forests exist within the present institutional framework (Table 6), The first is the forests outside the RFD-administered permanent forest area. (Permanent forests cover a wider area than reserves, yet they are only supported by a Cabinet resolution, whereas reserves are protected by law.) This is a category of public land that can avoid the involvement of the forestry patrol because it is mostly under the supervision of the Department of Land rather than the RFD. If registered properly, forests in this category can be protected by Article 1304 of the Civil and Commercial Code and the Land Code mentioned earlier.

TABLE 6
Distribution of Lands based on RDF Zoning

Category of Land	*Area (millions of rai)*	*Percentage*
National Forest Reserves	147.34	45.9
Conservation forests (C zone)	88.23	27.5
Good forests	71.56	22.3
Forests for rehabilitation	7.85	2.4
Other land uses	8.82	2.8
Economic forests (E zone)	51.89	16.2
Good forests	8.82	2.8
Forests for rehabilitation	15.46	4.8 (to ALRO)
Other land uses	27.61	8.6 (to ALRO)
Land reform areas (A zone)	7.22	2.2
Good forests	0.16	0.0
Forests for rehabilitation	0.4	0.0
Other land uses	7.2	2.2
Land outside forest reserves	173.35	54.0
Good forests	4.89	1.5
Forests for rehabilitation	1.44	0.4
Other land uses	167.02	52.1

Source: Ministry of Agricultural Cooperatives and Royal Forestry Department, Thailand forestry sector master plan, vol. 5: Subsectoral plan for people and forestry environment (Bangkok: RFD, 1993), p. 29.

According to the latest available information, there are 17,000 sites (totalling 1.08 million rai) in this category, with the largest portion registered as grazing land. In 1997, those registered as community forests extended over 116,000 rai, and the area is increasing, according to the officer responsible for registration in the Land Department.[31] RFD can assert its claim even over trees standing on land outside its jurisdiction. However, land outside its territorial control is implicitly outside the purview of the Forest Reserve Act, meaning that there is less policing by the forest guards. Moreover, those who are in reality highly dependent on forests, such as the hill people, mostly reside inside the RFD land, thus making it difficult to apply this strategy.

The second and most common option is the informal use of RFD forests. In many locations, local RFD officials and villagers have reached an informal arrangement that allows people to collect forest products not only on a subsistence basis (firewood, herbs, small animals) but also as a source of supplementary income (such as mushrooms and bamboo shoots.[32] These apparently flexible and informal arrangements, however, are vulnerable in the sense that the system can be taken away at any time, since there is no legal foundation to back them up. In addition, this kind of forest use does not have the potential to develop into an advanced form of community forestry including commercial enterprise.

A third possible option for promoting community forestry involves lands transferred from the RFD to the ALRO for land reform. According to the 1995 agreement between the two agencies, remnant forests in land reform areas should officially be returned to the RFD. Again, however, the definition of what constitutes a 'forest' is arbitrary, and it is up to the local officials to decide what to return and what to keep. Since the original idea of the '20 per cent agreement' was to plant trees on the land reform area as community forests, the treatment of remnant forest stands is vague, providing room for local people to take advantage of the ambiguity. Under this scheme, small but locally useful patches of forest may be placed lawfully under local control.

From a conservation point of view, clearing forest for agricultural purposes entails some risk, but it is up to the local community to handle this problem. Perhaps more importantly, in the land reform areas people are given legal title to land for cultivation, which provides a degree of stability not enjoyed by those living inside the RFD land. In other words, there is a possibility for local people to obtain both private and communal resources jointly.[33] The problem remains, however, that since the best forests are the first to be protected by the RFD, it may be difficult for the ALRO to obtain forests in contentious areas such as the surrounding areas of wildlife sanctuaries and national parks.

It is unclear exactly how the new Community Forestry Bill will affect these practices, and many issues lie ahead. For example, the relationship between the Tambon (sub-district) Administrative Organisations (given the authority to manage natural resources under the 1995 Tambon Administrative Unit Bill) and the community forestry committees responsible for forest management has yet to be sorted out.[34] Moreover, land titles inside the protected forest require further consideration. Despite the risks and shortcomings, however, an institutional basis for community development clearly exists within the present system. Regardless of the final content of the bill, what remains crucial to the success of community forestry initiatives is to learn from these working examples.

CONCLUSION: PROSPECTS FOR COMMUNITY FORESTRY

State-owned lands in Thailand occupy about 50 per cent of its total land area. Management of this large portion of land not only has significant implications for the local villagers who depend on forests on a daily basis, it also affects broader domains such as energy, water supply, and conservation of biodiversity and the environment at the global level. To sustainably manage these various resources, social mechanisms to organise links between the government, village communities, and individuals become crucial. One cannot focus exclusively on a single component of a system while ignoring the others. With regard to the state, one must ask what kinds of resources are given to the people and what forces are affecting particular allocation, before asking how those resources can be managed in a sustainable and participatory fashion. With regard to an individual or a household, there needs to be attention not only to forest resources under collective use per se, but also to private prerequisites (such as adequate farm land) that enable people to effectively take part in communal activities.

This article has attempted to locate community forests within the existing legal framework to explicitly address the structural constraints and prospects for further development. It is argued that 'public land' as defined by the government has rarely been conceptualised as land for local people. Rather, it is considered as exclusively 'state land', and even when there are references to local people, the context is primarily protecting this land from their encroachment. The article has suggested that even without the Community Forestry Bill, there is a legal basis for community forestry if it only refers to subsistence use of forest resources.

Even so, there would seem to be positive roles for the bill to play. Since much of the community management of forests is taking place inside the C zones, the House version of the bill will certainly assist the villagers by stabilising and securing what they are already doing, given that any activity in such areas is considered illegal at present. This may discourage local people from engaging in a speculative abuse of resources such as the conversion of forests into farmland. Also, for those who are in the South where logging concessions for mangroves have expired, the new bill may help preserve the forest land from state confiscation as part of conservation zones or state plantations.[35]

TABLE 7
Existing forms of community forestry in Thailand

Administrative location	*Responsible Agencies*	*Form of Use*
Public land outside of the RFD territory	Department of Lands	Official
Forest reserves and protected areas	RFD	Unofficial
Land reform area	ALRO	Official

Administrative location	*Risk / Shortcomings*
Public land outside of the RFD territory	Marginal impact on forest dependent people who are mostly inside RFD territory
Forest reserves and protected areas	Unstable access, especially inside protected areas
Land reform area	Uncertainty of forest Status

The relationship among a rapidly changing economy, forests, people and the government requires a more systematic treatment. Official attempts to isolate people from forests by zoning and policing have naturally limited the numbers and skills of people who are most capable of managing the very forest that is meant to be protected. It is likely that economic development over the long run reduces people's direct dependence on forest resources.[36] However, this tendency is not homogeneous across regions or social categories. Unless legal recognition is given to those communities that have proven their capacity to care for their forests, community-based resource management will be devoid of its best models. The relationship between resources and people is after all one of competition, requiring a degree of mutual awareness and trust that has apparently been slow to develop in Thailand.

During the debate over the bill, one Senator who voted against Article 18 expressed his fear that 'if villagers were given access to protected areas, other people would follow them and exploit the forest.'[37] This tough but illuminating statement is a reminder that community forestry is not only about the poor living in the forests, but also the rich who do not live there yet have keen commercial interests there. If the new bill fails to protect the interests of the poor living in the forests and remains incapable of addressing the issue of power inequality, which fundamentally affects how resources are used, then public land for the people will never come about in Thailand.

NOTES

1. See, for example, Anan Ganjanapan, *Local control of land and forest: Cultural dimensions of resource management in Northern Thailand* (Chiang Mai: Chiang Mai University Faculty of Social Sciences RCSD Monograph Series, 2000).
2. The Thai government is undergoing a major reform, and the RFD was scheduled to move to the new Ministry of Natural Resources and Environment during the year 2002, while the ALRO will remain in the Ministry of Agriculture.
3. Samacha Khon Chon [Assembly of the Poor], *Samacha khon chon* (Bangkok: Samacha Khon Chon, 1997). On this movement see Chris Baker, 'Thailand's Assembly of the Poor: Background, drama, reaction', *South East Asia Research* 8, 1 (2000): 5-29. An overview of popular participation is in Shigetomi Shinichi, 'Noson kaihatsu seisaku' [Rural development policy], in Tai no keizai seisaku: Seido, soshiki, akuta [Economic policy in Thailand: The role of institutions and actors], ed. Suehiro Akira and Shigeki Higashi (Tokyo: Institute of Developing Economies, 2000), pp. 215-58.

4. Royal Forest Department, *Forestry statistics of Thailand* (Bangkok: Royal Forest Department, 1996). General discussions of this issue include Piers Blaikie, *The political economy of soil erosion in developing countries* (Harlow: Longman, 1985); William Ascher, *Why governments waste natural resources: Policy failures in developing countries* (Baltimore: Johns Hopkins University Press, 1999); and Michael L. Ross, *Timber booms and institutional breakdown in Southeast Asia* (New York: Cambridge University Press, 2001).
5. Chakrit Ridmontri, 'The pros and cons of the Bill', *Bangkok Post*, 19 June 1997.
6. Elinor Ostrom, *Governing the commons: The evolution of institutions for collective action* (Cambridge and New York: Cambridge University Press, 1990). For similar examples elsewhere in Thailand, see Jin Sato, 'People in between: Conversion and conservation of forest lands in Thailand', *Development and Change*, 31, 1 (2000): 155-77.
7. G. Johnson and T. Forsyth, 'In the eyes of the state: Negotiating a "rights-based approach" to forest conservation in Thailand', *World Development*, 30, 9 (2002): 1589-603. For a discussion in a regional context see Owen J. Lynch and Kirk Talbott, *Balancing acts: Community-based forest management and national law in Asia and the Pacific* (Washington, DC: World Resources Institute, 1995).
8. For the history of debates related to community forestry, see Johnson and Forsyth, 'In the eyes of the state' and M. Pearmsak, 'Forestland policy revisited: Opportunities for policy reform of Thailand', paper prepared during the International Writing Workshop on Community Management of Forestlands: Policy Frameworks for Enabling Successful Community Based Resource Management Initiatives, East-West Center, Honolulu, 2001.
9. The scrutinising panel was composed of twenty-seven members including representatives from NGOs; Secretariat of the Senate, Raingan khong Khanakammathikan Wisaman Phicharana rang Phraratchabanyat Pa Chumchon Pho. So . . . Wutisapa (Bangkok: Secretariat of the Senate, 2002). The House and Senate panels had

different members. Some say the hard lobbying at the Senate by opponents of the bill brought panel members who were basically against the idea of allowing community forest inside protected forests.

10. Kultida Samabuddhi, 'Senators add crucial clause before giving passage to bill', *Bangkok Post*, 16 March 2002.

11. Secretariat of the Senate, Raingan.

12. Rodolphe De Konick and Steve Dery, 'Agricultural expansion as a tool of population redistribution in Southeast Asia', *Journal of Southeast Asian Studies*, 28, 1 (1997): 15.

13. Royal Forest Department, *Forestry statistics of Thailand* (Bangkok: Royal Forest Department, 2000). On the technical and political biases of these government statistics, see Lynch and Talbott, *Balancing acts*.

14. General discussions of legal issues relating to land tenure are in David Feeny, 'The decline of property rights in man in Thailand', 1800-1913; *The Journal of Economic History*, 49, 2 (1989): 285-96; Jeremy Kemp, 'Legal and informal land tenures in Thailand'; *Modern Asian Studies*, 15 (1981): 1-23. Based on the latest available data on private land holdings, land with full ownership title amounted to 54 million rai, which is only about 30 per cent of all cultivated area. For the historical separation of usufruct and ownership rights, see Kitahara Atsushi, 'Kindai Tai no tochihosei: Senzen no tochi hotaikei ni kansuru ichishiron/ Land registration in modern Thailand: A sketch to [sic] the prewar system of land policy' (Tokyo: Institute of Developing Economies internal document, dated 1971). It is important to note that even full title to land does not include ownership of certain valuable trees on that land. According to the Forestry Act (1941), one is required to obtain permission from the local forestry official before cutting certain species such as teak and yang (Dipterocarpus), even those growing on one's registered land.

15. Donald Gienty, *Thailand's forest development and its effect on rural peoples* (Bangkok: United States Operations Mission, 1967).

16. Royal Forest Department, *Forestry statistics* (2000). The National Forest Reserve Act does stipulate (Article 16) that those who had lived there before demarcation can apply for permission to use land inside the reserve. However, the Act allows only 90 days after the demarcation to file an application, and it is unlikely that villagers in remote areas could meet this deadline.

17. Royal Forest Department, *Forestry statistics* (1996).

18. Chiefs of wildlife sanctuaries and national parks as well as regional forest offices covering multiple provinces are not required to report to the governor of their respective province. Provincial forestry offices, on the other hand, are officially under the authority of the governor, who is in turn under the Ministry of Interior. See also the discussion in Peter Vandergeest, 'Mapping nature: Territorialization of forest rights in Thailand', *Society and Natural Resources*, 9 (1996): 159-75 and idem., 'Property rights in protected areas: Obstacles to community involvement as a solution in Thailand'; *Environmental Conservation*, 23, 3 (1996): 259-68.

19. Krishna Ghimire, 'Parks and people: Livelihood issues in national parks management in Thailand and Madagascar', *Development and Change*, 25 (1994): 195-229. Achara Rakyutitham, 'Forest fire: A history of repression and resistance', *Watershed*, 6, 2 (2001): 35-42 gives an insightful analysis of how firefighting has served to justify the RFD's suppression of shifting cultivators who use fire.

20. Under new regulations implemented since 2000, those who are granted the permits have to pay a royalty of 7,220 baht per rai as compensation for the damage to the land and the cost of restoration. For mining projects the royalty will be three times as much; Royal Forest Department, Banthuek khokhwam Ko. So 0704.5w 16374, 3 July 2002.

21. Scott R. Christensen, and Akin Rabibhadana, 'Exit, voice and the depletion of open access resources: The political bases of property rights in Thailand', *Law and Society Review*, 28, 3 (1994): 639-55. Owen Lynch and Janis B. Alcorn, *Empowering local forest managers: Towards more effective recognition of tenurial rights, claims and*

management capacities among people occupying 'public' forest reserves in the Kingdom of Thailand (Washington, DC: World Resources Institute, 1991). Larry Lohmann estimates the area of this category of land at about 5,600 [km.sup.2]', which is approximately 10 per cent of the total land area; Larry Lohmann, 'Freedom to plant: Indonesia and Thailand in a globalizing pulp and paper industry', in *Environmental change in South-East Asia: People, politics and sustainable development*, ed. Michael Parnwell and Raymond Bryant (London: Routledge, 1996), pp. 23-48.

22. Pasuk Phongpaichit, *The army's land redistribution programme in forest reserves: Case study of the active exclusion of poor villagers in Northeast Thailand* (Bangkok: Chulalongkorn University Faculty of Economics, 1995). The main cause of resistance was not the environmentally harmful nature of fast-growing eucalyptus plantations, but rather the locations which the government chose for planting. Even those lands long cultivated by local villagers were assigned as plantation areas, and in many cases natural forests were destroyed to make room for the monocrop plantation sites.

23. Many of these projects took place inside or next to forest reserve areas. Forest villages, self-help settlements, and land allotment projects that began during the late 1960s and 1970s were often tied to national security concerns, particularly Communist insurgency. Conservation and restoration of forests merely served as pretexts for mobilising local villagers to counter insurgents who were often hiding in remote forest areas. As a result, many of the forest village projects took place along the borders of Laos and Cambodia; James Hafner and Yaowalak Apichatvullop, 'Farming the forest: Managing people and trees in reserved forests in Thailand', *Geoforum*, 21, 3 (1990): 331-46. In short, these projects were derived from the political agendas of various state departments to enhance their bureaucratic status in the government and lacked coordination, which in many cases actually induced further forest clearance, despite the purported objective of environmental conservation; see Harald Uhlig, 'Spontaneous and planned agricultural settlement: A general view of the present clearing-colonisation in the

ASEAN Countries of Southeast Asia', in *Spontaneous and planned settlement in Southeast Asia: Forest clearing and recent pioneer colonization in the ASEAN countries and two case-studies in Thailand*, ed. Harald Uhlig (Hamburg: Institute of Asian Affairs, 1984), pp. 6-118.

24. Under this scheme, farmers can obtain the usufruct rights for up to 50 rai of land and the certificate can be used as a collateral to obtain credit from banks. In 1994, about 200,000 households received the ALRO certificate; Prasong Charasdamrong, 'The land of no return', Bangkok Post, 16 Feb. 1997. To be eligible for land reform, an area must (1) be state land (i.e., forest reserve); (2) not be covered by forest; (3) be generally suitable for agriculture; (4) not be vulnerable to soil erosion; and (5) contain a high proportion of landless farmers (including smallholders and farmers without any certificate); Thai Development Resource Institute, Identification of potential land reform areas in Chantaburi Province, final results, main report (Bangkok: TDRI, 1989), vol. I, p. 1414.

25. Prasong, 'Land of no return'.

26. Categories of land to be returned to the RFD are (1) land covered with forest; (2) land not suitable for agricultural production; (3) ecologically vulnerable areas; (4) areas to be protected as communal forests, (5) land with an average slope of more than 35 degrees; (6) watershed areas; (7) land that goes under the supervision of the RFD according to the law and regulations; (8) mangrove forests; and (9) degraded forests that have not yet been cultivated by farmers. See Royal Forestry Department and Agriculture and Land Reform Office, *Bantheuk khotoklong rawang Krom Pamai lae Samnakngan Pathrup Thidin* (Bangkok: RFD, 2538/1995).

27. Somtheep Lacharot and Theeparit Koyphokhaisawon, 'Pa kap khon', unpublished manuscript (Royal Forest Department, 1997).

28. Shigetomi Shinichi, 'Tai noson no "kyoyuchi" ni kansuri ichikosatsu' [Land tenure system on communal lands in rural Thailand], in *Tonan Ajia no keizai kaihatsu to tochi seido* [Economic development and land tenure in Southeast

Asia], ed. Shigetomi Shinichi and Mizuno Kozuke (Tokyo: Ajia Keizai Kenkyujo, 1997).

29. MOI (Ministry of Interior) document 9317/2699, May 2499/ 1956. The document also refers to the ecological importance of the forest in giving moisture to the soil in addition to its economic significance for the local people. This statement, though never formalised, may be considered one of the earliest explicit state acknowledgements of the function of community forests.

30. Somtheep and Theeparit, 'Pa kap khon', p. 27.

31. The 1997 figure is from ibid. The most recent data is in Department of Lands, Thidin thi prachachon chai prayot ruamkan thi ok nangsue samkhan samrap thiruang laew (Bangkok: Department of Lands, April 2541/1998). Idle land with no occupants is by legal definition 'forest' regardless of the actual tree cover. However, it can he registered either as 'degraded vacant land' or 'land to be used collectively by citizens' in accordance with the Land Code under the supervision of the Land Department. Because of the larger number of local staff, land under the RFD is strictly monitored. Thus, if given a choice, people tend to register their common land as non-RFD land. Villagers' room for manoeuvre in taking advantage of various state regulations is a promising agenda for future research.

32. *A detailed case study of this type of community forestry is in Community allies: Forest co-management in Thailand*, ed. Mark Poffenberger and Betsy McGean (Berkeley: Southeast Asia Sustainable Forest Management Network Research Report, 1993).

33. Because the ALRO certificate will be given to those who already occupy a piece of land to cultivate, it will not rescue those who are literally landless. Given the likelihood that these landless people are more dependent on forest resources, the rigid imposition of a land reform scheme (i.e., the demarcation of private land boundaries) may distort the informal arrangement often made among villagers to accommodate the poor.

34. Both House and Senate versions of the bill lack explicit statements regarding the connection between TAOs and community forests. Since a majority of the forest areas presently under the management of TAOs lie within reserves, it is natural to assume that the RFD will retain ultimate control over their use; Apichai Puntasen, 'Tambol organization and community forests', in *Seeing forests for trees: Environment and environmentalism in Thailand*, ed. Philip Hirsch (Chiang Mai: Silkworm Books, 1997), pp. 72-88.

35. The 1989 logging ban did not apply to mangrove areas in the South.

36. H.M. Gunatilake, 'The role of rural development in protecting tropical rainforests: Evidence from Sri Lanka', *Journal of Environmental Management*, 53 (1998): 273-92.

37. *The Nation*, 16 Mar. 2002.

5

POPULATION AND THE FAMILY IN SOUTHEAST ASIA

—Gavin W. Jones

DEMOGRAPHIC TRANSITION IN SOUTHEAST ASIA

The decade of the 1960s was one of growing concern among demographers with the acceleration of the world's population growth, resulting largely from the sharp decline in mortality rates in the early post-World War II period. The concern has become more selective in recent times, with the prospects for population stabilization becoming clearer in some countries and regions as a result of sharp declines in fertility, but with population growth rates continuing to cause great disquiet in others. Southeast Asia as a whole gives grounds for a somewhat sanguine assessment; its population growth rate is slowing as a result of quite spectacular declines in fertility in a number of major countries. But the situation is quite variable, and some countries maintain high rates of fertility and of population growth.

To be more specific, in Southeast Asia as a whole, mortality rates declined very rapidly during the 1950s, and population growth rates accelerated alarmingly. From the late 1960s on, mortality continued to decline steadily, but fertility also declined, faster than any observer would have imagined in 1960. The net result has been (because fertility and mortality declines have to some extent offset each other) a gradual decline in population growth rates since the late 1960s. But this overall trend disguises a wide range of country situations, from those where the demographic transition is nearing completion (Singapore and Thailand), through those where it is very advanced (Malaysia and Indonesia), and those where the transition is well along but lagging for various reasons (Philippines, Vietnam, Burma) to those where the transition is embryonic (Laos and Cambodia). It is the impact of large countries such as Indonesia and Thailand, in both of which fertility declines surpassed original expectations, that has resulted in the regional declines being quite impressive.

In a sense, the fertility decline in the region "had" to happen. The effect of the sharp mortality declines in the early postwar years was to accelerate rates of population growth, which if continued would have led to a "blowout" in population size that would have quickly become unsustainable. Population growth provides, in fact, an ideal illustration of the application of compound interest formulae to multiply an original endowment (in this case, of population).

Thus to invoke the "continuity and change" paradigm, continuity was no longer an option once massive postwar declines in mortality had finally put paid to the always precarious balance between fertility and mortality, and raised population growth rates to 2.5 per cent per annum by the late 1960s. Continuation of this rate would have doubled Southeast Asia's population from 287 million in 1970 to 574 million in 1997, and again to 1,178 million in 2025 and 2,356 million in 2053. Although the alarmist geometric growth of the Malthusian model was too draconian a way to view the situation, there was no doubt that adjustments of one kind or another would have to come into operation. It was in recognition of this that from the mid-1960s the "big league" players in the international development assistance field—the U.S. government from 1965, the United Nations from 1967 and the World Bank from 1969—began to give support to family planning programmes, and—not entirely co-incidentally—government policies to reduce fertility were introduced across a wide range of Southeast Asian countries. Though international pressures to adopt family planning programmes were certainly felt, there were home-grown reasons as well in all cases. A little-known fact is that the Democratic Republic of Vietnam was the first Southeast Asian country to adopt a specific policy to reduce population growth rates. This took place in 1963, followed by Singapore in 1965, Indonesia in 1968 and Thailand and the Philippines in 1970.[1]

The notable degree of consensus reached by 1970 was maintained through the decade, but by the early 1980s, it began to crumble, partly because demographic and developmental circumstances were changing, partly because perceptions of the issues were changing. In 1984, the Prime Minister of Malaysia stated the desirability of reaching a population size of 70 million, almost five times Malaysia's population at the time. In 1983, Singapore introduced selective pronatalist policies, aiming at raising fertility among the better-educated, and in 1987 adopted a generally pronatalism policy, incorporating a battery of measures aimed at increasing fertility, especially that of the better educated.[2] The Philippines changed its policy on population after the election of Corazon Aquino as President in 1987. This was not in recognition of circumstances making population growth less of a problem (because circumstances in this respect had not changed), but rather a direct result of the increased influence of the Roman Catholic hierarchy on the Aquino regime.

The Southeast Asian countries which stood firm on the need for reduction of population growth rates were Thailand, Indonesia and Vietnam. In Thailand, fertility has now fallen to replacement level and shows signs of going still lower. It is not surprising, then, that as in Singapore before, Thai planners are now considering possible modifications in population policy to avoid unnecessary pressures for further fertility decline.

Despite lowered fertility rates, population in the region will grow much larger before it can possibly be expected to level off. This is the result of an age structure highly conducive to further growth. Even in Indonesia, where replacement level fertility could be reached within a decade, population is expected to increase by at least 70 million, and probably by much more, before it stabilizes.

Commonly, official projections of population are slow to catch up with changing realities. For example, in the early stages of a fertility transition, it is often assumed that recorded fertility declines are in error. These declines, moreover, are recorded from survey data only some years after the event. Assumptions used in projections therefore tend to systematically overestimate fertility in the early stages of fertility decline. This was certainly true of many official national projections, and also of successive UN projections for Southeast Asia, Thailand and Indonesia. Those who prepared the projections conducted in 1973 and 1977 did not have access to conclusive data about the substantial fertility decline that was already under way. Consequently, they failed to allow for the speed of fertility decline, and their projections for Southeast Asia for the year 2000 overshot by some 70-87 million (or 13 to 17 per cent) the Southeast Asian totals for the same year according to projections conducted later, in the 1980s. The difference was even more marked in the case of Thailand, whose year 2000 population was projected to be some 20 to 23 per cent lower by the projections of the 1980s than by that of 1977.

CHALLENGES TO THEORY

Explaining fertility decline, or lack of it, remains the central challenge to population theorists. First of all, however, it should be noted that there are alternative measures of the fertility trends to be explained. Declines in fertility measured on a calendar-year basis (called period measures in demographic terminology) are sometimes only very roughly matched by declines in cohort fertility, since a given cohort can shift its childbearing patterns forward or backward in time to adjust to particular circumstances including economic difficulties, famines, or political upheavals. On a more mundane level, cohorts may delay childbearing compared to earlier cohorts because they have married later; where average age at marriage has risen sharply, this can temporarily lower period fertility without necessarily lowering cohort fertility. To some extent, this appears to have happened in Malaysia and Singapore, particularly among the Malays, when their fertility rates were falling sharply during the 1970s. In Singapore, the forces making for lower fertility were so strong that they continued to lower it once the rise in marriage age slackened; but in Malaysia, Malay fertility decline ceased in 1976 and fertility even rose for a time. Fertility was no lower in 1988 than it had been in 1976.

Demographic transition theory, for all its shortcomings, continues to provide the schema into which analyses of fertility trends tend to be fitted, and the intellectual underpinning for population projections performed by the United Nations and the World Bank. Briefly, the theory holds that urbanization and industrialization, along with the social changes that accompany these processes, reduce the incentive to bear and rear children, and that declines in infant and child mortality reinforce the idea that fewer children were enough. In general, trends in the region support this theory.[3] Countries or groups that have experienced the sharpest declines in fertility, including

Singapore, Thailand and the Chinese and Indian populations of Malaysia, also happen to be countries and groups that have been doing very well economically. The same holds, to a slightly lesser extent, for Indonesia.

On the other hand, the classical demographic transition theory has been challenged with regard to its ability to explain demographic trends of the nineteenth and twentieth centuries in Europe.[4] And it is argued that the speed of the fertility decline in some countries of Southeast Asia is evidence that something other than classic demographic transition theory is operating. Some caution is needed in accepting this argument, because mortality decline and the processes of economic and social development have also been proceeding faster in these countries than in Europe when it was undergoing its demographic transition. However, as noted below, there are certainly enough Southeast Asian cases that do not fit neatly into demographic transition theory for this region's experience to be used by some to challenge the theory.

In casting about for other explanatory frameworks for fertility decline, one obvious factor has been governmentally organized family planning programmes designed to make contraception more accessible to people (in both a physical and a psychological sense). Southeast Asia contains a number of countries where strong family planning programmes have been mounted in support of national aims of reducing population growth rates: Singapore, Thailand, Indonesia, and Vietnam, in particular. Fertility has come down sharply in the first three of these countries, but economic and social development has also been rapid. A great deal of research has gone into trying to estimate what proportion of fertility declines has been caused by the family planning programmes. Again, the range of answers is hardly satisfactory. Measures of gross programme impact (reduction of fertility attributable to the use of contraception obtained from programme sources) are usually quite impressive; but net programme impact (the reduction in fertility that is actually achieved by the presence of the programme) is harder to measure and typically much smaller.

A recent study[5] estimates that the following percentages of fertility decline are due to the net impact of the family planning programmes: Indonesia, 64 per cent; Malaysia, 45 per cent; Philippines, 45 per cent; Singapore 48 per cent; Thailand 52 per cent; and Vietnam 55 per cent. These estimates appear suspiciously large. Those who stress demand for children as the main underlying determinant of fertility argue that the methodology in such studies is flawed and that contraceptive supply in itself has little independent impact on fertility.[6] Perhaps the conclusion by Paul Gertler and John Molyneaux[7] is the crucial one: 75 per cent of Indonesia's fertility decline from 1982 to 1987 resulted from increased contraceptive use, but was induced primarily through economic development and improved education and economic opportunities for females. Even so, the dramatic impact of demand-side factors on contraceptive use was possible only because a highly responsive contraceptive supply delivery system was in place.

Family planning programmes should not be seen as merely supply-side interventions: they normally seek also to influence community norms, and people's perceptions of community norms, about ideal family size and acceptability of contraception. In some countries, they exert considerable pressure on people to conform to state ideology on appropriate family size. They can therefore be plausibly integrated into two alternative explanatory frameworks of Southeast Asian fertility decline: one stressing institutional factors[8] and the other stressing the role of "ideational factors".[9] From the institutional perspective, "family planning programs are necessarily enmeshed in the political and administrative systems of the respective countries, and assume a corresponding style and coloration. In particular, they reflect the nature of state-individual relations . . ."[10] The ideational framework stresses the transport and communications revolution that has served to break down the isolation of many villages and exposed people to the perspectives of urban people (indeed, of foreigners) and almost instantaneously to new ideas sweeping the society. In this context, traditional ideas that may serve to inhibit change have lesser powers of resistance.

No one theory has achieved universal acceptance, because the varieties of actual experience challenge them all.[11] For example, if economic determinism plays the main role, why have the Malays of Malaysia (the most prosperous group in the Malay world) experienced such a sluggish fertility decline, with a total fertility rate still above four, while their less affluent ethnic counterparts in Indonesia have a rate below three and the Southern Thai Muslims a rate not much above three?[12] If educational development is a major explanatory factor, why does the Philippines, whose educational levels were historically well above those in the rest of Southeast Asia (though Singapore and Malaysia are now catching up) have higher fertility than many other Southeast Asian countries? If family planning programmes are crucial, why has Burma experienced substantial fertility decline, despite government pronatalism and restricted access to contraceptive supplies? A comprehensive explanation of Southeast Asian fertility decline appears to remain beyond our grasp for the time being. Explanation of individual country declines requires nuanced understandings, taking sociopolitical and institutional factors into account, rather than application of grand theory.

CHANGING MARRIAGE PATTERNS, FAMILY STRUCTURES AND FAMILY RELATIONSHIPS

Some of the most dramatic manifestations of social and economic change sweeping Southeast Asia are with regard to family patterns and family relationships. A familiar line of argument promoted by Talcott Parsons, William Goode and John Caldwell is that family systems increasingly converge to the Western conjugal type as societies industrialize and urbanize. The theory has its critics,[13] but its particular difficulty in relation to family change in Southeast Asia is that Southeast Asian families, which followed a bilateral kinship system,[14] were always nuclear, or at least not as fully joint as in the Indian subcontinent. In Thailand, for example, where matrilineal ties are the most important, households have alternate stages of being nuclear and extended.[15] Men normally move into their wife's parents' household for a period of one to three years and then establish a separate, economically independent household. This pattern is also the traditional one among the Malays in Malaysia, in Indonesia and in the Philippines.[16] Extended family relations, however, are very close: Gelia Castillo refers to the Filipino household as "residentially nuclear but functionally extended".[17] Alfred McCoy argues that in the Philippines, where family-based oligarchies strongly influence the course of politics, "elite families, organized on complex patterns of bilateral kinship, bring a contradictory mix of unified kinship networks and a fissiparous, even volatile, factionalism into the political arena".[18]

There are a number of causes of changing family structures. One is simply the decline in fertility experienced in many Southeast Asian countries. As nuclear families are the norm throughout the region, when fertility declines, households are smaller. A recent study for Thailand[19] shows that average household size has fallen from 5.8 in 1970 to 4.6 in 1990, and is expected to continue falling steadily to

3.3 in 2015. Not only this, but the proportion of households that are single-headed or single-person in Thailand in 1990 was 17.4 per cent and 4.3 per cent respectively.[20] Extended family contacts will, of course, widen the network of interaction, but not to anything like the extent in the past, when each couple had an average of six children, and an average individual had five siblings, six children, thirty nieces and nephews, ten uncles and aunts, sixty first cousins, 120 first cousins of his parents, and 720 second cousins.

Social and economic changes are also making for changes in family structure and family relationships. In some major countries of the region, booming economies are leading to a diversification of job opportunities; a much higher proportion of women are working than formerly, and many young women are migrating to the cities to work, living there apart from their families. Increasing participation of women in the labour market is related, both causally and consequentially, to the lower fertility, and to the rise in marriage ages to be discussed in the following section. But it also means that arrangements for raising children are changing. Rising levels of education are a major factor in the re-alignment of conventions about the role of women.

Norms and values related to family structures and family relationships can also change because of the spread of alternative ideas. The communications revolution has been crucial in this, as well as the expansion of education, especially for girls. In Southeast Asian cultures which formerly favoured a secluded role for women, dramatic changes have occurred, to be discussed in the following section on marriage. A rise in individualism, as in the West, is often declared to be taking place, but hard evidence is lacking, just as it was for the controversial earlier characterization of Thai society as "loosely structured".[21]

Given the paucity of quality sociological analyses of the Southeast Asian family, there is something to be said for basing a brief survey of change on some fairly "hard" demographic information on aspects of the family. First, average age at marriage for women has risen almost universally in Southeast Asia since the 1960s.[22] Some of the most striking changes have been among the Malay-Muslim populations of Singapore, Malaysia and Indonesia.[23] In Peninsular Malaysia, the median age at marriage for Malay women rose by five years (from 17 to 22) over the twenty-three-year period from 1957 to 1980. In Indonesia, the rise has been slower, but nevertheless median age at marriage for women rose by two years over the twenty-year period 1970-90.

This rise in age at marriage is closely linked to increasing autonomy of young women in the choice of their spouse. The traditional degree of control by parents over the choice of spouse has varied greatly within Southeast Asia, being much greater in Indonesia or among Malaysian Malays than in the Philippines, Thailand, or among the Malaysian Chinese. It has been argued that where daughters are valued for their reproductive capacity, early marriage will be preferred. Where daughters are valued primarily for their productive contributions to the family, late entry to marriage is to the parents' advantage. Where marriages are considered important in forming alliances, early marriage will be preferred. If the "affective individualism" of daughters is valued, the resulting marriage timing may be moderately late because daughters may have to go through a lengthy search for a spouse.[24] It is the second of these—the valuing of daughters for their productive contributions to the household—as well as to some extent the fourth, that have come greatly to the fore among Malaysian Malays since the 1960s, and in a kind of "social contract" parents have abdicated their former control over their daughters' marriage choice.[25] Lita Domingo and Elizabeth King argue that delayed marriage in the

Philippines has much to do with daughters honouring their social contract with their parents, and thus being granted more freedom in their nuptiality decisions.[26]

Not only has the average age at marriage increased dramatically, but the tradition of universal marriage is on the way out. In most Southeast Asian populations, as few as 2 or 3 per cent of women remain never-married by the end of their reproductive period. It has been unthinkable for any able-bodied and sound-minded woman to remain unmarried. This situation is in the process of dramatic change. In 1990, about 15 per cent of women aged 30-34 remained unmarried in Peninsular Malaysia, over 14 per cent in Thailand and over 13 per cent in the Philippines. In the cities, the proportion remaining unmarried tended to be the highest. In both Singapore and Bangkok, the figure was well over 20 per cent for women aged 30-34, and even by age 40-44, about 12 per cent remained single. In Metro Manila, the proportions single at age 30-34 were slightly lower, at 19 per cent, and 11 per cent at age 40-44. In Jakarta, however, the proportion still single at 30-34 was still only 9 per cent, although this represented a substantial rise over earlier years.

It is impossible to say exactly what proportion of women currently in their thirties will remain unmarried at the end of their reproductive period. A decade from now, the evidence will be much clearer. But what is already clear is that a substantial proportion of women in the region are remaining unmarried well into their thirties; in many cities of the region, more than 10 per cent of women are already completing their reproductive period without ever having married; this figure will rise much higher over time; and in countries such as Thailand, we are reaching a situation where nationally, more than 10 per cent of women will remain unmarried by the end of their reproductive period.[27] This is not only driving fertility rates significantly lower, but also leading to major changes in living arrangements, with large numbers of single young women leaving their households to enter other living arrangements: living alone, sharing group housing with friends, and—though it elicits expressions of shock and horror from official circles—living with a male partner without marrying.

Among those who do marry, fertility is much lower than before. This is particularly true in Singapore, Thailand, Indonesia, and among the Chinese and Indian populations of Malaysia. It is also true to a lesser extent of the Philippines, Vietnam, and Burma, and the Malays of Malaysia. Fertility is lower in urban than in rural areas, and particularly low in the mega-cities of the region. In Bangkok fertility is far below replacement level, and the continuing growth of Bangkok's population is therefore the result of continued in-migration and the high proportion of the Bangkok population in the main reproductive ages, resulting in positive rates of natural increase despite the extremely low fertility. Fertility is also below replacement in Singapore and Jakarta, and much lower in Manila than elsewhere in the Philippines. The implication of this for family size and family life is hinted at by Singapore figures for 1990: 16 per cent of married women aged 40-44 are either childless or have only one child.

Along with the rising age at marriage (and not unrelated to it) have gone declining rates of divorce throughout Islamic Southeast Asia.[28] These declines have been quite spectacular. In the 1950s divorce rates were universally high throughout the Malay-Muslim world, though ranging widely within it. In Kelantan and West Java, divorce rates were probably the highest in the world. Yet today, divorce rates throughout the region are less than half those prevailing in Western countries. The main reason divorce rates plummeted at a time when they were rising steadily in the West was that young people were increasingly choosing their own spouse and marrying at a later age than before; they were therefore more mature at the time of marriage, had a much greater stake in the success of the marriage, and had no need for recourse to the formerly common practice of divorce as the way to escape an unsatisfactory arranged marriage.

But divorce trends are not downwards everywhere in Southeast Asia. The factors leading to rising divorce rates among the Malay-Muslim population are very specific to this cultural group. In the major cities of the region, divorce rates have been tending to rise, a rise paralleling that in many other parts of the world.[29] The causes of this rise have received little systematic study. It is reasonable to hypothesize that they are related to more individualistic attitudes emerging in rapidly industrializing and urbanizing societies, and the growing pressures on marriages in contexts where the pace of urban life is demanding, pressures on working women to perform the "double shift" of paid work and household duties leads to stress, and both spouses are interacting with many members of the opposite sex in the workplace.

Another notable consequence of demographic change in Southeast Asia is the lengthening period of adolescence, defined for our purposes as the interval between attaining sexual maturity and marriage. This contrasts with earlier times when in many parts of the region, in particular Islamic Southeast Asia, a girl's attainment of menarche sometimes postdated marriage or at least triggered a period of intensive activity by her family in arranging a marriage. Even in countries such as Singapore, the Philippines and Thailand, where ages at marriage have long been well above those in the main Islamic areas of Southeast Asia, the female age at marriage has increased further in recent decades.[30] Thus throughout the region, adolescence is an increasingly lengthy period. The implications, however, have sometimes appeared lost on policy-makers and researchers alike. Adolescents are living longer at home, in an unmarried state. At the same time, the traditional authority of parents is under challenge. This makes for major problems of readjustment of family relationships. Adolescent sexuality is a particularly sensitive issue. The fact is that adolescent sexual activity is very common and on the increase. In Thailand, half of young men have had sex before the age of eighteen, and their first sexual encounter is normally with a prostitute.[31] But many have sex, not only with commercial sex workers but also with non-commercial partners.[32] In Indonesia, there is evidence that between 13 and 28 per cent of first births are premaritally conceived,[33] suggesting an even higher level of premarital sexual activity. Two recent newspaper reports concerning Indonesia, lamenting the tendency for young men and women living in dormitories for factory workers (Lamphun) or boarding houses for students (Yogyakarta) to form sexual relationships with co-residents,[34] hint at the widespread prevalence of such patterns among mobile populations in Southeast Asia.

With rising levels of premarital sexual activity, pregnancy often triggers marriage, rather than the other way around. It has been noted that the ratio of teen-aged mothers to all mothers has been rising as completed fertility has fallen.[35] Yet researchers have been slow to adapt to the situation. Peter Xenos observes that, because of the selection criteria adopted in most surveys of fertility, "most of what we know about youth in this area is limited to the ever married (. . . an ever-dwindling segment of the under twenty-five population)".[36]

The final point to be noted in relation to the changing family is the trend towards ageing of the population. This is not yet very far advanced, except in Singapore. The next three decades will see a sharp increase in the share of the elderly in the population. For example, in Thailand, the proportion of the population aged 65 and over will rise from 3.9 per cent in 1990 to 6.6 per cent in 2010 and to 9.1 per cent in 2020. Ageing is caused more by fertility decline (which undercuts the lower section of the age pyramid) than by increased longevity, but the latter does play a part. As women outlive men, women are more numerous among the elderly. As men tend to marry wives younger than themselves (though not as much younger as in Middle Eastern countries or the Indian subcontinent), a substantial proportion of these elderly women are widowed. There is strong pressure in the region on elderly widowers to remarry, but no such pressure on elderly widows. Thus there is typically a ratio of between three and six women to one man among the Southeast Asian elderly who are currently widowed.

POLICY EMPHASES

Most Southeast Asian governments emphasize family cohesion and resilience as worthy features of their societies, in contrast to perceived undesirable features of family life in the West, including excessive individualism, materialism and neglect of the elderly. Article 2, section 12 of the Philippine Constitution of 1986 makes the defence of the family a basic national principle: "The State recognizes the sanctity of family life and shall protect and strengthen the family as a basic autonomous social institution". The family is being given considerable prominence in Indonesian official state ideology in the Sixth Five Year Plan, with "kesejahteraan keluarga" the catch phrase. It is emphasized that the term "kesejahteraan" means "wellbeing", a term hinting at not only material welfare but also a deeper, almost spiritual cohesion, rather than simply "welfare", a term which has the connotation of being amenable to a "quick fix" through policy measures. Malaysia is also placing emphasis on the family, replacing the National Family Planning Board with the National Population and Family Development Board, and initiating an annual family day, complete with speeches, family activities and competitions.

But family cohesion is seen as being under some threat.

In Singapore, the official Report of the Committee on the Problems of the Aged in 1984 argued that in the case of young people born during the 1960s and 1970s, "Their bonds with Asian family-oriented moral values of filial piety, and respect and reverence for the elderly and weak, would have been eroded by the influence of Western values of individualism and materialism". Recently, attention has been given by the Singapore legislature to the possibility of enforcing care of the elderly by recalcitrant family members, culminating in the passage of the 1994 Maintenance of Parents Bill.

The concern expressed in the Singapore committee report noted above is widely shared in Southeast Asia, but it is important to be sure that the issue is correctly perceived. The "continuity and change" paradigm might again be invoked. While it may be true that there are timeless elements of continuity and cohesion in family systems of Southeast Asia, it is hardly credible that the Southeast Asian family can avoid being deeply affected by the fast-changing social and economic milieu in which it is located. Changes to the Southeast Asian family, particularly in metropolitan areas, may be due much more to the inevitable consequences of industrialization, affluence and the pressures of urban living than to an insidious "Westernization".

The evidence of rising levels of premarital sexual activity has rarely resulted in imaginative programmes to deal with the need for counselling and contraceptive services for sexually active adolescents, despite the addition of HIV/AIDS to the problems of pregnancy and sexually transmitted diseases. Governments in the region appear to be universally opposed to making contraception available to adolescents without the consent of their parents. Indonesia's Minister of Population asserts that strengthening of the family, not programmes utilizing peers, is the way to deal with problems of adolescent sexuality.

There is some danger that government spokespersons will be convinced by their own rhetoric, and that a tendency (as in Indonesia) to assert that all programmes directed towards the problems of adolescents should operate through their families will leave substantial numbers of young people untouched by initiatives, for example on issues of adolescent sexuality, that are of vital importance to them. What does seem clear is that youth-oriented policies will receive considerable attention in the region, and that "family life education", "once a euphemism for informational and persuasive materials aimed at promoting fertility control"[37] will, for better or worse, increasingly take on a more literal meaning as governments in Asia edge their way towards true family policies: goal-directed government actions designed to mould the family system in ways perceived to be in the national interest.

NOTES

1. Gavin W. Jones, "Forms of Aid: Population Control", in *International Aid: Some Political, Administrative and Technical Realities*, ed. R.T. Shand and H.V. Richter (Canberra: Monograph No. 16, Development Studies Centre, Australian National University, 1979), pp. 212-34.
2. Paul P.L. Cheung, "Recent Changes in Population Policies: Malaysia and Singapore", in *International Population Conference*, New Delhi (Lige: IUSSP, 1989), vol. 1, pp. 133-42.
3. Gavin W. Jones, "Implementation Strategy for Achieving Replacement Fertility Level", in Senior Officials Meeting on Targets and Goals of the Bali Declaration on Population and Sustainable Development: Implementation Strategy, *Asian Population Studies Series* No. 127 (Bangkok: ESCAP, 1994).
4. Ansley J. Coale and Susan C. Watkins (eds.), *The Decline of Fertility in Europe: The Revised Proceedings of a Conference on the Princeton European Fertility Project* (Princeton: Princeton University Press, 1986).

5. John Bongaarts, "The Fertility Input of Family Planning Programmes" (New York: Working papers No. 47, The Population Council Research Division, 1993), pp. 19-20.
6. Lant H. Pritchett, "Desired Fertility and the Impact of Population Policies", *Population and Development Review* 20, 1 (1994): 1-56.
7. Paul J. Gertler and John W. Molyneaux, "How Economic Development and Family Planning Programs Combined to Reduce Indonesian Fertility", *Demography* 31, 1 (1994): 33-63.
8. John Cleland and Chris Wilson, "Institutional Analysis of Fertility", lecture presented in the series on *Population, Environment and Development*, Beijer Institute, Royal Swedish Academy of Sciences, Stockholm, 1993.
9. John Cleland and Chris Wilson, "Demand Theories of Fertility Transition: An Iconoclastic View", *Population Studies* 41, 1 (1987): 5-30.
10. Geoffrey McNicoll, review of Richard Leete and Iqbal Alam (eds.), *The Revolution in Asian Fertility: Dimensions, Causes and Implications, Population and Development Review* 20, 1 (1994): 215-19.
11. See John C. Caldwell, "The Asian Fertility Revolution: Its Implications for Transition Theories", in *The Revolution in Asian Fertility: Dimensions, Causes and Implications*, ed. Richard Leete and Iqbal Alam (Oxford: Clarendon Press, 1993), pp. 299-316; John Cleland, "Different Pathways to Demographic Transition", in *Population—The Complex Reality*, ed. Sir Francis Graham-Smith (Colorado: North American Press, for the Royal Society, 1994), pp. 229-47.
12. Gavin W. Jones, "Fertility Transitions among Malay Populations of Southeast Asia: Puzzles of Interpretation", *Population and Development Review* 16, 3 (1990): 507-537.
13. Peter McDonald, "Convergence or Compromise in Historical Family Change?", in *Family Systems and Cultural Change*, ed. Elza Berquo and Peter Xenos (Oxford: Clarendon Press, 1992), pp. 3-14.

14. Anthony Reid, *Southeast Asia in the Age of Commerce 1450-1680*, vol. I: The Lands Below the Wind (New Haven: Yale University Press, 1988), p. 126.
15. Kerry Richter and Chai Podhisita, "Thai Family Demography: A Review and Research Prospects", *Journal of Population and Social Studies* 3, 1-2 (1992): 1-19.
16. Belen T.G., Medina, *The Filipino Family* (Diliman: University of the Philippines Press, 1991), pp. 16-23.
17. Gelia T. Castillo, *Beyond Manila: Philippine Rural Problems in Perspective* (Ottawa: International Development Research Centre, 1979), p. 116.
18. Alfred W. McCoy, *An Anarchy of Families: State and Family in the Philippines* (Madison: Centre for Southeast Asian Studies, University of Wisconsin, 1993).
19. Andrew Mason, Mathana Phananiramai and Nipon Poapongsakorn, "Households and Their Characteristics", in *The Economic Impact of Demographic Change in Thailand, 1980-2015*, ed. Burnham O. Campbell, Andrew Mason and Ernesto M. Pernia (Honolulu: University of Hawaii Press, 1993), p. 70.
20. *Ibid.*, p. 71.
21. Jack M. Potter, *Thai Peasant Social Structure* (Chicago: University of Chicago Press, 1976).
22. Peter Xenos and Socorro Gultiano, "Trends in Female and Male Age at Marriage and Celibacy in Asia", *Papers of the Program on Population*, no. 120 (Honolulu: East-West Center, 1992).
23. Gavin W. Jones, *Marriage and Divorce in Islamic Southeast Asia* (Singapore: Oxford University Press, 1994).
24. A.J. Cherlin, P.C. Smith, T.E. Fricke, L.J. Domingo, S.M. Adioetomo, A. Chamratrithirong and S. Syed, "Family Influence on the Timing of Marriage: Evidence from Four Asian Societies", paper presented at *Workshop on Changing Marriage and the Family in Asia*, Pattaya, Thailand, February 1985.
25. Jones, *Marriage and Divorce*, chs. 5 and 6.

26. Lita J. Domingo and Elizabeth M. King, "The Role of the Family in the Process of Entry to Marriage in Asia", in *Family Systems and Cultural Change*, ed. Elza Berquo and Peter Xenos (Oxford: Clarendon Press, 1992).

27. Philip Guest and Joo Ean Tan, "Transformation of marriage patterns in Thailand", working paper, Institute for Population and Social Research, Mahidol University, Thailand, 1994. Thailand in this respect is following the lead of Japan, where female age at marriage is now among the highest in the world, and roughly 12 per cent of women can be expected to reach the end of their reproductive period without marrying. See Naohiro Ogawa and Robert D. Retherford, "The Resumption of Fertility Decline in Japan: 1973-92", *Population and Development Review* 19, 4 (1993): 703-741.

28. Jones, *Marriage and Divorce*, chs. 5 and 6.

29. William J. Goode, *World Changes in Divorce Patterns* (New Haven: Yale University Press, 1993).

30. Peter Xenos, "Extended Adolescence and the Sexuality of Asian Youth: Observations on Research and Policy", East-West Center reprints, *Population Series* No. 292 (Honolulu: East-West Center, 1993), Table 1.

31. Weerasit Sittitrai, Praphan Phanupak, Jean Barry and Tim Brown, Report of the Survey of Partner Relations and Risk of HIV Infection in Thailand, 1990 (Bangkok: Thai Red Cross Society and Institute of Population Studies, Chulalongkorn University, 1992).

32. Napaporn Havanon, Anthony Bennett and John Knodel, "Sexual Networking in Provincial Thailand", *Studies in Family Planning* 24, 1 (1993): 1-17.

33. David Sly, Chingsa Wu and Abdul Rahman, "HIV Transmission Risk Implications of Estimates of Premarital Conceptions: The Case of Indonesia", forthcoming.

34. Bangkok Post, "Lamphun Residents Face a Social Crisis", 19 Jun. 1994; Jakarta Post, "'Urban Culture' Triggers Sexual Promiscuity", 12 Aug. 1993.

35. Katherine F. Darabi, Susan Gustavus Philiber and Allan Rosenfield, "A Perspective on Adolescent Fertility in Developing Countries", *Studies in Family Planning* 10, 10 (1979): 300-303.

36. Xenos, "Extended Adolescence", p. 65.

37. *Ibid.*, p. 56.

6

THE INTERNATIONAL POLITICAL ECOLOGY OF INDUSTRIAL SHRIMP AQUACULTURE AND INDUSTRIAL PLANTATION FORESTRY IN SOUTHEAST ASIA

—Derek Hall

During the 1980s and 1990s, industrial shrimp aquaculture and industrial plantation forestry took their places in the long history of 'boom' natural resource sectors in Southeast Asia. The development of these two sectors has been marked by a number of similarities beyond the timing of their emergence. First, these new crops were tied to growing affluence in Eastern Asia. The Japanese 'bubble economy' of the 1980s and the upward revaluation of the yen led to rapid growth in the market for shrimp, and indeed Japan has come close to monopsony with respect to the production of some countries in the region. During the 1990s, rising incomes in the rest of the region and exports to Europe and the United States helped to keep shrimp aquaculture viable as Japanese consumption stagnated. Industrial plantations of fast-growing tree species suitable for pulping, meanwhile, have been encouraged by rapidly rising demand for high-quality paper and for packaging. Second, the foreign exchange potential of these sectors has meant that regional governments and bi- and multilateral aid organisations have assiduously promoted them. Shrimp farms and tree plantations have become increasingly important to Southeast Asian political economies, and have been taken up as primary examples of the regionalisation and globalisation of natural resource sectors in the region.

More fundamentally, there has been a critical shift in the shrimp and forestry sectors away from a 'hunting-and-gathering' model towards one based on agriculture. Until the 1980s, most internationally-traded shrimp originated in the capture fishery, while the trees harvested in Southeast Asian forestry came largely from more or less 'natural' forests, teak plantations being an important exception.[1] The origins of these shrimp and trees were thus largely independent of the production and trade circuits in which they later became enmeshed. With the rise of aquaculture and tree plantations, however, the supply of living organisms has become decreasingly tied to, for instance, coastal shrimp population dynamics, and increasingly related to human stocking and planting decisions. In Karl Polanyi's terms, shrimp and trees were previously 'fictitious commodities' in that while they were not 'objects produced for sale on the market,' they were subject to market mechanisms as though they had been so produced. Now, however, they have become real commodities: the very existence of these shrimp and trees is a consequence of their having been grown-out or planted for eventual sale.[2] Shrimp and trees are here part of a broader deepening of the incorporation into capitalist production of inputs that were once harvested from nature.[3] This process derives from the responses of capitalist firms to ecological scarcity (as the availability of natural stocks drops) and the benefits (homogeneity, control over species selection, and so forth) to be gained from newly available techniques of monocultural farming.

Over the last two decades, then, both the shrimp aquaculture and tree plantation sectors have been characterised by state, corporate and donor agency efforts to transform extensive areas of Southeast Asia into new and intensely managed ecosystems in order to pursue foreign exchange earnings. There have also been key differences between these sectors, however—both in the way they have been organised and in the extent to which reality has measured up to the often breathless plans of the promoters. While this article will outline a number of these differences, among the most important has been the variation in the overall trajectories of the two sectors. Shrimp aquaculture, at both the local and to a lesser degree the national levels, has been characterised by a pattern of sudden booms in production followed by equally spectacular crashes. While tens of thousands of people in Southeast Asia have tried their hands at shrimp farming, the mercurial quality of the sector has meant that their efforts have often collapsed almost immediately. Industrial tree plantations, in contrast, have faced their biggest difficulties in getting off the ground in the first place. Opposition to the sector, which has been most intense in Thailand but has taken place in other parts of the region as well, has imposed a brake on plantation expansion. These two sectors have thus been 'boom crops' in quite different senses. To use the puns beloved of headline writers, the shrimp boom has largely followed a 'prawndike' pattern of dramatic production rises followed by equally devastating crashes, while the difficulties that enthusiastic governments and corporations have faced in trying to promote an industrial tree plantation boom have led some to write the sector off as 'pulp fiction'.

This article will use the similarities and variances between these sectors to explain the different kinds of 'booms' they have experienced, as well as the ways in which they have interacted with surrounding communities and the characteristic political alliances that have formed around them. The discussion has been guided by work done in the now well-established field of political ecology, which foregrounds the relations between human beings and the natural world, or what Marx called the 'human-nature metabolism.'[4] The specific approach taken here differs from most work in political ecology, however, in not being based on close, detailed fieldwork at one or two locations. Rather, the article takes a comparative perspective, examining both the differences between shrimp aquaculture and plantation forestry and the differences within these sectors across nations (in particular, Indonesia, the Philippines and Thailand) and localities.[5] The analysis begins by identifying what might be called the 'sectoral environmental particularities' of industrial shrimp aquaculture and plantation forestry—that is, the characteristic requirements and problems of the new and heavily managed ecosystems created by these sectors. Rather than arguing for a kind of sectoral determinism, however, the article contends that attention must be paid to the ways these sectoral environmental particularities have interacted with different local and national conditions. The objective is thus largely to identify 'translocal' regularities and variations in these interactions.

The analysis will be divided into four sections. After a brief description of the technical characteristics of each sector, the discussion will examine the establishment of shrimp ponds and tree farms in terms of the range of viable farm sizes, local tenure relations and the methods through which land is acquired. It will then canvass the implications of the operation of shrimp and tree farms for local areas, including the ways they are integrated into local communities and economies, the problems of 'self-destruction' with which they have to grapple and their biological characteristics. These various processes have influenced the politics of these sectors, including the political alliances in which they are embedded, the way each sector and each commodity is represented, and typical forms of social conflict. Throughout the analysis, the importance of the interaction between the political-ecological characteristics of different sectors and changes in the communities that surround them is highlighted.

THE MOVE TO AN AGRICULTURAL MODEL

Although the capture fishery dominated the international trade in shrimp until the 1980s, shrimp aquaculture has been practiced for centuries in some parts of Southeast Asia, notably in Indonesia and the Philippines, where shrimp has been a subsidiary crop in milkfish ponds.[6] Traditional or 'extensive' aquaculture relies on tidal action for the provision of food and shrimp fry, and requires as inputs mainly the labour involved in impounding low-lying areas along bays and tidal rivers where the shrimp can be grown to market size. Modern Asian shrimp farming, which is based on techniques developed in Japan and Taiwan between the 1930s and 1970s and focuses on the species Penaeus monodon (black tiger shrimp), is far more capital- and input-intensive than traditional aquaculture.[7] Semi-intensive ponds are stocked not by the tides but by trawler-caught postlarval shrimp or by hatcheries. Similarly, pumps replace tides as the source of water exchange, and feeds are artificial. Yields are much higher, ranging from 50 to 5,000 kg per hectare, as against 50 to 500 kg for extensive farming.

Intensive aquaculture involves even closer management. The system uses small ponds (0.1 to 1.5 ha) and is able to densely stock shrimp through a combination of heavy feed inputs, waste removal and aeration. Yields range from 5,000 to 20,000 kg per hectare.[8] In both semi-intensive and intensive shrimp aquaculture, large amounts of fresh and salt water (which are mixed together to create the brackish water preferred by the shrimp), agricultural chemicals, feeds and farm machinery are brought together to form an artificial ecosystem that, in Peter Riggs' words, 'no more mimics the mangrove forest or the coastal estuary in which it is situated than would a parking lot.'[9]

Industrial tree plantations have mushroomed worldwide for many of the same reasons and through many of the same processes as shrimp farms. Just as overfishing has led to plateauing catches of natural shrimp, deforestation, environmental regulation and protest have reduced access to natural or second-growth trees. Technical advances have also contributed to making plantations more viable. By 1993, 95 per cent of Chile's industrial wood production, 93 per cent of New Zealand's and 60 per cent of Brazil's were derived from plantations.[10] Southeast Asia's move towards tree plantations has been driven by the same forces but was given extra impetus by the rapid growth of regional markets for paper products in the 1980s and 1990s. Different fast-growing species have been chosen for their suitability for local conditions, with Eucalyptus camaldulensis dominating in Thailand and various Acacia species most popular in Indonesia. Ricardo Carrere and Larry Lohmann have pithily described industrial tree plantations as follows:

> [they] are much closer to an industrial agricultural crop than to either a forest as usually understood, a traditionally-managed coppice, or a traditional farm plot. Usually consisting of thousands or even millions of trees of the same species, bred for rapid growth, uniformity and high yield of raw material, and planted in even-aged stands, they require intensive preparation of the soil, fertilisation, regular spacing of trees, seedling selection, intensive weeding using machines or herbicides, use of pesticides, thinning, mechanised harvesting, and in some cases, pruning.[11]

While this article will focus on the environmental particularities of shrimp and tree farming, it is important to note certain biological aspects of each species in order to understand the ways in which these sectors differ. Three differences should be highlighted between shrimp and fast-growing tree species: their respective harvest cycles, how quickly the harvested crop needs to be brought to market, and the potential for selective breeding. The fact that shrimp grow from post-larval to harvestable size in just two to three months has contributed to the often fly-by-night, 'slash-and-burn' characteristics of the industry. It is not necessary to make a long-term investment in shrimp farming in order to make returns that, in the words of the Bangkok Post, 'relative to outlay, can probably be bettered only by dealing in illicit drugs.'[12] Farmed trees, on the other hand, require at a minimum five and more often seven or eight years to reach harvestable size, and thus require a longer time commitment and the ability to assess risks over a period of more than a decade. With respect to transportation, the biological characteristics of shrimp are much more exacting than are those of trees. They must be moved from harvest to freezing/processing as quickly as possible—some farms in Indonesia manage this in under 20 minutes—and deteriorate significantly in quality each time they are unfrozen; this feature has tended to keep the farming and processing of shrimp quite close together. Logs and wood chips, however, are not nearly so delicate, a fact that has allowed widely dispersed siting of raw materials and processing. Finally, while tree scientists are making efforts through hybridisation and genetic engineering to develop hardier and faster-growing trees with better fibre content, shrimp have not in fact been fully domesticated in Asia. The post-larval shrimp that stock Asian ponds are either caught from the ocean (a form of fishing with an extremely high bycatch rate, i.e. the quantity of marine life caught inadvertently when fishing for something else) or grown out in hatcheries from wild broodstock. Because economically important shrimp species like black tiger cannot yet be bred in captivity, breeding and genetic engineering cannot be harnessed to address the problems of shrimp farming, although intense efforts to bring the life cycle of these shrimp under human control are underway in Asia.[13]

ESTABLISHMENT

One of the most important aspects of the move from hunting-and-gathering to an agricultural model in the shrimp and forestry sectors has been the necessity of gaining secure access to land. The establishment of both shrimp ponds and tree farms has involved significant shifts in land relations across Southeast Asia. These shifts have happened in different ways, depending in part on the ways in which shrimp and trees have moved from being 'fictitious' to 'real' commodities. In particular, land relations have depended upon the size of the farms being established, pre-existing tenure relations in the areas in question and the methods through which land has been acquired.

Shrimp farms are virtually always much smaller than tree plantations. While they can contain a number of individual ponds and vary in size, the dominant tendency in Asia has been towards clusters of small to medium-sized farms ranging from under one to five hectares. Tree plantations have tended to be much larger, generally on the order of hundreds or thousands of hectares. Given the difference in size between shrimp and trees, this disparity is hardly surprising; however, it can only partly be explained by the technical and biological characteristics of shrimp and tree farming. One study has argued that shrimp farming is either scale-neutral or else provides advantages to small-scale farming, and that large-scale corporate contract farming arrangements are not well suited to the sector. The authors state that:

> In a highly unstable disease environment, small farmers are better able to micromanage, have a more detailed knowledge of local ecologies, and can take advantage of a trial and error approach. Studies based on data obtained from large numbers of farmers in different parts of [Thailand] consistently show that small owner-operated farms are more efficient than medium and large farms operated by hired workers.[14]

This argument, however, is weakened by the existence of large-scale contract-farming arrangements in Indonesian shrimp aquaculture. Indeed, the study goes on to provide a number of other explanations for the tendency towards small shrimp farms in Thailand that derive more from political economy than they do from the nature of shrimp farming itself. These factors include the cost, availability and pattern of control over land; the dense canal networks that already exist in much of coastal Thailand and reduce the cost of establishing farm infrastructure; and government policies forcing banks to lend to farmers. It is thus not clear that there is any inherent optimal size for a shrimp farm.[15] The large size of tree plantations, however, is linked much more tightly to the nature of the sector. One reason for this is that while the stocking density in a shrimp pond can vary dramatically, on a tree plantation the range of optimal tree spacings is quite small. Anyone wishing to make a significant investment in tree farming is thus obliged to plant at least a few hundred hectares of land, while shrimp farmers can limit their attentions to a few hectares and still turn a profit. In addition, economies of scale on tree plantations (for instance, in land clearance and pesticide application) clearly point towards the benefits of scale. In Indonesia, it has been estimated that the optimal area for an industrial tree plantation is on the order of 30,000 to 50,000 hectares.[16] Similarly, in Thailand large-scale plantations have tended to be more profitable than smaller ones, and a Japanese survey team in the

Philippines estimated that the 2248 ha available at the former site of Clark Air Force Base would be insufficient for an optimally-sized tree plantation.[17] In Thailand, the turn to contract farming of eucalyptus and other industrial tree species has clearly been a second-best response of corporations that have been unable to establish large-scale plantations, as will be discussed below.[18] The tree plantation sector thus differs from shrimp aquaculture in that investors in the former always prefer large operations.

Both shrimp aquaculture and industrial tree plantations in Asia have largely been established in areas that did not previously have clearly defined property relations in land. Both sectors have tended towards land such as coastal areas or reserved forests that, while legally claimed by the state, is actually inhabited, in some cases by communities that have existed for centuries. This pattern has meant that the establishment of both shrimp and tree farms has often been predicated on the sometimes violent dispossession of these communities and the effective enclosure and expropriation of their land. Here again, however, there has been variation, particularly in the case of shrimp farming. The Asian shrimp aquaculture boom of the last twenty years has contributed to raising the price of coastal land that was not previously of much economic value. As a result, governments and corporations have developed an interest in land which had previously been left to be managed by local communities and/or was still covered in mangrove forests. Along both coasts of Thailand, for instance, most coastal land was legally the property of the government, a fact that worked to the disadvantage of fishing communities as investors moved in to enclose ponds. Similarly, while along the north and east coasts of Java it was possible for fishpond owners to claim title to land once they had invested a certain minimal level of labour in it, most areas were still marked by unclear tenure relations at the beginning of the shrimp boom.[19]

In both Indonesia and Thailand, however, local people have been very much involved in shrimp aquaculture, a fact that has complicated the politics of enclosure, as will be discussed further below. It should also be noted that in some of the major centres of Asian shrimp farming, such as Negros (in the Philippines), the area just inland of the eastern coast of southern Thailand, and the Chao Phraya River basin, shrimp farming has been established in areas that already had well-institutionalised capitalist land relations.[20] Land for shrimp ponds in these areas has largely been acquired through either the use of the farmer's own land, purchase, or lease.

In the case of tree plantations, again much of the area targeted for the sector—whether forest land, degraded scrub or villages and farmland -has been under the de jure control of the state. In Thailand, for instance, most of the push to establish plantations in the 1980s took place in the government-owned reserve forests, while plantation establishment in Indonesia has largely occurred through government awards of concessions on the outer islands.[21] The scale of operation favoured by forestry companies has meant that purchasing or leasing sufficiently large chunks of contiguous land from private owners has generally been impossible in Southeast Asia. However, this has not been the case for Japanese companies setting up tree plantations in Australia, and it seems that purchase and lease have been the primary means of establishment of pine plantations in the Araucania region of Chile.[22]

In practice, of course, these concessions on nominally state-owned land in Southeast Asia come into conflict with the claims of the inhabitants. In Indonesia, this conflict has mostly been with communities practicing swidden agriculture, in part because many companies in Indonesia have sought plantation concessions in forested areas primarily in order to cut and sell the standing timber.[23] In Thailand, conflict was with denser and more settled communities which were producing export crops for the world market and which had in some cases been encouraged by the state to settle in the reserve forests in the 1960s and 1970s as part of the war against the Communist Party of Thailand. Given the common pattern of eviction, and the close involvement of the military with tree plantations, it is not surprising that Tasaka Toshio has modified Marx's description of enclosure in England to say that in Thailand 'trees eat people'.[24] It should be noted, however, that in some cases the move to farming of trees has actually facilitated the ability of peasants to claim more secure land tenure. Peasants engaged in contract tree farming in Thailand have been able to use the presence of trees on their land as an argument for being granted better tenure certificates, and indeed the role of trees in asserting land claims has been identified in many parts of the world.[25]

OPERATION

The above section has outlined the similarities and differences in the establishment of shrimp farming and tree plantations. This section will briefly discuss the characteristic patterns in the ways that these two sectors interact with the political economies and ecologies around them once they are up and running. One striking difference is the extent to which shrimp farming and tree plantations are integrated into local political economies. As noted above, shrimp farms in Asia have generally been quite small, and while participation by urban and corporate capital has certainly been significant, the major farming centres have mostly seen a mix of absentee and local ownership. Local participation in the sector, whether through ownership or employment, has thus tended to be fairly high. Industrial tree plantations have displayed the opposite pattern. These projects have almost all been owned by large corporations and staffed by workers brought in from outside; in addition, tree plantations have (as already mentioned) tended to displace pre-existing land uses on a wide scale. Local ownership has been close to non-existent and local employment relatively insignificant in comparison to the opportunities destroyed by plantations.[26] There have, of course, been exceptions to both of these broad patterns. Indonesian transmigration projects have staffed shrimp farms of hundreds or thousands of hectares with transmigrants from Java with little integration into local economies. Conversely, contract tree farming in Thailand has seen both smaller farms and more participation from local people than have large-scale plantations. For the most part, however, shrimp farms have been much more closely integrated into local communities than have tree plantations.

Just as shrimp farms and tree plantations have brought socio-economic changes to local communities, so environmental change has also been central to the fate of the two sectors. The most remarked-upon aspect of the problems that shrimp farming causes for local people has been the destruction of mangrove forests. Shrimp aquaculture demands that existing ecosystems be obliterated to make way for ponds, which has often meant the destruction of mangroves. These forests, which grow along tropical coasts and brackish waterways, provide a number of vital ecological services, including preventing coastal erosion and storm damage, filtering upstream pollutants before they enter the ocean (and thus protecting other ecosystems), serving as a breeding and feeding ground for countless fish species, and cycling and storing nutrients. Mangroves are under intense pressure throughout tropical Asia and the ecosystemic services they provide may soon be permanently lost. The role of shrimp aquaculture in mangrove destruction, however, is unclear. Activists, scholars and governments have all claimed that shrimp farming is the primary cause of mangrove destruction in many Asian countries, while industry sources have rejected these claims. Whatever the damage done in the past, the industry is now moving away from mangrove zones because of controversy and tighter regulation, and because mangrove soil chemistry is 'sub-optimal' for semi-intensive production and 'unsuitable' for intensive production.[27] To the extent that shrimp farms have been responsible for mangrove loss, however, they have contributed through the destruction of habitat and breeding grounds to the decline of coastal fisheries on which local people had previously relied for much of their income and food.[28]

Shrimp farming has also caused significant problems for local communities, and for agriculture in particular, through its thirst for water. Excessive exploitation of groundwater has led to the drawing down of local aquifers and in some cases to salinisation (as seawater moves in to take up the space previously occupied by underground fresh water). In some of the worst affected regions there has been extensive ground subsidence, with buildings in Taiwan sinking a storey or more. Farmers who have leased land to shrimp farms have also objected to the salt deposits left behind in their fields, rendering them unsuitable for agriculture.[29] Another issue related to water usage has been the dumping of shrimp farm effluent into communal waterways, which degrades the water available for local agriculture.

Similarly, tree farms have continued to cause problems for their neighbours even after they have been established, for two major reasons. First, compared to mixed forests tree plantations have quite different ratios of (a) water intercepted by foliage to that reaching the ground, (b) runoff to water infiltrating the soil, and (c) evapotranspiration to water reaching the subsoil.[30] Eucalypts, in addition, absorb water from further underground than do other trees and plants. Plantations thus destabilise water cycles, with results including reduced water flow throughout the year, the disappearance of streams during the dry season, and damage to other ecosystems facing reduced access to water. Farming, irrigation, livestock and fishing in areas around plantations all suffer. A second reason is that even when locals are not evicted from their land, monocultures of eucalyptus afford none of the ecological benefits which mixed forests provided to people living nearby—for instance, grazing land, fodder and firewood, and intercropping.[31]

With respect to the long-term viability of these sectors, it must be noted that while environmental sources of conflict with local communities have been important in both cases, shrimp farming confronts intense difficulties even in the absence of such conflict. While shrimp aquaculture has been criticised for the damage it does to mangroves, the environmental issues which most concern the industry are those which make shrimp farming prone to undermining its own conditions of existence. Modern shrimp aquaculture has faced four major environmental problems that have made the sector prone to sudden crashes in production levels and long-term malaise.[32] First, shrimp are highly sensitive organisms, and as such are particularly vulnerable to upstream pollution (for instance, industrial effluent or agricultural runoff) entering their water supply. Second, shrimp ponds themselves produce sizable amounts of effluent; and when water intake and outflow systems in areas crowded with farms are not well-designed, there is a strong tendency for farms to pollute each other's water supply. Third, the industry uses fresh water in sufficiently large quantities that it has often depleted local supplies.

A final issue is that dense monocultural stocking of shrimp in conjunction with intraregional flows of broodstock and the transfer of water from farm to farm have left industrially-farmed shrimp highly susceptible to disease outbreaks. No country in Asia has been immune to these, and the industry has devoted hundreds of millions of dollars to efforts to control them. The disease-induced crash that hit Ecuador in 2000, which is estimated to have cost the country $1 billion in export revenues and half a million jobs, is only the most recent of the spectacular declines in production that have plagued shrimp aquaculture.[33] In these four ways, participants in industrial aquaculture are forced to confront some of the environmental consequences of their production choices in the form of declining profits or even bankruptcy. Tree farm monocultures, on the other hand, while also faced with disease problems, have generally not been overwhelmed by them.

POLITICS AND REPRESENTATION

The above sections have discussed the ways in which the particularities of the capitalisation of nature in shrimp aquaculture and tree farming have shaped the organisation of each of these sectors and their interaction with the political economies and ecologies that surround them. The patterns identified above have in turn affected the ways these sectors have been represented ideologically, the types of political alliances that have formed around them and the forms of conflict that have attended these farms. An analysis of the politics of these sectors highlights first, the critical influence that contention has had on their respective trajectories and second, a fascinating disjuncture between the degrees of opposition they have provoked at the domestic and international levels.

Shrimp have long been associated with wealth and longevity in many parts of Asia; in Japan, for instance, the idea that shrimp look like venerable old men has made them a staple of New Year's parties. That shrimp have been something of a luxury good underlined this image. In Southeast Asia during the late 1980s and early 1990s, the incredible amounts of money that could be made from shrimp farming transformed the sector into a symbol of economic boom times. In particular, the possibility of people from the middle class or even below hitting the jackpot with a couple of hectares of shrimp ponds meant that shrimp became associated with getting rich quick. Proponents of shrimp farming have thus been able to draw on both the association of the shrimp itself with luxury and longevity and on the proliferation of Horatio Alger success stories associated with the sector.

The regional pulp and paper industry, meanwhile, has made much of the comparatively low rates of per capita paper consumption in Southeast Asia in arguing that tree plantations are essential for bringing the benefits of modernity and information economies to the region. However, the lack of positive associations with eucalyptus and the dearth of cases of poorer people doing well out of tree farming has meant that there is much more space for negative representations of tree plantations. In Thailand, eucalyptus has been perceived by farmers as a 'selfish tree' or a 'tree of hell.' One of Amare Tegbaru's informants in Thailand made explicit the connection between the qualities of eucalyptus and the infringement by the state onto local lands, arguing that 'eucalyptus is like the state. It sucks and takes everything for itself. It competes with other plants and trees, and grows by undermining everything around it. The same is true of the state. It has become rich and powerful while we remain weak and poor'.[34]

The stronger negative connotation associated with tree plantations has manifested itself in the local—though not the global—NGO politics of the respective sectors. Local NGOs in Indonesia, the Philippines and Thailand, while generally critical of industrial aquaculture, have tended not to become involved in active resistance, likely because of the sector's complicated politics and the divisions it brings about in local communities. It is notable in this context that the most intense conflict over shrimp farming in Thailand—the seesawing fight over the banning of low-salinity aquaculture in inland rice farming areas—has been primarily a battle between shrimp and rice farmers and their respective political patrons.[35] Perhaps the main example of NGO involvement in Asian shrimp politics has been the work of human rights groups in Indonesia to support calls for better working conditions by workers at the giant shrimp estates in southern Sumatra, but this battle has had more to do with labour relations than with shrimp farming per se. With respect to tree plantations, however, local NGOs have had no such reservations, and have engaged wholeheartedly in struggles in Thailand and Indonesia. As noted above, tree plantations in Asia have often been established through the militarised dispossession of local people who are subsequently unable to find employment on the new plantation and derive few to no benefits from it. While states in the region have attempted to mobilise images of reforestation and paper consumption as symbols of development, in practice the sharp distinction between elite benefit and local impoverishment associated with tree plantations has motivated NGO opposition.[36]

Internationally, interestingly enough, the situation has been reversed, with shrimp farming attracting more opposition than plantation forestry. Industrial shrimp farming has seen the organisation of international opposition movements and boycott campaigns that have responded mainly to the destruction of mangrove forests.[37] Globally, shrimp's image as a luxury product has worked to encourage opposition to industrial aquaculture, given the perception of developed-world luxury consumption ravaging coastal Asian environments. The issues that have been most prominent in Western and local NGO critiques of shrimp farming have been quite different, however. In a response to environmentalist critiques of shrimp farming, the Shrimp Council (an industry organisation) has focused almost entirely on issues such as mangroves, turtle excluder devices, and bycatch in the trawling of shrimp larvae—the main concerns of Western groups—rather than addressing local concerns such as access to land, water pollution, salinisation, ground subsidence and violence.[38] International opposition to industrial plantation forestry has been slower to develop, likely because the association with reforestation initially increased the appeal of the sector for some Western environmental groups. However, concern about industrial plantations has been growing in recent years, stimulated by the anti-plantation campaign of the World Rainforest Movement and by the sudden rise to prominence of the sector as a possible source of carbon sinks under the Kyoto Protocol.[39]

While a good deal of conflict has certainly surrounded shrimp aquaculture in Asia, it is perhaps surprising that there has not been more, given the damage that the industry has done to fishing and farming in the areas that surround it. The industry has seen much more contention and violence in other countries, including Honduras and India.[40] While the range of factors that work together to explain the eruption or otherwise of social conflict is obviously very large, a comparison with the industrial tree plantation sector suggests some possible explanations for the difference. In particular, the comparatively small size of individual shrimp farms, the integration of local people (particularly elites) and the potential for windfall profits associated with the sector have meant that united opposition to the sector at the community level in Indonesia, the Philippines and Thailand has been fairly rare. Indeed, what protest has occurred often seems to have been against absentee owners.[41] Local-level opposition thus appears to have been restricted for the same reasons that local NGOs have found it difficult to get involved in conflicts over shrimp farming.

Tree plantations, which like shrimp farms have been associated with dispossession and damage to local agriculture, have differed on most of these points. They are very large, poorly integrated into local communities, and provide little opportunity for local elites beyond the prospect of being bought off by corporate or state actors.[42] Furthermore, while the land for both sectors has been acquired in a variety of ways in Asia, tree plantations have seen a more consistent pattern of de facto enclosure, often with military participation. These conditions have united communities against tree plantations and made it easy to demonise the sector and the trees themselves, as noted above. Thus, Tasaka argues that the wave of peasant resistance to plantations that swept the Northeast of Thailand in the mid-1980s was triggered by a highly militarised attempt by the Thai government and corporate actors to relocate peasants living in the reserve forests.[43] The militarisation of forest policy can be seen most clearly in the Khor Jor Kor resettlement project, initiated under military rule in March 1991 and described as one of the military's 'most ambitious money-making programs.'[44] The project, which was cancelled in June 1992 after Thailand's return to democracy, sought to resettle 250,000 families from reserve forests between 1991-6 and to sell the newly-vacated land for eucalyptus plantations. Intense resistance to these projects has more or less brought the industry to a standstill in Thailand, where frustrated pulp and paper companies have turned to contract farming of eucalyptus as a second-best alternative now that it is clear that large areas of land for plantations will not be forthcoming.[45] In Indonesia, the Finnantara company, which has attempted to defuse resistance to plantations by taking a more conciliatory approach to local concerns, is instead being abandoned by investors and government officials frustrated with the time required to run 'kinder, gentler' industrial tree plantations.[46]

CONCLUSIONS

This article has moved from the more local and technical to the more political and larger-scale in explaining the differing success of industrial shrimp farming and industrial tree plantations in Southeast Asia. The organisation of these sectors, the way they interact with the political ecologies around them, and the politics and contention that they have inspired are, it is argued, rooted in good part in the particularities of the ways in which they have moved away from hunting-and-gathering techniques towards methods which are more agricultural. As peripatetic sectors have become sedentary, the control over land required in order to establish production has meant that these sectors have been associated with enclosure and dispossession, and the day-to-day operations have caused significant environmental problems for local farming and fishing. However, the ways in which these broad similarities have translated into oppositional politics in shrimp and tree farming have varied, in part because of such factors as economies of scale and integration into local communities.

While the politics of shrimp farming in Southeast Asia have been complex and important, they have not ultimately posed a major threat to the sector's perpetuation in the region. Only in the Chao Phraya basin in Thailand has a ban been imposed on shrimp farming (as was done in India) because of the damage that it does to local communities, and even that ban may well be revoked.[47] The primary threat to shrimp aquaculture in the region has been not protest but the sector itself, as water pollution, salinisation and particularly disease epidemics have wiped out billions of dollars worth of production in massive crashes. Industrial tree plantations have also been susceptible to disease, but their spread in Southeast Asia has primarily been slowed by opposition from people who have been dispossessed by their establishment or whose livelihoods are threatened by their very existence. Interestingly, while Japanese corporations have been scouring the world for the last 15 years looking for locations for industrial tree plantations and have invested heavily in the sector in Australia, their initial interest in Southeast Asia quickly dissipated when they came to understand the politics of tree plantations in the region.[48] At present, there is only one Japanese tree plantation in Southeast Asia—in Vietnam. While this article has not been able to address all of the relevant factors—variations in state support, for instance, have been critical in both cases—it has emphasised that the confluence of sectoral particularities, community responses and political alliances has been central in shaping the 'prawndike' and 'pulp fiction' trajectories of these two sectors.

NOTES

1. See, for instance, Nancy Lee Peluso, *Rich forests, poor people: Resource control and resistance in Java* (Berkeley: University of California Press, 1992) and Raymond Bryant, *The political ecology of forestry in Burma, 1824-1994* (London: Hurst & Company, 1997). 'Capture fisheries' have fish caught in the wild, as opposed to fish farms.
2. Karl Polanyi, *The great transformation: The political and economic origins of our time* (Boston: Beacon Press, 1957). This is not entirely true of shrimp, as we will see later.
3. Martin O'Connor, 'On the misadventures of capitalist nature', in *Is capitalism sustainable? Political economy and the politics of ecology*, ed. Martin O'Connor (New York: Guildford Press, 1994), pp. 125-51.
4. On political ecology, see *Third World political ecology*, ed. Raymond Bryant and Sinead Bailey (London and New York: Routledge, 1997). 'Human-nature metabolism' is discussed in John Bellamy Foster, *Marx's ecology: Materialism and nature* (New York: Monthly Review Press, 2000).
5. An increasing amount of comparative work is being done in political ecology; see, for instance, Susan C. Stonich and Peter Vandergeest, 'Violence, environment, and industrial shrimp farming', in *Violent environments*, ed. Nancy Lee Peluso and Michael Watts (Ithaca, NY: Cornell University Press, 2001), pp. 261-86.
6. Chairul Muluk and Conner Bailey, 'Social and environmental impacts of coastal aquaculture in Indonesia', in *Aquacultural development: Social dimensions of an emerging industry*, ed. Conner Bailey et al. (Boulder: Westview Press, 1996), pp. 193-209; Michael A. Rice and Arthur Z. DeVera, 'Aquaculture in Dagupan City, Philippines', *World Aquaculture*, 29, 1 (1998): 18-24.

7. Yamauchi Kageki, *Sakana to Nihonjin* [Fish and the Japanese] (Tokyo: Chikuma Shinsho, 1997).
8. Bob Rosenberry, *World shrimp farming 1997* (San Diego: Shrimp News International, 1997), pp. 165-8.
9. Peter Riggs, 'Commodities, certification, and value: A social and environmental perspective on shrimp aquaculture' (Unpublished paper, Tufts University School of Veterinary Medicine, 1998), p. 8.
10. Ricardo Carrere and Larry Lohmann, *Pulping the South: Industrial tree plantations and the world paper economy* (London: Zed Books, 1996), p. 49; an overview of these developments is in Alexander Mather, 'Global and globalizing trends in wood production', *Geography*, 80 (1995): 355-66.
11. Carrere and Lohmann, *Pulping the South*, p. 4.
12. 'High-risk industry roars better than ever', *Bangkok Post*, 18 May 1998.
13. Jasper Goss et al., 'Agri-food restructuring and Third World transnationals: Thailand, the CP Group and the global shrimp industry,' *World Development*, 28, 3 (2000): 513-30.
14. Peter Vandergeest et al., 'A political ecology of shrimp aquaculture in Thailand', *Rural Sociology*, 64, 4 (1999): 584-5.
15. *Ibid.*, pp. 585-6. On Indonesia, see Dan Murphy, 'Deeper into the morass', *Far Eastern Economic Review*, 1 June 2000. A general discussion of shrimp farming is in Derek Hall, 'Explaining the diversity of Southeast Asian shrimp aquaculture', paper presented to the annual meeting of the Rural Sociology Association, Albuquerque, New Mexico, 18 Aug. 2001.
16. From a report by the consulting company Jaakko Poyry cited in Wahana Lingkungan Hidup Indonesia (WALHI) and Yayasan Lembaga Bantuan Hukum Indonesia (YLBHI), Mistaking plantations for Indonesia's tropical forest (Jakarta: WALHI, 1994), p. 27.
17. Moriyama Hiroshi, 'Watashitachi ga tsukau kami o ODA ga sodateru!? Tai nado' [ODA pays for the paper we use!?

Thailand, etc.], in *Nihonjin no kurashi no tame datta ODA* [ODA was in aid of Japanese livelihoods], ed. Fuke Yosuke and Fujibayashi Yasushi (Tokyo: Commons, 1999), pp. 12-43; Kaigai Sangyo Shokurin Senta, *Firipin kyowakoku ni okeru shokurin tekichi chosa hokokusho* [Report on afforestation in the Philippines] (Tokyo: Kaigai Sangyo Shokurin Senta, 2000), p. 51.

18. Roger Clapp has argued, however, that there is likely to be an increase in contract tree farming in Chile for reasons connected closely to the nature of the sector; Roger Alex Clapp, 'Regions of refuge and the agrarian question: Peasant agriculture and plantation forestry in Chilean Araucanla', *World Development*, 26, 4 (1998): 585.

19. Miriam Huitric, 'The Thai shrimp farming industry: Historical development, social drives and environmental impacts' (M.A. thesis [Examensarbete 1998: 13], Stockholm University, 1998); George W Chamberlain, 'Shrimp farming in Indonesia 1: Growing techniques', *World Aquaculture*, 22, 2 (1991): 14.

20. See Mark Flaherty and Peter Vandergeest, '"Low-salt" shrimp aquaculture in Thailand: Goodbye coastline, hello Khon Kaen!', *Environmental Management*, 22, 6 (1998): 817-30; and Mike Polioudakis, 'Synopsis of results of research on Southern Thai shrimp farming: Some recommendations' (unpublished paper, 2000).

21. WALHI and YLBHI, *Mistaking plantations*.

22. Hisada Mutsuaki, 'Wagakuni minkan kigyo no kaigai sangyo shokurin no doko' [Trends in our country's private overseas industrial tree planting], Kokusai Noringyo Kyoryoku [International agriculture and forestry cooperation], 22, 8 (2000): 18-28; Clapp, 'Regions of refuge'.

23. Lesley Potter and Justin Lee, *Tree planting in Indonesia: Trends, impacts and directions* (Bogor, Indonesia: Center for International Forestry Research, 1998), p. 16.

24. Tasaka Toshio, *Yukari bijinesu: Tai shinrin hakai to Nihon* [Eucalyptus business: Japan and forest destruction in Thailand] (Tokyo: Shin Nihon Shuppansha, 1992). On dispossession in Indonesia see Potter and Lee, 'Tree planting in Indonesia', p. 45.

25. Pearmsak Makarabhirom, 'A study on contract tree farming in Thailand' (Ph.D. diss., Tsukuba University, 1998); Richard A. Schroeder, 'Shady practice: Gender and the political ecology of resource stabilization in Gambian garden/orchards', *Economic Geography*, 69, 4 (1993): 349-65.

26. Potter and Lee, *Tree planting in Indonesia*, report that 'villagers seem to view a rubberwood estate more favourably than a pulp or timber plantation because of the opportunity to work felling the trees before they are ready for felling' (p. 18); industrial tree plantations are discussed on pp. 36, 39.

27. Bob Rosenberry, *World shrimp farming* 1996 (San Diego: Shrimp News International, 1996), p. 166; Imre Csavas, 'Important factors in the success of shrimp farming', *World Aquaculture*, 25, 1 (1994): 43. See also Piamsak Menasveta, 'Mangrove destruction and shrimp aquaculture', *World Aquaculture*, 28, 4 (1997): 36-42.

28. Huitric, 'Thai shrimp farming industry'.

29. On groundwater see, for instance, 'Prawn farms threaten Mindanao's water supply', (Manila) *Sunday Chronicle*, 22 Aug. 1993, and Philip Liu, 'Water supply in peril', *Free China Review*, August 1993. Salt deposits are mentioned in Flaherty and Vandergeest, '"Low-salt" shrimp aquaculture', p. 827.

30. Carrere and Lohmann, *Pulping the South*, pp. 64-5.

31. See also 'Eucalyptus a bad experience for farmers: Harms nearby crops, kills water sources', *Bangkok Post*, 6 Sep. 1999.

32. Tania Li describes a similar boom pattern in the cocoa sector in her 'Local histories, global markets: Cocoa and class in upland Sulawesi', *Development and Change*, 33, 3 (2002): 419.

33. 'Ecuador: State of emergency declared over lost shrimp revenue', http://www.shrimpaction.com/News/Ecuador5.html

34. Amare Tegbaru, 'Forests, farmers and the state: Environment and resistance in Northeastern Thailand' (Ph.D. diss., Stockholm University, dist. Almqvist & Wiksell International, 1998), pp. 160-1.

35. 'A change of heart', *Bangkok Post*, 23 July 1998; 'Govt walks minefield in shrimp-paddy battle', The Nation, 22 Dec. 1998. On NGO involvement see Flaherty and Vandergeest, '"Low-salt" shrimp aquaculture' and Li, 'Local histories', p. 430.

36. Larry Lohmann, 'Visitors to the commons: Approaching Thailand's "environmental" struggles from a Western standpoint', in *Ecological resistance movements: The global emergence of radical and popular environmentalism*, ed. Bron Raymond Taylor (Albany: SUNY Press, 1995), pp. 109-26; WALHI and YLBHI, Mistaking plantations; and Tasaka, Yukari bijinesu. There are NGOs in the region that support tree plantations; see 'Philippines tree-growers, others oppose total log ban' *Asia Pulse*, 1 Dec. 1999.

37. Susan C. Stonich and Conner Bailey, 'Resisting the blue revolution: Contending coalitions surrounding industrial shrimp farming', *Human Organization*, 59, 1 (2000): 23-36.

38. Rosenberry, *World shrimp farming* 1996, p. 146.

39. World Rainforest Movement, Climate change convention: Sinks that stink (Montevideo, Uruguay: World Rainforest Movement, 2000).

40. Stonich and Vandergeest, 'Violence'.

41. Flaherty and Vandergeest, '"Low-salt" shrimp aquaculture', p. 827.

42. On this last point see Potter and Lee, 'Tree planting in Indonesia'.

43. Tasaka, *Yukari bijinesu*, p. 171.

44. Stan Sesser, 'The course of corruption', *Mother Jones*, 93 (1993): 67.

45. Permsak, 'Study on contract tree farming in Thailand'.

46. Potter and Lee, 'Tree planting in Indonesia', pp. 16-9.
47. 'Government to relax shrimp farming restrictions', (Bangkok) *Business Day*, 18 Jul), 2001; 'Shrimp ban remains for now', *Bangkok Post*, 1 Aug. 2001.
48. Morimoto Taiji, 'Parupu-zai no shorai tenbo' [Future direction of pulp materials], Kami-pa Gikyoshi [Paper-pulp technical cooperation], 47, 1 (1993): 45; and Derek Hall, 'Environmental change, protest, and havens of environmental degradation: Evidence from Japan-Southeast Asia relations', *Global Environmental Politics*, 2, 2 (2002): 20-8.

7

SOCIAL ASPECTS OF FORESTRY IN SOUTHEAST ASIA: A REVIEW OF POSTWAR TRENDS IN THE SCHOLARLY LITERATURE

—Nancy Lee Peluso, Peter Vandergeest, Lesley Potter

This article examines the major trends since the 1950s in social science writing on forest management in Southeast Asia. Southeast Asia is simultaneously rich in and dependent on natural resources, both for local and national use or sale. Among renewable resources, forest products have played critical roles in the region's national, provincial, and local economies before, during, and after colonialism - for as long as two millennia. Their importance in international trade illustrates that Southeast Asia's forests linked the region to other parts of the world for quite some time, dispelling myths that parts of the region such as Borneo were "remote", "primitive", or "pristine".[1]

Though only 12 per cent of the world's tropical rainforests lie in Southeast Asia, mostly in the Philippines, Sumatra, and Borneo,[2] Indonesia and Malaysia share some

80 per cent of the global tropical timber trade.[3] Since the colonial period, forest products and forested land have helped fuel economic growth in Indonesia, Malaysia, Thailand, and the Philippines. Particularly since the end of World War II, the exploitation of Southeast Asian tropical timbers used for construction, framery and plywood, most from the Dipterocarpaceae family,[4] has stimulated periodic booms in many Southeast Asian economies.[5] Luxury woods such as rosewood (Dalbergia spp.), teak (Tectona grandis), ebony (Diospyors ebonaster), and mahogany (Switenia spp.) have been traded in international markets from colonial times, generating considerable revenue for both colonial and contemporary states. Regionally important non-timber forest and agro-forestry products include rattans, fruit, bamboos, natural latexes, gums, resins, birds nests, incense woods, camphor, and animal skins, meat, other animal body parts, and living wildlife. Throughout Southeast Asia, forest products of all types have also played a role in financing resistance movements and revolutions, or helping people subsist during social upheaval.

Because of their local and regional importance, many groups have staked claims and managed forest resources in Southeast Asia. Local people throughout the region cultivate, encourage, or protect products crucial to their livelihoods, despite some perceptions that they simply extract a "subsidy from nature".[6] The urge to control and produce these valuable products has also had a major influence on states' land use policies throughout the region.[7] For example, the Royal Forestry Department in Thailand, which controls land rights in almost half the national territory, was created to control production and the extraction of teak. While most of Java's teak production is sold on the domestic market, government teak plantations occupy some eight per cent of the Java's total land area. Nearly a quarter of this densely populated, rapidly developing island is under government forest of one kind or another.[8] State control of forest lands here is both a legacy of the colonial period and a clear indicator of the wealth contained in the region's forests.

The myths that forested areas are remote and primitive derive in part from the distinction often made between so-called lowland and upland areas in Southeast Asia. The major states - those with which European, Chinese, Arab and Indian traders had the most immediate contacts - were based on lowland wet-rice agriculture and control of access to river trade. Upland areas were understood as forested and less accessible regions. In fact, lowland forests have been important throughout Southeast Asia, and in insular Southeast Asia many of the remaining forests are still in the lowlands. Both colonial and postwar state-building efforts included major programmes by lowland-based states to take control of upland and forested areas. States sought this control in order to claim and use resources to finance colonialism and economic development, and in some cases, to neutralize potential security threats from upland peoples. Somewhat contradictorily, such control strategies were intended to incorporate upland populations into the national states on one hand, and to keep the uplands as "frontiers" for the resettlement of lowland people marginalized by the commercialization of agriculture on the other.

Despite some largely undisputed facts about the history of Southeast Asian forests, several wholly different types of analyses, as well as debates about the benefits and unintended consequences of resource exploitation, have characterized the scholarly literature on forest management and forest peoples of the region since the end of World War II. The remainder of this paper will be divided roughly into three 10-15 year periods, each characterized by the initiation of particular types of analytic focus and debate. These are first, the early development era, from the 1950s to the mid-1960s, during which local and macro approaches to understanding forest management were largely divorced from one another; second, the mid-1960s to mid-1970s when research attention to lowland rice systems dominated and attention to upland and forested areas was driven by international and civil wars and by internal security concerns; and finally, the mid-1970s to the present, when attention to environmental issues in general, many of which are connected to forests and forest peoples, has exploded. This periodization is a general guide only; as will be apparent, traditions initiated in one period often continued well into subsequent periods. In the final section, we discuss some of the differences between the literature on mainland and insular Southeast Asia, gaps in these literatures, and mention some current research trends.

1950S TO MID-1960S: THE EARLY DEVELOPMENT ERA

During the 1950s, two distinct writing traditions on forest management were initiated, both of which have continued to the present, albeit with some changes. The first was that of development and forest economists, both practitioners and academics. Many of these economists were working for or with the Food and Agricultural Organization of the United Nations (FAO), the World Bank, or bilateral aid agencies, such as the U.N. Economic Commission for Asia and the Far East.[9] They were interested in forests as a source of "fuel" for economic growth and development. Major themes of this literature included specifying maximum rates of sustainable timber exploitation in "natural" forests, the creation of plantation or industrial forests, and the potential for development of forest industries based on tropical products such as tree resins, latexes, timbers, and so on.[10]

During this early period in the development literature, economists were influenced by theories of economic growth such as that of W.W. Rostow.[11] Realizing that poor countries would have difficulty obtaining initial investment capital,

Rostow argued that it could be generated from a society's land and natural resources, where quick productivity increases at low costs were possible. Thus forestry was often treated, as in John Furnival's work,[12] as a source of state revenue, and the claims of local inhabitants were either ignored or treated as a threat to government revenue. Forested lands were also examined for the contribution they could make to economic growth in other sectors such as agriculture and hydroelectricity.

The emphasis on the economic role of forests is illustrated by reports of the FAO and World Bank missions to Thailand which recommended the demarcation of at least 40 per cent of national territory into protected and production forests. The protected forests were justified as necessary for watershed regulation, given that hydroelectric and irrigation projects dependent on river flow were deemed economically more important than commercial timber exploitation, while the production forest area was supposed to be sufficient to supply timber and fuelwood needs. Although the accelerated demarcation which followed these reports represented a massive land expropriation on the part of state, the reports did not consider that local people might also have claims to these resources. On the contrary, they depicted local inhabitants as threats to the forests. The World Bank recommended that the Forestry Department increase penalties and enforcement for "encroachment" on the public domain, and that the government devote more funding to reforestation and government land claims through forest reservation.[13] Analyses which ignored or deplored local people's forest claims and uses were also produced in Indonesia and Malaysia, and they continue to influence current studies throughout Southeast Asia.

Also in this vein, economic historians such as James Ingram and T.H. Silcock for Thailand discussed the expansion of upland crops in terms of volume, value, and export earnings, but they failed to mention the possible effects of this expansion on forests and forest dwellers.[14] Today, many environmentalist critics blame the subsequent loss of forests in Thailand (from over 50 per cent of land area at the time to 10-15 per cent at present) on the government policies demarcating the forests while simultaneously encouraging the expansion of permanent upland agriculture.[15]

The second tradition initiated during the 1950s was that of anthropologists and human geographers who initiated the study of forest use and management from a local perspective. Partly because of the anthropologists' preference for seeking out "isolated" groups to study, some of this period's classic ethnographies were of forest-based peoples. By treating forest dwellers as active managers of the forest, they took a giant step beyond the travelogues and diaries of earlier "naturalists" and "explorers", which, particularly in Borneo, had perceived forest-dwelling peoples as a part of the tropical landscape rather than as land managers. Besides naturalists, Catholic and Protestant missionaries also preceded anthropologists in documenting some of the agricultural and forest-related activities of forest-based peoples throughout Southeast Asia. Some anthropologists and other researchers began their careers as either missionaries or members of church-sponsored groups working among tribal and other forest-dependent peoples.[16]

Although the style and scope of the ethnographers' work distinguished them from forest management macro-economists, there were many implicit connections. Some studies were contracted by the remaining colonial governments (for example, in Sarawak), while anthropologists often acted as advisors for the new national governments. Nevertheless, and as discussed further in the next section, many of these studies became standard works on particular groups as well as on variations of swidden cultivation.

Karl Pelzer's classic study of land settlement early in the postwar period was one of the first to pay attention to the ecological effects of upland agriculture and land settlement.[17] His work has had something of a prophetic quality, since one of the most important phenomena affecting forest management during the postwar period has been land settlement. Resettlement has been widely encouraged and even organized by most Southeast Asian governments as a solution to landlessness, "overpopulation", and resource pressure, often as an alternative to the more politically difficult alternative of local land redistribution.[18] These policies and programmes have created exactly the kinds of crowding that Pelzer and other students of swidden agriculture warned would make upland agriculture unsustainable.[19] Although Pelzer argued that swidden cultivation was not destructive if the population density were low, he suggested measures to force a shift to permanent cultivation where population density exceeded that limit. In common with the colonial writers who preceded him, Pelzer seemed unaware of the ecological barriers to permanent cultivation in some upland areas which had been converted from forest.[20]

The classic work on swidden cultivation as a method of land and forest management is Harold Conklin's study of the Hanunoo in the Philippines.[21] Later research which integrated ecology with anthropology included J.S. Spencer's work comparing swidden systems of Southeast Asia[22] and Peter Kunstadter's studies in Northern Thailand, discussed in the next section. Unlike other contemporary ethnographers who looked only at agriculture or social organization,[23] these authors painstakingly detailed the ways that local people transformed mature forest into productive agricultural systems that both differed from the region's lowland wet-rice production systems, and comprised a portion of a larger pattern of forest change and succession. Indeed, some of this work formed part of the baseline for what subsequently became known as the "indigenous knowledge" literature.

Conklin was the first to use detailed research to dispel many detrimental myths about shifting cultivation, including its destructiveness, the alleged preference of swiddeners for "primary" forest, the haphazardness of locating swidden plots, the lack of fire-control by swiddeners, the uniformity of swidden agricultural techniques throughout Southeast Asia, and the erosion and loss of soil fertility in swidden plot.[24] He also identified key features of swidden systems that later became major themes in the study of local forest management.

Not all studies of this period agreed that swidden was not destructive; Derek Freeman, for example, called the Iban of Borneo "forest eaters" and was extremely critical of swidden agriculture.[25] Other influential writers of the period wrote critically about swidden cultivation and had a significant negative influence on thinking about that agricultural system at the time and since.[26] Nevertheless, since the 1950s many students of swidden cultivation have expanded on and reworked Conklin's ideas in other parts of Southeast Asia and the world, continuing the scholarly project of refuting detractions of swidden cultivation as the sole or most significant cause of forest degradation.[27] Some of the key ideas which emerged during the 1960s and 1970s in this tradition included: the variation in swidden systems from one group to another; the preference of many swiddeners to clear in secondary rather than primary forest areas; the need to calculate swidden farming's efficiency by calculating yield per unit of labour not unit of area; the multiplicity of crops produced in swiddens; the importance of looking at all crop cycles as part of the agricultural productivity of these lands rather than just the rice-fallow rotations; the importance of grasses (especially Imperata cylindrica) to an agrarian economy even though in some contexts they are noxious pests; and the fact that swidden farmers usually know the ecological limits and impacts of many or most of their practices.[28]

These ethnographies illustrate the range of variation in local people's agroforestry strategies (although the term agroforestry was not yet in vogue at the time). They also demonstrate the importance of site-specific studies because of the wide range of ecological impacts and market involvements that the many peoples of Southeast Asia called "swiddeners" or "shifting cultivators" could have. Some also provide baseline data on local systems prior to the serious constraints on access to land and forests caused by government land use planning and by spontaneous and planned migrations to and from forested areas.

MID-1960S TO MID-1970S: THE TWO REVOLUTIONS

The successes and failures of various types of development strategies continued to influence Southeast Asian scholars during the 1960s and 1970s. Two revolutionary events, however, began to play a major role in research and publishing.

The first was the development of new food production technologies for lowland agriculture, the so-called Green Revolution. Governments and development agencies devoted considerable efforts to promoting the adoption of new rice varieties and of cash crops such as maize. The technological revolution led to major revolutions in social organization, and the distribution of resource control (especially land). As a result, many anthropologists and rural sociologists turned toward studying the impacts of these changes in wet-rice growing areas - both in support of them and as a critique.[29] The new emphasis also affected economic and social historians, whose histories focused on lowland areas.[30]

The exceptions included a number of studies of Dayak and other indigenous groups in Indonesia and Malaysia carried out at this time, some of which examined the relations between swidden agriculture and hunting and gathering as parts of larger ethnographies.[31] Early work on home gardens as important ecological and economic systems also began to appear in this period. Housegardens were found to produce things which were once available from the forest, provided more than half the family income, and gave higher returns to land and labour than the "modernized" rice fields, while being operated in a manner the authors in one study described as "technically careless".[32] An important study toward the end of this period was James Fox's Harvest of the Palm,[33] which compared Timorese shifting cultivators unfavorably with Rotinese lontar-palm tappers. (Later, however, Fox changed his mind about the Timorese.) The study was unusual for the period as it focused on the social organization and production of a multi-purpose tree, rather than on a grain. With these few exceptions, the focus on lowland rice agriculture and the Green Revolution drew attention away from developments in the forests.

The second revolutionary event was the Indochinese war and spread of peasant insurgencies through much of Southeast Asia. The Vietnam war, and the success of the North Vietnamese and Chinese peasant-based revolutions, drew the attention of many social scientists who set out to explain the reasons for these peasant movements. Although most studies of agrarian unrest were based on cases in wet-rice areas,[34] war and peasant insurgency did draw some attention to upland and forested areas.

During this period, anthropologists were enlisted to the cause of stemming the spread of communism in Southeast

Asia during the Cold War, and thus also to the cause of incorporating these people into the region's emerging nation states.[35] The Tribal Research Center in Northern Thailand is particularly notable in this regard: it was set up in 1964 with the help of William Geddes to assist the Department of Public Welfare's efforts to develop "tribal" peoples,[36] and many important publications on forest-dependent peoples were produced by researchers working out of the Center or in volumes resulting from meetings organized through it.

Many anthropologists carried out their research in the hope that they could represent forest-based or upland people to the government, in order to promote a more sympathetic approach by government agencies to the incorporation of minority peoples.[37] Others used the results of their research to defend local practices against criticisms of their ecological destructiveness. Moreover, despite their funding sources, many researchers had no intention of linking their studies to national security issues. As a result, some of the studies which resulted from this effort carried on the tradition of Conklin in their examination of different swiddening practices and their ecological effects in North Thailand, even though the intentional and unintentional uses of such research during the Vietnam war were hotly debated at the time and subsequently. These studies are even more important in some ways today because Burma, Laos, Vietnam, Cambodia and South China became nearly inaccessible for research during this period.

This research culminated with the publication in 1978 of Farmers in the Forest, arguably the most important work of the period on local-level forest management in mainland Southeast Asia. In the introduction, Kunstadter and Chapman lay out the four types of upland cultivation/ forest conversion which now form the basis of most analyses of swidden systems in mainland Southeast Asia, while the individual chapters document these systems and their ecological effects in detail.[38] In particular, Kunstadter and

Chapman distinguish between the "short cultivation, long fallow" (or what they call rotational swidden) systems practised by mid-slope groups, especially the Karen and the Hill Lua and the "long cultivation, very long fallow" (or what they call primary swidden) practised in the higher elevations, especially by the Hmong. Moreover, they also point out that the disproportionate attention given to "hilltribes" obscures the fact that the majority of swiddeners were in fact "Northern Thai". They go on to distinguish two types of swidden cultivation among Northern Thais: "short cultivation, short fallow", and "permanent field tree crops" especially tea gardens.

A second kind of security and resource control concern took shape around the cultivation of opium poppies and production of opium by some forest-based people in mainland Southeast Asia. Although some U.S. government agencies promoted the production and trade of drugs,[39] other U.S. agencies put increasing pressure on the Thai government to halt opium production through crop substitution. The Hmong were held responsible for destroying watershed forests by their swidden practices and were also held responsible for most opium production, increasing already intense government and academic scrutiny and drawing enormous amounts of research and development funds to these regions.[40]

The exception to the unavailability of studies in Indochinese countries is Gerald Hickey's work in the Central Highlands of Vietnam, not published until 1982.[41] In his ethnohistories, Hickey mentions how the use of bombing, long range artillery, agent orange and other defoliants, in addition to forced labour and resettlement, destroyed forests and forced people into new settlements where they shortened fallows to cope with lack of land.[42] The war thus radically disrupted swiddening and forest management practices, and transformed local and regional ecologies in Vietnam, Cambodia, and Laos. Since the war, rapid forest conversion and assimilation policies resembling those of Thailand have continued to circumscribe the livelihood activities of Vietnam's forest-based groups.[43]

Similar rearrangements of forest-based populations were spurred by security concerns in Peninsular Malaysia, Sarawak, and Indonesia, in response, respectively, to the "Emergency" (which produced insurgency in forested areas of the Malay Peninsula) and to the "Confrontation" between Malaysia and Indonesia along international borders in Borneo. Very little has been written on the impacts of these events on forest use, as research permission for border areas has been difficult to obtain.

Overall during this second period, lowland agricultural and peasant revolutions drew attention away from upland and lowland forests in much of the region, although some important research continued to be published in the two traditions initiated during the first period. By the end of this period, the new environmental "threat" had already begun to draw the interests of a new generation of researchers migrating into forest areas throughout Southeast Asia.

LATE 1970S TO THE PRESENT: THE MOVE INTO THE FOREST

The late 1970s marked the beginning of the surge in the social analysis of environmental change. Although ideas like "sustainable development" are hardly new,[44] the mid-1970s was the point at which a more critical concern over the environment and resources joined development as a dominant theme in scholarly research and writing. Whereas environmental themes had previously emphasized the value of natural resources for fueling economic growth, the new generation of writers imparted value to the preservation of forests and wildlife as such, sometimes in contradiction to economic growth objectives. New debates also emerged about the past, present, and future roles of forest-dependent peoples in forest production and protection.

Environmental change is often equated with the fate of the forests, and during this period there was considerable attention to forest management, and intense debate on the subject. In Southeast Asia, research interests and development funding first moved uphill from the lowlands because downstream flooding and siltation in grain-exporting lowlands were attributed to deforestation in upland watersheds.[45] Later the loss of forests was deplored because of the greenhouse effect and loss of biodiversity, both of which affect rich countries as well as poor. The perception of a global threat of environmental collapse still causes industrial country donors to pour enormous quantities of funding into research and conservation programmes in Southeast Asia's forested areas.

Already by the early 1970s, researchers who later became major voices in the forest literature of the 1980s and 1990s had initiated fieldwork on which their later work was based.[46] Some writers began to conduct interdisciplinary research across the biological and social sciences. One notable effort was Man and the Biosphere project no. 1, "Interactions between People and Tropical Forests in East Kalimantan", headed by A.P. Vayda and Kuṣwata Kartawinata. The studies conducted under the rubric of this and a subsequent Man and the Biosphere project were intended to marry biological and human ecological/anthropological fieldwork.[47] One objective of the project was to challenge some widely-held assumptions about interactions between people and forests, especially the insistence that forest clearing is a singular result of poverty. This trend to interdisciplinary research may have been encouraged by the simultaneous increase in biologists' and ecologists' documentation of the nature and state of Southeast Asian forests. For example, books by T.C. Whitmore[48] and Peter Ashton[49] were widely read outside of their disciplines, as were those of their predecessors from the colonial period.[50]

A more recent attempt to apply an interdisciplinary perspective to forest management has been that of the Australian "team" of Harold Brookfield, Lesley Potter, and Yvonne Byron. They have highlighted the roles of cyclic drought and flood in forest dynamics which result from the anomalies in tropical Asia-Pacific circulation patterns known as ENSO (El Nino Southern Oscillation). Droughts are likely to be especially severe in Indonesia during an extreme ENSO event, and these are sometimes accompanied by extensive burning of the rain forest. This happened during 1982-83, when up to 3 million hectares were reported to have been burned in East Kalimantan, with similar conflagrations in neighbouring areas of Sabah and elsewhere. One of the aims of subsequent research has been to establish methods of predicting severe events, which would enable farmers to adjust their behaviour in advance.[51] Other studies have documented the human cost of drought, in terms of lost crops and prevalence of disease.[52]

From the mid-1980s, political economy and political ecology (see below) writers took an interest in the origins of deforestation and environmental degradation. Their investigations moved beyond site-specific local studies or nationally oriented policy studies initiated in earlier periods. These scholars have drawn connections between changing international and national markets, state policies, the actions of state bureaucracies, the activities of local and national private interests, and the practices of local people who manage forests and use forest products.

An important new aspect of the 1990s literature, following from such multi-scaled analyses, is the debate over environmental change and the human rights of local people. Much of this discussion has not yet moved from the popular and NGO (non-government organization) literature.

Critics have chastised governments for over-riding the rights and cultures of these minorities and disregarding their resource management practices.[53] Public discussion of these issues has been made possible by changes in the region's national political climates beginning only as recently as the mid-1980s.[54]

Another major recent event has been the relative easing of access to Vietnam, Laos, and Cambodia. However, most research in these areas remains limited to natural sciences. With the exception of some popular environmental writing and assessments by international agencies, these countries remain out of the mainstream of forest-people writing.[55] An exception to this silence is Raymond Bryant's work on Burma, although he focuses primarily on the colonial period.[56]

In the remainder of this section we will elaborate on the new political ecology approaches, and some of the debates surrounding local versus state forest management rights in Southeast Asia.

THE POLITICAL ECONOMY AND POLITICAL ECOLOGY OF FOREST MANAGEMENT

During the 1970s, critics of economic development and the Green Revolution developed a political economy approach to understanding both macro (national/world systems) and micro (agrarian) social transformations.[57] What we call political ecology refers to the effort of more recent writers to combine this political economic approach with more ecological or human-ecological understandings of people-environment interactions. The attention to ecology and human ecology forces researchers to include locally and regionally-grounded analyses of forest management practices. At its best, this approach uses multiple scales (micro to macro) of analysis to look at interacting cycles of social and ecological change. Both political economy and political ecology emphasize a historical perspective or multiple perspectives on history to understand contemporary environmental circumstances.[58]

At the macro level, the attention of many scholars has turned to how the region's government resource agencies and militaries have aggressively pursued land and resource control. In particular, national governments have given state resource agencies great freedom to claim and administer access to natural resources. Government ministries or parastatal corporations managing mining and forest resources have become "golden ministries". In many countries, management agencies work directly or indirectly with military units who enforce agency resource claims and often participate in harvesting concessions.[59] These policies were promoted and supported by international agencies such as the World Bank and FAO. In Burma and Cambodia, both government and insurgent militaries have appropriated control of valuable forest resources in territories they control.

The question of state formation and the extension of state control into upland and forested areas, so prominent in the literature on Northern Thailand during the 1960s, reappeared during the 1980s, but with a much more critical flavour. One of the features of some recent studies is that they try to understand state formation and control from the point of view of historical village studies rather than from the centre. Village studies can be used as a window through which to view the variety of ways colonial states took control of forests. They also can be used to show how colonial and contemporary states' attempts at forest control have created struggles between state agencies and villagers trying to reclaim these forests.[60]

In Southeast Asia, the consolidation of state power involved a switch from species and labour control to territorial control, a transition that is particularly clear in the study of forest policy.[61] These processes of "territorialization" involve an increasingly detailed demarcation of national territory into land use zones, including various categories of forest.[62] In colonial Burma, forced conversion of forest into rice land reorganized settlement patterns and consolidated colonial state control over land, labour, and resource management.[63] In Burma, Java and Thailand, state-sponsored forestry and reforestation by the taungya system[64] not only reinforced the colonial state's control over teak, but also facilitated the expansion of state control of land into the forests.[65] Many times, colonial forest policies succeeded where pre-colonial states failed in incorporating local peoples' lands and labour into state systems of agricultural or forest production.[66]

A major theme in the political economy and political ecology literature, given the rapid depletion of forests in some parts of Southeast Asia, has been the attempt to explain deforestation. Although writers emphasize different aspects of the nexus of factors leading to deforestation and degradation, most agree on several points. One is that state control of forests has been a major if not the primary cause of environmental degradation and the deterioration of the well-being of forest-dependent peoples. A second is that national elites of one form or another - inside the state or out - often manipulate the legal systems and bureaucracies to their personal economic advantage but to the detriment of forest resources and local people. A third point of agreement is that "local" or "forest-dependent" rural peoples are the most directly and immediately threatened by the "onslaught on the forests".[67]

That both local and national elites benefit from deforestation and aggressive forest exploitation has been shown for the Philippines,[68] Indonesia,[69] Malaysia,[70] and Thailand[71]. The processes have unraveled in different configurations in different countries because of their varied social and political histories. In the Philippines, powerful interests in the oligarchic state and society are so intertwined that these elites have had unprecedented opportunities to control the extraction of forest resources, simultaneously shoring up a heavily indebted state and enriching individual members of this elite.(72) In Malaysia and Indonesia, similar linkages exist between state and entrepreneurial elites,[73] with the addition of even heavier-handed state security forces than in the Philippines. In Indonesia, forest control has involved a major military component in both the allocation of access to forest concessions and their protection.[74] Although the military has not played a direct role in Malaysia, the state is equally strong and has invoked its Internal Security Act in disputes over forest access and control.[75] As in the Philippines, writers on Malaysia and Indonesia have often attributed state claims on forests to the colonial legacy of state forest control for production, although during their respective colonial periods, this interest and control was felt primarily in the forests of Java for Indonesia[76] and on the peninsula for Malaysia.[77]

In contrast, work on Thailand shows that despite formal state control of forests, forest exploitation has often been driven by local, regional, and national private interests comprising groups such as logging companies, wealthy farmers, sugar planters, eucalyptus interests, agricultural middlemen, and land speculators, and even politicians and military units.[78] These local groups use privately organized violence and the threat of violence to pursue their interests, often with the collaboration of local government officials. Some writers focus on the inability of the Royal Forestry Department to overcome these local obstacles to achieve stable forest management.[79] Others have placed the blame for deforestation and the displacement of forest dependent people squarely on the government and its policies, citing, for example, the undermining of local management regimes through forest reservation, the logging orientation of the

Royal Forestry Department, corruption, promotion of cash crops, dam and road construction, and inequity caused by misguided development policies.[80] Similar debates have emerged in the Philippines: some writers contend that an oligarchic, externally-oriented state has shaped forest use,[81] while others take a more nuanced view of the differences between state and local perspectives on land use and the tensions arising as the state penetrates more deeply into forest community life.[82]

An important result of rising global, regional, and national attention to the fate of Southeast Asian forests is intense pressure on governments to increase forest conservation, sustainable management, and the integration of local people into management plans. This pressure and its effects, themselves partly the outcome of intense scholarly attention, have become a theme in the critical scholarly and activist literature. In discussions of production and protection forest policy in the "Outer Islands" of Indonesia, for example, changes in forest policies and practices are increasingly seen as responses to the nation's growing economic prosperity and subsequently to public pressure from the middle class and NGOs. These changes include greater willingness to impose some restrictions on loggers, bans on logging or log exports, and the assignment of protected status to extensive forest areas. According to this view, some Southeast Asian governments have grown more tolerant of conservation partly because of rising international concerns with environmental protection - especially of "charismatic mega-fauna" such as the Javanese rhinoceros, native tigers, and orangutans—and the increasing interest in genetic resources for medical and agricultural science.[83] Because they have major economic benefits associated with them, the preservation of these megafuana and of biodiversity is advocated by diverse and otherwise opposed groups, including major international environmental groups, World Bank economists, and academics who are generally critical of government policies.[84]

Many international organizations have invested financial and human resources into government conservation measures. For example, the Indonesian Department of Nature Conservancy was created in the 1970s with support from the World Wildlife Fund (WWF), while the establishment of the first Indonesian national parks in 1988 was partly the result of lobbying and financial assistance by international organizations including WWF, FAO, and the International Union for the Conservation of Nature (IUCN). Despite these "unholy alliances", many scholars have faith in the ability of international organizations, NGOs, and people's organizations to save the region's forests, wildlife, and endangered habitats, a feeling they share with many in the rich countries and the Southeast Asian middle classes.[85]

In a more recent theme, following from these trends, some writers have argued that the support given by international NGOs may be more likely to increase the capacity of the state to enforce its own claim to resources against local users than actually save the forest. In Java and elsewhere, certain NGO alliances with government forest agencies support militaristic, exclusionary means of forest conservation and production.[86] In Thailand, the government banned logging in 1989, accelerated the demarcation of National Parks, Wildlife Sanctuaries, expanded "Sensitive Watershed Areas",[87] and stepped up the enforcement of strict forest regulations on the occupation and use of these areas with the help of the military and paramilitary Border Control Police.[88] However, many observers are just as critical of these forest protection policies as of older policies devoted to resource extraction, since demarcation is often followed by attempts to relocate local forest users.[89]

The optimism of writers who believe in the capacity of states or international NGOs to slow forest extraction and improve local people's well-being is also tempered by some scholars who embed their analyses of local forest issues within larger political economic frameworks. Michael Dove, for example, has suggested that the main reason that policy fails (and will continue to fail) is that government officials have created a set of official myths about villagers' forest management which block their capacity either to see things from forest villagers' viewpoint or to formulate more equitable policies such as bottom-up management, community involvement in decision-making, or co-management strategies.[90] Moreover, official classifications of forest land, with their implied restrictions on human usage, tend to ignore realities on the ground and are in turn largely ignored by forest people. As a result, many of their activities are considered illegal.[91]

Local NGOs have recently jumped on the biodiversity bandwagon, arguing that villagers, not the state and international organizations, are the real defenders of biodiversity, and that local people should be given forest management rights.[92] This leads us to the final two topics of this period: recent research on local management, and publications based on projects which try to "implement" local participation in forest management.

THE CONTINUING INFLUENCE OF LOCAL PERSPECTIVES ON FOREST MANAGEMENT

Much of the current literature that addresses itself to local people's impacts on the forest is divided into two camps - one that blames local or indigenous people for destroying or degrading the forest, and one that sees local people as stewards of the environment. Those who blame local people often call upon the notions that unmitigated rural population growth is largely to blame for pioneer settlement of forested areas, that shifting cultivation is nothing but an unorganized, destructive, land extensive farming system, and that "squatting" on forest lands by longtime rural inhabitants and recent migrants are the primary "motors" of deforestation.[93] While some of these claims may be true in some sites, there are numerous studies disproving their ubiquity. However, this perspective continues to underlie the analysis of many government and international economists for whom economic growth remains the fundamental policy priority. Some in this group have tempered their analyses with policy suggestions aimed at trying to turn rural land users into good land managers, usually by allotting property rights to forest inhabitants, while retaining major areas as protected or productive state forest.[94] Others still argue that some kinds of swidden destroy natural resources and that the sensible solution is to replace swiddening with permanent agriculture.[95]

On the other end of this spectrum are two kinds of literature that focus on local people's forest management. One of these is the most recent version of cultural or human ecological approaches, focusing on local agroecosystems or forest and forest product management systems. Such studies generally look at local sociological and ecological variables and argue for integrating these into forest and agroforestry policy. This group maintains the argument that swiddeners use a variety of strategies for land and forest management with positive or negative impacts on the environment. Christine Padoch, for example, documents the management techniques of a forest-dwelling group in West Kalimantan, and their creation of extensive tracts of forests filled with economic species.[96] Many writers have also aimed to document indigenous knowledge to show that forest peoples have a sophisticated knowledge of the local ecology and the impacts of their actions, whether such actions are good or bad for the forest.[97] Some authors argue that mixed ecosystems, i.e., those which combine mature forests with intensively managed agroforestry systems, are most likely to secure the welfare of tropical people.[98] Like other regional writers, they note that indigenous people have traditionally enriched fallows or created forests from fallows as sources of food, wood, resin, and many other amenities.[99]

Other work examines the relationship between the timber industry and swidden agriculture, e.g., that the timber industry employment of young males has led to more intensified working and subsequent degradation of swidden land close to the longhouses because of the shortage of labour. Local people tolerate the problem because they view the benefits and disadvantages of timber industry employment as temporary.[100] In rapidly developing areas of Sarawak, land devoted to hill rice relates directly to prices available for cash crops such as rubber and pepper, so that shifting cultivation may decline significantly when prices are high. Contrary to government pronouncements and some scientific predictions, yields per unit of land in many areas have been shown to remain stable over time, despite population increases.[101]

Writing in French by anthropologists and other social scientists has remained somewhat inaccessible to many English-speaking readers. No discussion of local people-forest interactions, however, can ignore the important work by Bernard Sellato on the Bukat nomads of West Kalimantan.[102] Sellato combines extensive knowledge of the history and ethnography of some of Borneo's nomadic or formerly nomadic groups with research on forest peoples' modern myths and changed lifestyles. Sellato has unrivalled experience of a variety of remote Dayak swiddeners and hunter-gatherer groups, and is very critical of the thesis that hunter-gatherers, such as the Punan, have developed from agricultural societies.[103]

The second type of literature on the impacts of local people's activities on the forest revolves around questions of carbon sequestration and climate change. The results of studies on these issues are used to justify a variety of activities and programmes.[104] Nevertheless, the complexity of the causes and effects of these global problems are still being debated. For example, the World Resources Institute's publication of estimated CO_2 releases resulting from tropical deforestation[105] provoked some contentious Third World comment.[106] However, evaluation of the effects of shifting cultivation (and industrial logging) in tropical forests is complicated by the fact that new growth absorbs carbon at a faster rate than old growth forest.[107] Again, much of this discussion has not yet been debated in the scholarly literature.[108]

INSTITUTIONAL AND APPLIED APPROACHES TO FOREST MANAGEMENT

A final literature worth mentioning is based on local studies and development projects in forest management. Most foreign funding given to research and development in land and forest management is channelled through local universities and non-affiliated research institutions. Many of these projects result in reports not published in the international literature,[109] but in some places they comprise the bulk of new research on forest management and have become a crucial resource for researchers.[110] Projcct reports and working papers are also published by non-local implementing organizations such as the East-West Center.[111]

Applied scientists often try to re-orient local management systems to fit changing political-economic and environmental contexts and to demonstrate systematically that there are ecologically acceptable alternatives to coercive resettlement. Notable in Thailand have been participatory forestry/land use projects in Chiangmai and Khon Kaen.[112]

Another major producer of both "grey" literature and published volumes is the Southeast Asian Universities Agroecosystem Network (SUAN), an association of university-based research groups working on rural resource problems in Indonesia, the Philippines, and Thailand which was established in 1982. The major features of the SUAN approach are agroecosystems analysis, a "systems" human ecology perspective; and Rapid Rural Appraisal as the facilitating technique.[113] The problems the original group took on included the comparative production of nutrients for humans from home gardens, upland and lowland fields, farmers' uses of indigenous genetic resources, and the roles of traditional agroforestry systems in preventing soil erosion.[114] Many agroecosystem case studies were conducted in the three regions. By SUAN's fourth regional symposium in 1988, South China was added to the "core" group of countries. In 1989, SUAN expanded to Vietnam and Laos. SUAN's publications have started providing basic data on agroecosystems and swidden in previously little-studied regions of Southeast Asia, although at a very localized level.[115]

CONCLUSION: GAPS AND NEW DIRECTIONS

Common themes and approaches have been pointed out above. In this final section, we discuss briefly some of the gaps in research and differences between data on mainland and insular Southeast Asia. Some of these differences may be attributed to the lumping together of local areas and whole regions with very different histories into a contemporary political category called Southeast Asia. Forest-related research in Southeast Asia has tended to cluster around specific places. Some of the reasons for this are obvious, relating, as they do, to the location of the forests. Other reasons are less obvious, having to do, for example, with security, the changing value of particular forest resources, and anthropological and political interest in the peoples living in these forests. This is true both across the region and within countries.

With the exception of Thailand, minimal published research exists concerning the countries of mainland Southeast Asia. Within Thailand, a majority of research on forests and forest-based peoples has been focused on the "hilltribes" in Northern Thailand.[116] These groups comprise less than two per cent of Thailand's population and are a small minority of its forest-dependent peoples. In addition, a small body of literature on the forests and forest-dependent peoples of Northeastern Thailand has begun to appear more recently.[117] Nevertheless, almost all our information about "local forest management" in mainland Southeast Asia is based on a small and non-representative sample of places and peoples.

In Indonesia, the greatest attention to forest issues has been in Kalimantan, followed by Java and widely disparate areas of Sumatra. Overall, despite this vast island's extensive forests and the relative openness of research opportunities, publications on Sumatra are surprisingly scarce.[118] Within Kalimantan, the most research has been conducted in East Kalimantan with a recent surge in West Kalimantan in the past five years. While this is partially because of the province's vast forest resources, the concentration is also largely due to difficulties of research access in West and Central Kalimantan until very recently; national security issues have also precluded access to research opportunities in West Irian as well. The Malaysian literature on forests and forest peoples is dominated by studies in Sarawak. As in Indonesia, sociological studies in Peninsular Malaysia and Sabah have been restricted by difficulties in gaining research permission, and similar problems arise in Vietnam, Cambodia, and Laos.

Another regional disparity occurs in the nature and extent of forests remaining within various countries. In Thailand, the Philippines, and much of Vietnam, exploitable forests are largely gone. In the first two countries, government policy and scholarly attention are now focused on conservation and rehabilitation of degraded lands. This is also a direction being taken in initial forest research in Vietnam. The governments of Indonesia and Malaysia do not intend to stop logging or converting forest to other land uses. Forests in Burma, Cambodia, and Laos have been virtually under siege for several decades, but whether or not policy makers and planners in these countries will try to avoid mistakes made in other parts of the region remains to be seen.

Some of the "gaps" in research on Southeast Asian forests and people, at least in comparison to research being conducted in other parts of the world, are beginning to be filled by studies just getting underway. One critical gap is the study of resource tenure and overlapping statutory/ customary systems for forest management. Given the wealth of ethnic groups and their tendencies to migrate and assimilate across the region, studies of the interactions between diverse local systems and national legal codes meant to homogenize the legal treatment of forest access promise to provide many research opportunities for decades.

Similarly, only recently have scholars attempted to document the multitudinous varieties of managed forests and agroforests of the region. These types of studies are ideal for collaboration between scholars of different disciplines. Some of the cases cited above illustrate how ecological research can support the findings of sociological studies and the reverse. One interesting question in this regard is found in the social origins of old growth forests once believed to be largely "pristine". This notion has been called into question not only by evidence of the early role of forest products in the region's thriving international trade, but also by the discoveries of social scientists documenting local people's management techniques, including planting, protecting, and encouraging various species of Dipterocarps and other difficult to grow forest trees such as Borneo ironwood (*Eusideroxylon zwagerii*) and damar (*Shorea, spp.*).

In addition to more case studies, regional comparisons of the many issues and themes mentioned throughout this paper are extremely limited, although, again, some comparative projects are underway. Comparative studies are needed, for example, of the region's French, British, Dutch, and American colonial forest services, laws and policies, and their interactions with local groups. No comparative or cumulative accounting of the damages wrought by the Japanese occupation in every Southeast Asian nation has been made. The toll taken on people and forests by localized insurgencies and uprisings has begun to be documented only for Vietnam, although most other Southeast Asian nation-states have experienced periods of civil or revolutionary war which have affected both the forests themselves and thc patterns of their use.

Many opportunities for further research thus remain for current and future generations of Southeast Asia scholars. While we might argue that the past two decades of change in the structure and extent of the region's forest resource base have been the most significant ever, the twenty-first century will reveal new ways of intensive forest management by local people and government. These ways will include some of the region's relatively new political actors - local and international environmental NGOs - which themselves will inevitably undergo major transformations in structure, political allegiences, and effectiveness. The contradictions between the life-styles and power of swiddeners and hunter-gatherers and the world's most wealthy entrepreneurs, many of whom have strong interests in Southeast Asian forests, will continue to occupy the international news media. Larger, more urbanized, and more cosmopolitan populations, with different means of valuing forest resources, will also play new roles in unfolding forest dramas. Issues of human rights will move squarely into the arena of the values and politics of forest control. Clearly, sociological research on Southeast Asian forests is poised at an intellectual frontier.

NOTES

1. O.W. Wolters, *Early Indonesian Commerce* (Ithaca: Cornell University Press, 1967); Kenneth Hall, *Maritime Trade and State Development in Early Southeast Asia* (Honolulu: University of Hawaii Press, 1985); Lesley Potter, "Indigenes and Colonizers: Dutch Forest Policy in South and East Borneo (Kalimantan) 1900 to 1950", in *Changing Tropical Forests: Historical Perspectives on Today's Challenges in Asia, Australasia and Oceania*, ed. John Dargavel, Kay Dixon and Noel Semple (Canberra: Centre for Regional and Environmental Studies, 1988), pp. 127-54; Nancy Lee Peluso, "The Political Ecology of Extraction and Extractive Reserves in East Kalimantan, Indonesia", *Development and Change* 23, 4 (1992): 49-74.
2. *World Resources Report* 1994 (Washington D.C.: World Resources Institute, 1994).
3. Bangkok: *The Nation*, 1 July 1994.
4. One notable exception is the softwood timber "ramin" (Gonystylus bancanus) which experienced a boom in Sarawak and West Kalimantan during the first two decades after the war.
5. Robert Repetto and Malcolm Gillis, *Public Policies and the Misuse of Forest Resources* (New York: Cambridge University Press, 1988).
6. Lesley Potter, "Land Degradation, Innovation, and Social Welfare in the Riam Kiwa Valley, South Kalimantan Indonesia" in *Land Degradation and Society*, ed. Piers Blaikie and Harold Brookfield (London: Methuan, 1987), pp. 164-96; Nancy Lee Peluso, "The Ironwood Problem:

(Mis-)management and Development of an Extractive Rainforest Product", *Conservation Biology* 6, 1 (June): 210-19; Christine Padoch, "Woodlands of Tae: Traditional Forest Management in Kalimantan", in *Forest Resources and Wood-based Biomass Energy as Rural Development Assets* (New Delhi: Oxford and IBH Publishing Co., 1994); cf., S.B. Hecht, A.B. Anderson and P. May, "The Subsidy from Nature: Shifting Cultivation, Successional Palm Forests, and Rural Development", *Human Organization* 47, 1 (1988): 25-35.

7. R. Cribb, "The Politics of Environmental Protection in Indonesia" (Working Paper 48, Centre for Southeast Asian Studies, Monash University, 1988); Mark Poffenberger (ed.), Keepers *of the Forest: Land Management Alternatives in Southeast Asia* (West Hartford, CT: Kumarian Press, 1990); Eduardo Tadem, "Land-based Resources in ASEAN Countries", in *Conflict over Natural Resources in the Asia-Pacific Region*, ed. Lim Teck Ghee and Mark Valencia (Singapore: Oxford University Press, 1990).

8. Nancy Lee Peluso, *Rich Forests, Poor People: Resource Control and Resistance in Java* (Berkeley: University of California Press, 1992).

9. In addition, some colonial or former colonial foresters remained in Southeast Asia and continued to influence forest policy in the initial postwar period.

10. Some examples include Leong Hing Nin, "Highlights of Forestry During the First Decade of Independence in West Malaysia", *The Malayan Forester* 31 (1968): 3-14; Florencio Asiddao, "Natural versus Artificial Reproduction of Dipterocarp Species", *Philippine Journal of Forestry* 7 (1950): 63-77; Juan Utleg, "Contribution of Forest Industrialization to the Economic Development and Improvement of the Country", *Philippine Journal of Forestry* 21 (1965): 1-11; Tan Chein Hoe, "One Hundred Years of Forestry in Burma", *Burmese Forester* 6, 1 (1956): 45-53; S. Mahaphol, *Teak in Thailand* (Bangkok: Royal Forest Department, 1956); F.K.M. Steup, "Enkele Desiderata Betreffende Bosonderzoek en Bospolitiek in Indonesia", *Tectona* 43 (1955): 265-77; A. Ottow, "De Opzet

van Boschexploitatie-Bedrijven in de Buitengewesten, Meer Speciaal in Oost-Borneo", *Tectona* 42 (1952): 175-281.

11. W.W. Rostow, *The Stages of Economic Growth: A Non-Communist Manifesto* (Cambridge: Cambridge University Press, 2nd ed., 1971).

12. See, e.g., John Furnival, *Netherlands India: A Study of Plural Economy* (Cambridge: The University Press and the Macmillan Company, 1944), and *Colonial Policy and Practice, A Comparative Study of Burma and Netherlands India* (New York: New York University Press, 1956).

13. *Food and Agriculture Organization of the United Nations*, Report of the FAO Mission for Siam (Washington, D.C.: FAO, 1947). *International Bank for Reconstruction and Development, A Public Development Program for Thailand* (Baltimore: Johns Hopkins Press, 1959), pp. 82-83.

14. James C. Ingram, *Economic Change in Thailand 1850-1970* (Stanford: Stanford University Press, 1971); T.H. Silcock, *The Economic Development of Thai Agriculture* (Ithaca: Cornell University Press, 1970).

15. For example, Shalardchai Ramitanondh, "Forests and Deforestation", pp. 23-51 in *Culture and Environment in Thailand*, ed. The Siam Society (Bangkok: The Siam Society, 1989).

16. We are indebted to David Thomas for reminding us of this important point.

17. Karl Pelzer, *Land Settlement in Southeast Asia* (New Haven: Yale University Press, 1948).

18. See, for example, Jonathon Rigg, *Southeast Asia: A Region in Transition* (London: Unwin Hyman, 1991); Harold Uhlig (ed.), *Spontaneous and Planned Settlement in Southeast Asia* (Hamburg: Institute of Asian Affairs, 1984).

19. Special Issue on the Indonesian Transmigration Program, *The Ecologist*, 16, 2/3 (1986).

20. See, e.g., Pelzer, *Land Settlement*, p. 189.

21. Harold Conklin, *Hanunoo Agriculture* (Rome: FAO, 1957), and "An Ethnoecological Approach to Shifting Agriculture",

Merrill-Bobb Reprint service, 1957, first published in *Transactions of the New York Academy of Sciences* 17 (1954): 133-42.

22. J.S. Spencer, *Shifting Cultivation in Southeastern Asia* (Berkeley: University of California Press, 1967).

23. For example, H.A. Bernatzik, *Akha and Miao: Problems of Applied Ethnography in Farther India* (New Haven: HRAF, 1970, translated by Alois Nagler); Vinson H. Sutlive, *The Iban of Sarawak* (Arlington Heights, II: AHM Publishing Corporation, 1978); E.R. Leach, *Political Systems of Highland Burma* (Cambridge, Mass: Harvard University Press, 1954).

24. Conklin, "Ethnoecological Approach", pp. 140-41.

25. Derek Freeman, *Report on the Iban* (Kuching: HMS Printing Service, 1957).

26. See, e.g., Clifford Geertz, *Agricultural Involution* (Berkeley: University of California Press, 1963); Pierre Gourou, *The Tropical World: Its Social and Economic Conditions and its Future Status* (London: Green and Co., 1953); and F.J. Ormeling, *The Timor Problem: A Geographical Interpretation of an Underdeveloped Island* (Groningen and Djakarta: E.J. Wolters, 1956).

27. For example, Spencer, *Shifting Cultivation*, Peter Kunstadter in *Farmers in the Forest*, ed. Kunstadter, E.C. Chapman and S. Sabhasri (Honolulu: University of Hawaii Press, 1978), and later work by Christine Padoch [e.g., *Alternatives to Migration among the Iban of Sarawak* (Leiden: Martinus Nijhoff, 1983)]; Terry B. Grandstaff, *Shifting Cultivation in Northern Thailand* (Tokyo: United Nations University, 1978); and Michael R. Dove [see especially, "Theories of Swidden Agriculture, and the Political Economy of Ignorance", *Agroforestry Systems* 1 (1983): 85-99].

28. See Conklin, "Ethnoecological Approach", pp. 140-41.

29. For example, Gillian Hart, *Power, Labor, and Livelihood* (Berkeley: University of California Press, 1976); Frans Husken, "Landlords, Sharecroppers, and Agricultural

Labourers: Changing Labour Relations in Rural Java", *Journal of Contemporary Asia* 9, 2 (1979): 140-51; Michael Moerman, *Agricultural Change and Peasant Choice in a Thai Village* (Berkeley: University of California Press, 1968). Note that many of these arguments are reexamined and built upon in a 1986 volume edited by Gillian Hart, Benjamin White and Andrew Turton, *Agrarian Transformations: Local Processes and the State in Southeast Asia* (Berkeley: University of California Press, 1986).

30. David Feeny, *The Political Economy of Agricultural Productivity: Thai Agricultural Development 1880-1975* (Vancouver: University of British Columbia Press, 1982). Also, Lim Teck Ghee, *Peasants and their Agricultural Economy in Colonial Malaya, 1874-1941* (Kuala Lumpur: Oxford University Press, 1977).

31. See, e.g., A.B. Hudson, *Padju Epat, the Ma'anyan of Indonesian Borneo* (New York: Holt, Rinehart, and Winston, 1972); Douglas Miles, *Cutlass and Crescent Moon* (Sydney: Center for Asian Studies, University of Sydney, 1976); and Terry Rambo, "Human Ecology of the Orang Asli: A Review of Research on the Environmental Relations of the Aborigines of Peninsular Malaysia", *Federations Museums Journal* 24 (1979): 39-71.

32. David Penny and Meneth Ginting, "House Gardens-the Last Resort? Further Economic Arithmetic from Sriharjo", in *Indonesia: Australian Perspectives*, ed. J. Fox, R. Garnaut, P. McCawley and J. Mackie (Canberra: Research School of Pacific Studies, The Australian National University, 1980), pp. 487-99. See also Ann Stoler, "Garden Use and Household Economy in Rural Java", *Bulletin of Indonesian Economic Studies* 14, 2 (1975): 85-101.

33. James Fox, *Harvest of the Palm: Ecological Change in Eastern Indonesia* (Cambridge, Mass.: Harvard University Press, 1978).

34. See, for example, Ben Kerkvliet, *The Huk Rebellion* (Berkeley: University of California Press, 1977); and Michael Adas, *Prophets of Rebellion: Millenarian Protest Movements Against the European Colonial Order* (Durham: North Carolina University Press, 1979).

35. See especially the two volume set edited by Peter Kunstadter, *Southeast Asian Tribes, Minorities, and Nations* (Princeton: Princeton University Press, 1967). This trend resembled what government anthropologists were doing in the 1950s, as mentioned above.

36. See William Robert Geddes, *Migrants of the Mountains* (Oxford: Clarendon Press, 1976), pp. vi-vii.

37. See comments by William Robert Geddes, "The Tribal Research Center, Thailand", in *Southeast Asian Tribes*, ed. Kunstadter, pp. 553-81.

38. They reject Conklin's distinction between integral and partial as inappropriate for understanding the different types of resource use in Northern Thailand.

39. Alfred McCoy, *The Politics of Heroin in Southeast Asia* (New York: Harper and Row, 1972).

40. A few of the many examples include Geddes, *Migrants of the Mountains*, and Robert Cooper, *Resource Scarcity and the Hmong Response: Patterns of Settlement and Economy in Transition* (Singapore: Singapore University Press, 1984). Perhaps because of the interest in replacing opium with other cash crops, these studies seldom analyze swidden agriculture in relation to forest management.

41. For example, Gerald Canon Hickey, *Free in the Forest: Ethnohistory of the Vietnamese Central Highlands, 1954-1976* (New Haven: Yale University Press, 1982); see also his *Shattered World* (Philadelphia: University of Pennsylvania Press, 1993).

42. Hickey, *Shattered World*, pp. 260ff.

43. *Ibid.*, p. 264.

44. For example, governments and resource economists have long planned carefully for sustainable timber production, even if these plans were locally undermined. See Raymond L. Bryant, "Shifting the Cultivator: The Politics of Teak Regeneration in Colonial Burma", *Modern Asian Studies* 28, 2 (1994): 225-50; Peluso, Rich Forests, *Poor People*.

45. Cf. Larry Hamilton, "Forward", in L.A. Bruijnzeel, *Hydrology of Moist Tropical Forests and Effects of*

Conversion: A State of Knowledge Review (Paris: UNESCO International Hydrological Programme, 1990); John McKinnon, "Structural Assimilation and Consensus: Clearing Grounds on which to Rearrange our Thoughts", in *Hill Tribes Today*, pp. 303-359. Both question the "established knowledge" that forest conversion or swidden agriculture necessarily cause flooding, land degradation, erosion, and sedimentation, and note that forest policies have often been based on this "knowledge". The physical impacts of land use change are still being hotly debated; see, D. Alford, "Streamflow and Sediment Transport from Mountain Watersheds of the Chao Phraya Basin in Northern Thailand. A Reconnaissance Study", *Mountain Research and Development* 12 (Aug. 1992): 257-68.

46. For example, Christine Padoch, Michael Dove, Terry Rambo and Jeff Romm.

47. For an explanation of the study's intentions and some of its results, see A.P. Vayda, Carol Colfer and M. Brotokusumo, "Interactions between People and Forests in East Kalimantan", *The Impact of Science on Society* 30, 3 (1980): 179-90; and Kuswata Kartawinata and A.P. Vayda, "Forest Conversion in East Kalimantan, Indonesia: The Activities and Impacts of Timber Companies, Shifting Cultivators, and Migrant Pepper and Others" in *Ecology in Practice: 1. Ecosystem Management*, ed. F. di Castri, F.W.G. Baker and M. Hadley (Paris: UNESCO, 1984), pp. 98-126.

48. *Tropical Rainforests of the Far East* (Oxford: Clarendon Press, 1975).

49. *Ecological Studies in the Mixed Dipterocarp Forests of Brunei State* (Oxford: Clarendon Press, 1964).

50. For example, I.H. Burkhill, *The Economic Products of the Malay Peninsula* (Kuala Lumpur: Published on behalf of the Governments of Malaysia and Singapore by the Ministry of Agriculture and Cooperatives, 1935); F.W. Foxworthy, *Timbers of British North Borneo and Minor Forest Products and Jungle Produce* (Sandakan: Government of British North Borneo, Department of Forestry, 1916).

51. N. Nicholls, "ENSO, Drought and Flooding Rain in Southeast Asia", in *Southeast Asia's Environmental Future*, ed. Brookfield & Byron, pp. 154-75.

52. For example, Potter combines Dutch and British historical sources from Borneo's severe drought of 1877-78 and others occurring up to 1941, with recollections of contemporary informants, newspaper reports, and field observations to analyze ENSO's impact on forests and human populations. Lesley Potter, "Drought and Fire: Hazards Leading Toward Endangerment", in In *Place of the Forest: Environmental and Socioeconomic Transformation in Borneo and the Eastern Malay Peninsula*, ed. Harold Brookfield, Lesley Potter and Yvonne Bryon (Tokyo: United Nations University Press, 1995). See also, Nicholas Salavsky, "Drought in the Rain Forest", *Climate Change* 27, 4 (1994): 373-96.

53. See, for example, Lim Teck Ghee and Alberto Gomes (eds.), *Tribal Peoples and Development in Southeast Asia* (Special Issue of Manusia and Masyarakat, Department of Anthropology and Sociology, University of Malaya, 1990).

54. See, for example, the exchange between Wanat Bhruksasri ("Government Policy") on one hand, and John McKinnon ("Structural Assimilation") and other contributors to the volume *Hill Tribes Today*.

55. See, e.g., Stephen Bass and Elaine Morrison, *Shifting Cultivation in Thailand, Laos, and Vietnam: Regional Overview and Policy Recommendations* (London: International Institute for Environment and Development, 1994); Do Dinh Sam, Shifting Cultivation in *Vietnam: Its Social, Economic, and Environmental Values Relative to Alternative Land Use* (London: International Institute for Environment and Development, 1994); and others in the same series.

56. Raymond C. Bryant, "Shifting the Cultivator". Note that although Hickey's work was published in the 1980s and 1990s, his fieldwork was done several decades earlier, as discussed above.

57. Contributors to Hart, et al., *Agrarian Transformations*, apply a political economy approach to site-specific agrarian relations across much of Southeast Asia.

58. For some definitions and theoretical treatment of political ecology analyses by Asianists, see Piers Blaikie and Harold Brookfield, *Land Degradation and Society* (London: Methuan, 1987), especially chapters 1 and 2; see also, Raymond Bryant, "Political Ecology: An Emerging Research Agenda in Third World Studies", *Political Geography* 11, 1 (1992): 12-36.

59. Richard Robison, *Indonesia: The Rise of Capital* (Asian Studies Association of Australia, Southeast Asia Publications Series, no. 13; Sydney: Allen & Unwin, 1986).

60. See, e.g., Nancy Lee Peluso, *Rich Forests, Poor People*; Lesley Potter, "Indigenes and Colonisers: Dutch Forest Policy in South and East Borneo", in *Changing Tropical Forests*, ed. John Dargavel, et al. (Canberra: ANU, 1988), pp. 127-53, and "Environmental and Social Aspects of Timber Exploitation in Kalimantan, 1967-1989", in *Indonesia: Resources, Ecology and Environment*, ed. Joan Hardjono (Singapore: Oxford University Press, 1991), pp. 177-211; and Philip Hirsch, *Development Dilemmas in Rural Thailand* (Singapore: Oxford University Press, 1991).

61. Peluso, *Rich Forests, Poor People*; Peter Vandergeest and Nancy Lee Peluso, "Territorialization and State Power in Thailand", *Theory and Society*, Vol. 24 (1995).

62. Pieces such as Ulig, *Spontaneous and Planned Settlement*; Lesley Potter, "The Onslaught on the Forests in Southeast Asia", in *South-east Asia's Environmental Future: the Search for Sustainability*, ed. Harold Brook field and Yvonne Byron (Kuala Lumpur: Oxford University Press, with United Nations University Press, 1993); Vandergeest and Peluso, "Territorialization"; Peter Vandergeest, "Mapping Nature", *Society and Natural Resources*, forthcoming; and Nancy Lee Peluso, "Counter-mapping Forest Territories of Kalimantan, Indonesia", *Antipode*, forthcoming; show how governments used forest clearing and land settlement to extend territorial administrative control into upland and forested areas.

63. Michael Adas, "Colonization, Commercial Agriculture, and the Destruction of the Deltaic Rainforests of British Burma in the late 19th Century", in *Global Deforestation and the Nineteenth Century World Economy*, ed. Richard P. Tucker and John F. Richards (Durham, N.C.: Duke University Press, 1983), pp. 95-110; Uhlig, *Spontaneous and Planned Settlement*.

64. "Taungya" is a reforestation system used in teak and other forest types, in which peasants are allowed to plant agricultural crops between rows of teak. The peasants retain access to the land for crops for two or more years, depending on the local rules set by the forestry service. Teak then dominates the land use for the remaining years of its 60-100 year life cycle.

65. Bryant, "Shifting the Cultivator"; Peluso, *Rich Forests, Poor People*; Pragtong and David Thomas, "Evolving Management Systems in Thailand", in *Keepers of the Forest*.

66. See, e.g., Michael Dove, "Agroecology and the Mythology of the Javanese", *Indonesia* no. 39 (1985): 1-35; Jan Palte, *Upland Farming on Java, Indonesia: A Socio-economic Study of Upland Agriculture and Subsistence Under Population Pressure* (Amsterdam & Utrecht: Koninklijk Nederlands Aardrijkskundig Genootschag & Geografisch Instituut Rijksuniversitet Utrecht, Nederlandse Geografische Studies, 1989); and Robert W. Hefner, *The Political Economy of Mountain Java* (Berkeley: University of California Press, 1990).

67. Lesley Potter's phrase from "Onslaught".

68. David M. Kummer, *Deforestation in the Postwar Philippines* (University of Chicago Geography Research Paper no. 234, Chicago: University of Chicago Press, 1992); R. Pineda-Ofreno, "Debt and the Environment: The Philippine Experience", in *Southeast Asia's Environmental Future*, ed. Harold Brookfield and Yvonne Byron (Tokyo: United Nations University Press, 1993), pp. 221-34; Germelino M. Bautista, "The Forestry Crisis in the Philippines: Nature, Causes, and Issues", *The Developing Economies* 28, 1 (1990): 67-94.

69. Shannon Smith, "The Politics of Indonesian Rainforests" (Clayton, Australia: Monash University, Center for Southeast Asian Studies Working Paper 76, 1992); Potter, "Onslaught"; Peluso, *Rich Forests, Poor People*.

70. Evelyn Hong, *Natives of Sarawak: Survival in Borneo's Vanishing Forests* (Penang: Institut Masyarakat, 1987).

71. Philip Hirsch, *The Political Economy of Environment in Thailand* (Manila: Journal of Contemporary Asia Publishers, 1993), and Hirsch, *Development Dilemmas*; Larry Lohman, "Peasants, Plantations, and Pulp: The Politics of Eucalyptus in Thailand", *Bulletin of Concerned Asian Scholars* 23, 4 (1991): 3-18. For a regional perspective, see Lim and Gomes (eds.), *Tribal Peoples and Development*.

72. Pineda-Ofreneo, "Debt and the Environment".

73. On Malaysia see Hong, *Natives of Sarawak and Lim and Gomes* (eds.), *Tribal Peoples*; on Indonesia see Charles V. Barber, Nels C. Johnson and Emmy Hafild, *Breaking the Logjam: Obstacles to Forest Policy Reform in Indonesia and the United States* (Washington: World Resources Institute, 1994); Joan Hardjono, *Indonesia: Resources, Ecology, and Environment*; Smith, "Political Economy"; and, less comprehensively, Robison, *Indonesia*.

74. Barber, et al., *Logjam*; Robison, *Indonesia*.

75. Hong, *Natives of Sarawak*; Robert S. Aiken and Colin H. Leigh, *Vanishing Rainforests: The Ecological Transition in Malaysia* (Oxford: Clarendon Press, 1992).

76. Peluso, *Rich Forests, Poor People*.

77. Aiken and Leigh, *Vanishing Rainforests*.

78. Hirsch, *Political Economy*, p. 67; Lohman, "Peasants".

79. David Feeny, "Agricultural Expansion and Forest Depletion in Thailand, 1900-1975", in *World Deforestation in the Twentieth Century*, ed. John F. Richards and Richard P. Tucker (Durham: Duke University Press, 1988), pp. 112-43; Hafner, "Forest and Policy Issues"; Pragtong and Thomas, "Evolving Management Systems".

80. This is the prevailing opinion among Thai NGOs, expressed, for example, in Shalardchai, "Forests and Deforestation".

81. For example, Kummer, Deforestation; Pineda-Ofreneo, "Debt and the Environment".

82. Percy Sajise and Elizabeth Omegan, "The Changing Upland Landscape of the Northern Philippines", in *Keepers of the Forest*, ed. Poffenberger.

83. On Indonesia, see, e.g. Smith, "Political Economy"; Cribb, "Politics of Protection"; and Otto Soemarwoto, "Human Ecology in Indonesia: the Search for Sustainability in Development", in *Indonesia: Resources, Ecology and Environment*, ed. Joan Hardjono.

84. See, for example, arguments for increasing the area under National Parks and Wildlife Sanctuaries in Thailand, by Anat Arbhabirama, *Thailand: Natural Resources Profile* (Singapore: Oxford University Press, 1988).

85. See, e.g., Robin Broad and John Cavanaugh, *Plundering Paradise: The Struggle for the Environment in the Philippines* (Berkeley: University of California Press, 1993); James Rush, *The Last Tree: Reclaiming the Environment in Tropical Asia* (New York: The Asia Society, 1991); Shalardchai, "Forests and Deforestation".

86. Nancy Lee Peluso, "Coercing Conservation: The Politics of State Resuurce Control", *Global Environmental Change* 3, 2 (1993): 199-218.

87. As of 1994, the goal was to increase this "Protected Area System" to an astonishing 25 per cent of national territory.

88. MIDAS Agronomics Company Ltd., *Study of Conservation Forest Area: Demarcation, Protection and Occupancy in Thailand*, Volume III (Bangkok). [Published in Thai by the Local Development Institute, Chermsak Pinthong (ed.), under the title Wiwatanaakaan kong kaan bukberk thiidin tham kin, 1991.]

89. Much of this discussion has not yet moved out of the NGO literature and popular media, but see, for example, newspaper articles on the controversy associated with plans associated with the Global Environmental Facility to move

a Karen village out of a National Park (such as "Nowhere to Run", *Bangkok Post*, 24 July 1994).

90. See, e.g., Dove, "Political Economy of Ignorance" and several other pieces on this and related themes, including "A Revisionist View of Tropical Deforestation and Development", *Environmental Conservation* 20, 1 (1993): 17-24. Some contrasting views are found in William D. Sunderlin, "The Resistance of the Poor and the State's Call to Equity: A Perspective through Social Forestry in Java", paper presented at the Annual Meetings of the Rural Sociological Society, 19-21 Aug 1991, Cincinnati, Ohio; Poffenberger (ed.), *Keepers of the Forest and in Brookfield* and Byron (eds.), *Southeast Asia's Environmental Future*.

91. Jill M. Belsky, "Soil Conservation and Poverty", *Society and Natural Resources* 7, 5 (1994): 429-44; see also, Potter, "Onslaught".

92. Larry Lohmann, "Who Defends Biological Diversity: Conservation Strategies and the Case of Thailand", *The Ecologist* 21, 1 (1991): 5-9.

93. Examples of this outmoded approach include Ooi Jin Bee, "Depletion of Forest Resources in the Philippines" (Singapore: Institute of Southeast Asian Studies, Asian Economic Research Unit Field Report Series No. 18, 1987) and *Tropical Deforestation: The Tyranny of Time* (Singapore: Singapore University Press, 1993); Raj Kumar, *The Forest Resources of Malaysia: Their Economics and Development* (Singapore: Oxford University Press, 1986).

94. Examples include publications by the World Bank group led by Gershon Feder, "Land Ownership Security and Farm Productivity: Evidence from Thailand", *Journal of Development Studies* 24 (1987): 16-30; and Tongroj Onchan (ed.), *A Land Policy Study* (Bangkok: The Thailand Development Research Institute, 1990).

95. Wanat Bhruksasri, "Problem Solving Through Understanding", in *Hill Tribes Today*, ed. John McKinnon and Bernard Vienne (Bangkok: White Lotus-Orstom, 1989), pp. 227-48; A. Terry Rambo, *Primitive Polluters' Semang Impact on the Malaysian Tropical Forest Ecosystem* (Ann

Arbor: The University of Michigan, 1985). Rambo challenges the assumption that "primitives" live in harmony with their environment.

96. Christine Padoch, "The Woodlands of Tae"; other examples will be found among the sources cited above.

97. See, e.g., Terry Rambo, K. Gillogly and Karl Hutterer (eds.), *Ethnic Diversity and the Control of Natural Resources in Southeast Asia* (Ann Arbor: University of Michigan Press, 1988).

98. S. Brown and A.E. Lugo, "Tropical Secondary Forests", *Journal of Tropical Ecology* 6 (1990): 1-32.

99. Christine Padoch and Charles Peters, "Managed Forest Gardens in West Kalimantan, Indonesia", in C.S. Potter, et al., *Perspectives on Biodiversity: Case Studies of Genetic Resource Conservation and Development* (Washington D.C.: AAAS, 1993); G.M. Michon and J.M. Bompard, "The Damar Forests of South Sumatra", in *Proceedings of the Third Round Table Conference on Dipterocarps*, ed. A.J.G.H. Kostermanis (Paris: MAB/UNESCO, 1987), pp. 3-17; Chin See Chung, *Agriculture and Resource Utilization in a Lowland Forest Kenyah Community* (Kuching: Sarawak Museum Journal 35, Special Monograph no. 4, 1984).

100. Francis Jana Lian, "On Threatened Peoples", *Southeast Asia's Environmental Future*, ed. Brookfield and Byron, pp. 322-37.

101. R.A. Cramb, "Shifting Cultivation and Sustainable Agriculture in East Malaysia: A Longitudinal Case Study", *Agricultural Systems* 42 (1993): 209-226; see also his piece "Shifting Cultivation and Resource Degradation in Sarawak: Perceptions and Policies", *Borneo Research Bulletin* 21, 1 (1989): 22-49.

102. Bernard Sellato, *Nomades et Sedentarisation a Borneo: Histoire Economique et Sociale* (Paris: Editions de l'EHESS, Etudes Insulindiennes/Archipel 9, 1989). Some of the flavour of the original may be glimpsed in his paper "Myth, History and Modern Cultural Identity Among Hunter-Gathers: A Borneo Case", *Journal of Southeast Asian Studies* 24, 1 (1993): 18-43.

103. See Carl Hoffman, *The Punan: Hunters and Gatherers of Borneo* (Ann Arbor: University of Michigan Research Press, 1986); and Sellato's comments in the *Borneo Research Bulletin* 20, 2 (1988): 106-120. See also Peter Brosius, "A Separate Reality; Comments on Hoffman's The Punan: Hunters and Gatherers of Borneo", *Borneo Research Bulletin* 20, 2 (1988): 81-129.

104. See, e.g., Thailand Development Research Institute and Thailand Environment Institute, *Preparation of a National Strategy on Global Climate Change: Thailand* (Bangkok: Thailand Development Research Institute, 1993).

105. *World Resources Report* 1990-91 (Washington, D.C.: World Resources Institute, 1991).

106. See, e.g., A. Agarwal & S. Narain, *Global Warming in an Unequal World: a Case of Environmental Colonialism* (New Delhi: Center for Science and Environment, 1990).

107. Harold Brookfield, "Environmental Colonialism, Tropical Deforestation, and Concerns other than Global Warming", *Global Environment Change* (June 1992): 93-96.

108. But see Brookfield, Potter and Bryon (eds.), *In Place of the Forest*.

109. However, these reports are sometimes published by donor or other international organizations such as the FAO's Forest, Trees, and People and the Community Forestry monograph series.

110. Some of the many examples from Thailand include publications out of the Tribal Research Center, the Regional Community Forest Training Center, the Social Research Institute and the Resource Management and Development Program at the University of Chiangmai University, the Northeast Thailand Upland Social Forestry Project in Khon Kaen University, Kasetsart University, the Thailand Development Research Institute, and local NGO publishers such as the Local Development Institute.

111. See the series edited by Jefferson Fox, *Voices from the Field*, 5 vols. (Honolulu: East West Center, 1989-93).

112. See Uraiwan Tan-Kim-Yong, "Participatory Land-Use

Planning as a Sociological Methodology for Natural Resource Management", *Regional Development Dialogue* 14, 1 (1993): 70-83, and other publications by the Resource Management and Development Program, Chiangmai University. In Khon Kaen see Lert Chuntanaparb and Henry I. Wood, *Management of Degraded Forest Land in Thailand* (Khon Kaen: Northeast Thailand Upland Social Forestry Project, 1986).

113. Percy Sajise, "Agroecosystem Analysis: the SUAN Approach", in *Agroecosystem Research for Rural Development*, ed. Kanok Rerkasem and A.T. Rambo (Chiangmai: Multiple Cropping Center, Faculty of Agriculture, Chiangmai University and SUAN, 1988), pp. 9-31.

114. See various papers in Otto Soemarwoto and Terry Rambo, *Impacts of Development on Human Activity Systems in Southeast Asia: Selected Papers from the First SUAN/EAPI Regional Research Symposium* (Chiangmai: Chiangmai University Multiple Cropping Center, 1987).

115. SUAN, *Swidden Agroecosystems in Sepone District, Savannakhet Province, Lao PDR* (Khon Kaen, Thailand: The Southeast Asian Universities Agroecosystems Network Regional Secretariat, Khon Kaen University, 1991).

116. An important exception being Hirsch, *Development Dilemmas*, which is about people of "Thai" ethnicity.

117. See, e.g., David E. Thomas, "Village Land Use in Northeast Thailand: Predicting the Effects of Development Policies on Village Use of Wildlands" (Ph.D. diss., University of California, Berkeley, 1988). Other materials include the SUAN publications produced at Khon Kaen University.

118. A few exceptions being Thomas M. Psota, "Forest Souls and Rice Dieties: Rituals in Hill Rice Cultivation and Forest Product Collection", pp. 30-51, in *The Rejang of Southern Sumatra* (Centre for South-East Asian Studies at the University of Hull, Occasional Papers no. 19, 1992); Jill Belsky, "Household Food Security, Farm Trees, and Agroforestry: A comparative Study in Indonesia and the Philippines", *Human Organization* 52, 2 (1993): 130-41.

8

INDIGENOUS URBANISM: CLASS, CITY AND SOCIETY IN SOUTHEAST ASIA

—Richard A. O'Connor

While Southeast Asia revolves around its cities, scholarship spins off into disciplines that ignore this fact. In a region that has known cities for two millennia, where even remote peoples have shaped themselves to or against urban rule, research goes on as if the city were an alien entity, easily factored out and best forgotten. So village studies represent these city-centred nations, and few wonder if the entrepreneurs and middle class who now explain so much might themselves be explained as urban. Our disciplines divide so deeply that no one addresses how the city organizes society and shapes the region.

My paper takes the city's centrality as a given and focuses on how urbanism works and what it means as a social and cultural order. Urbanism, Louis Wirth tells us, is "a way of life".[1] His now classic phrase suggests an inherited form but to him urbanism was less what the past bequeathed than what the present dictated. Urbanism was a response to urban conditions. Such conditions might be historical or cultural but to Wirth, an urban ecologist, the determining conditions were economic or functional. Today, a half century later, urban research has reduced itself to detailing material conditions—the demographic, economic or political facts—as if urbanism were a reflex of the market. Against this naive reductionism, I assume that urbanites are just as cultural and social as any group. Their pattern, urbanism, has a life of its own.

Understanding urbanism's privileged place requires a conceptual shift from our rural/urban dichotomy to Southeast Asia's city/society dyad. Splitting rural from urban distorts how the Southeast Asian city is at once a centre and the whole. In effect, city and society function as what Louis Dumont calls a hierarchical opposition.[2] Just as right and left are at once opposed (right vs. left), ranked (right is culturally superior to left) and presume a larger whole (the body) that the superior part represents (the right hand betokens the person), so too is the Southeast Asian city distinct from, superior to and yet representative of society.[3]

My paper starts broadly and works inward in three steps. The first section argues that urbanism is only one of several indigenous structural arrangements that "organize life". In this light the city is not an alien imposition but an indigenous construction. The second section takes up how this one arrangement has come to dominate the region. Urbanism, I argue, is a historical and cultural complex that grows by elaborating status distinctions that create meaning and structure society. As city life generates the distinctions that govern society, an urban autocracy arises. The final section looks at the modern era where today's new nations ideally supersede the city's well institutionalized dominance. Three complexes—the nation, the state and the middle class illustrate how earlier ideologies and institutions constrain present arrangements. My larger conclusion is that to understand the region we must study urbanism culturally, historically and comparatively.

URBANISM AND SOCIETY

Southeast Asia's cities have always brought diverse peoples and societies together. Urbanism is neither the sum of this diversity nor its common denominator but a society of societies, a culture of cultures. It encapsulates difference much as written Chinese encompasses spoken diversity. By encapsulating, urbanism reifies lesser wholes—a people or village, an entourage or occupation—so that they become fixed parts of a still higher city-centred whole. In its simplest sense urbanism is just one of many indigenous relations of parts, and the fact of its great success does not change its nature.

Urbanism's nature—its function and meaning—arises from how it relates to society. As we shall see, urbanism is neither alien to society nor the antithesis of rural life but the essence of societal ordering. What gives urbanism its distinctive character is how it fits amid the region's other indigenous orders. All of these are "relations of parts" that assume the still more fundamental process whereby groups first constitute themselves as wholes. One consequence of this self-conscious "society-making" is a localism that pervades Southeast Asia.

Localism: Scholars divide Southeast Asia into hundreds of ethnic groups or a handful of national cultures, but the older and firmer reality is localism. To describe, say, Indonesia, people by people[4] imposes a higher order grouping on villages and even households that are already ritually complete, each a whole unto itself. Such intense localism typifies the region's prehistory[5] and history[6] as well as its present where the uplands can fragment into "village-level ethnicity"[7] and lowland states have localities doting on difference.[8]

Localism is not just the diversity that accumulates from drift and isolation, but an active principle of symbolic differentiation. Consider, for example, how the Vietnamese colonized rice plains. A people who expanded from a common core onto accessible and undifferentiated land should create a homogenous countryside, but because each Vietnamese village sought its own craft or skill monopoly, they created an intricate specialized web.[9] While Vietnamese differentiated by village and craft, other groups manufacture diversity on ethnic or moral lines, by culinary nuance or ceremonial style. The idioms vary from place to place but everywhere nearby groups align their differences. Indeed, on the Malay Peninsula each group changes not just on its own but with a "tacit understanding" of its neighbours,[10] while for Balinese villages "no two do things exactly alike; [and] if they find that they do, one of them changes something".[11] None of this is new. Going back three or four millennia nearby mainland sites differ so greatly in pottery and ritual culture that archaeologists would assume isolation were it not that metallurgical techniques and materials show wide linkages.[12] Here localism suggests not isolation but interacting societies, and the larger symbolic differentiation suggests a Durkheimian organic solidarity between societies.[13]

"Society-Making" Rules: The region's localism arises from how its societies self-consciously represent themselves by rites, rules and customs. While these society-making sets are diverse—ethnicity,[14] etiquette, ritual language,[15] ritual interdictions[16] as well as local customs and royal rites—our interest lies in their similarity in societal function and cultural meaning. All such sets are taken to be consequential, order-imposing and pragmatic strictures. We may state these characteristics as three indigenous principles.

First, society-making rules are directly consequential. A body of custom does not merely represent a group that already exists but its discipline creates that group. It is not as if "the People . . ." create a constitution that creates a nation, but rather that such rules create not just a polity but a people. Such rule-making has the radical and direct effectiveness often attributed to ritual but need imply no religious belief and may be as mundane as an agricultural practice.[17]

Second, society-making rules impose order lest chaos reign. Chaos is so readily imagined that rules are justifiably rigid.[18] Even if such rules arise openly from practice, once established their authority comes from outside of everyday life. This "outside" need only be the wisdom of elders or the legacy of ancestors but it is never just what people do. Southeast Asian society, it seems, is better than the people in it, better even than its own practice. Conceived as exogenous strictures, such discipline appears as good-to-have[19] but hard-to-keep rules whose very rigidity leaves the rest of life rather loose.[20] It not only creates "systems in which the 'individual' has a notable measure of autonomy vis-a-vis the 'social structure'"[21], but as A. W. Macdonald says, society can be so generally open because its specific points of closure are so clear and uncontested.[22]

Third, society-making rules are formulated openly and changed pragmatically. Southeast Asians adjust inherited forms almost as freely as democracies write and revise laws. So society is neither god-given laws nor ancestral custom, but rather working arrangements wherein gods, ancestors and humans adjust their unfolding interests.[23] In the islands this consensual arrangement, adat, may constitute a group literally out of words whereas on the mainland chthonic cults do the same symbolically out of ancestors, but both act as working sets that adapt an inheritance pragmatically by treating the ancestors as mentors, not law-givers. In effect the dead guide the living just as any elder guides the young.[24]

Negotiable customs let Southeast Asians live pragmatically and localize freely. How can a group openly adjust the customs that create the group? "Changeable customs", a seeming oxymoron, are perfectly consistent wherever practical rituals constitute a group. As the group or its needs change, so must custom. In effect, authority is anchored locally in an ongoing group and not displaced categorically from the living to the dead, humans to gods, or present needs to eternal truths. In this rule-making, where "society seems sedimented . . . out of the pragmatic interests of its acting subjects", the region joins what Marshall Sahlins calls an entire "family of cultures" that organize life by performative rather than prescriptive structures.[25] Such unfolding structures are how localism prospers and how urbanism arises within the conditions that localism creates.

"Higher" Orders: As each group makes rules to create itself and keep distinct from neighbours, a great variety of higher order arrangements arise. Such arrangements may be as self-conscious as the ritual that organizes polyethnic Lao states[26] or as consciousness-deciding as the ethnic differentiation wherein Malay, Senoi, and Semai construct each other out of their differences? State coercion may create some orders as a collectivity of local cults[28] while others such as the marriage systems[29] and competitive feasting[30] arise spontaneously. Varied as they are, what these arrangements share is that they not only preserve but require diversity.[31] All encapsulate self-consciously distinct groups that thereby function as parts of larger wholes.

Urbanism: Urbanism is one such larger whole. It appears to be a radical break, thanks to its foreign symbols and how thoroughly it has displaced rival wholes, but Southeast Asian urbanism functions as a supra-local and supra-ethnic order just as upland feasting or coastal trading do. Its symbols are foreign—Indic, Sinitic, Arabic or

Western—but their indigenous role requires this "outside" origin. Were the urban not conspicuously foreign, it could not stand categorically above the ethnic and the local; and yet were it not effectively indigenous it could not dominate these lesser orders deeply. Indeed, the city's dominance is so deep precisely because it is a grander version of whatever localism might oppose it. After all, an alter ego is far harder to resist than an alien imposition. Urbanism, we must conclude, is a typically indigenous response to localism as a distinctively regional condition.

Southeast Asian urbanism's distinguishing features are urban rule and foreign idioms. All society-making imposes order but urbanism's regime presumes a ruling centre a king, palace, capital or government—whose power institutes higher rites and rules that order a realm of lesser peoples and places. Just as fifteenth century Pegu brought the Mon realm's local chthonic cults together in the capital's Buddhist cult,[32] the current Indonesian government represents its realm's once remote peoples as ethnic pieces of a national whole.

Urbanism requires conspicuously foreign idioms. Society-making rules always come from outside of everyday life, but for localism this exogeny need be no more than the ancestors or the past. For urbanism or indeed any higher order this will not do. If they are to order localism as it orders everyday life, then these higher orders require a still more distant idiom. Once begun, pursuing the outside culminates in either asceticism or foreign borrowings. Asceticism, the ultimate trump, plays off of society's representations to stand beyond not just localism but urbanism too.[33] Crucial as it is to current politics, asceticism cannot create a polity and thus it is the other "outside", foreign borrowings, that best explains how urban rule works.

Where India abhorred the outside as polluting and China disdained it as barbaric, Southeast Asia appropriated foreign borrowings as the idiom of urban rule. Examples abound but consider how Manila's elite has favoured foreign tongues—once Malay, then Spanish and lately English[34]—just as Siamese rulers have followed Khmer, Western and now international styles. Speaking broadly, the idiom is always changing—Indic, Arabic, Sinitic, modern—but there is continuity in the way foreign symbols set the city and its elites above the countryside and commoners. In effect, what begins as a foreign fad becomes an indigenous hierarchy; and what appears as exogenous change—Indianization, Sinicization, modernization—functions as an indigenous urbanization that breaks down the local only to build up the urban. Where society's structure arises performatively, the outside is a perpetually valuable resource.

Whatever its origins,[35] the outside's ongoing function is that it meets a structural need created by localism. Here, in its own ideology, urbanism averts the chaos that localism creates. Where groups live together and each represents its motives by localism, internecine struggle always seems only a moment away. Set against this incipient anarchy, urbanism represents itself as the cool reason and objectivity that only the outside offers. The fact that such dramas sometimes play themselves out for real should not disguise the abiding symbolic interdependence whereby localism's supposedly parochial claims on the person strengthen urbanism's "civilizing" authority over society. Urbanism's ostensibly exogenous order requires a chaos that comes from within the society it rules.

In this section we have seen how urbanism is not an alien imposition but an indigenous arrangement whose structural equivalence to localism lets the city epitomize society. Were the urban opposed to the rural or equated with the market, then its dominance would be circumscribed. Yet Southeast Asia lacks—or lacked—these limits. Constructed as a hierarchical opposition, the city becomes that part whose superiority lets it represent the whole. In this setup urban authority reaches deeply into social life. It is to this cultural dominance that we turn now.

URBANISM AS A HISTORICAL AND CULTURAL COMPLEX

While urbanism is just one way Southeast Asian societies arrange themselves structurally, it is the dominant arrangement in most of the region. Today's urban behemoths are primate cities whose wealth and power dwarf other towns and dominate their societies.[36] The sheer size of Bangkok or Jakarta may be new but such centrality is as old as Angkor or Srivajaya. We might as easily imagine the United States without capitalism as think of Southeast Asia without urban dominance.

Urban Dominance: So obvious and decisive a feature would seem to demand some explanation and yet urban dominance is left largely unexplained. True, some scholars measure population flow or material conditions as if today's balance must abide by timeless laws of economic efficiency, but they are assuming conditions of intense and continual competition that hardly exist. Any selective pressure operates slowly if at all because a primate city creates monopoly conditions. It forces society to adapt to it. Like any monopoly, it can be inefficient or even self-destructive and yet survive for centuries. To assume the city's size, wealth or power represents some higher economic logic or hegemonic reason merely imposes an adaptationist teleology on the data.[37] Such tautologies aside, we are left to explain urban dominance as either purely historical or "rational" within cultural conditions that require their own explanation. Either way history and culture require examination.

If history holds the answer, then the region's early cities established patterns that structured later events. In this explanation urbanism's sheer self-interested mass would perpetuate itself by creating the conditions that decide what is economically viable and politically effective. While this is plausible for the Tai as well as the region,[38] the historical evidence is not strong enough to stand alone and thus we must consider the cultural pattern this history presumes.

A cultural explanation for urban dominance focuses on how society represents itself in symbols that presume a centre. A culture can have what Sahlins calls "a privileged institutional locus . . . whence emanates a classificatory grid imposed upon the total culture".[39] In the West, he argues, that locus is the economy. In Southeast Asia it is the city.[40] A locus rules its region by creating conditions that colour experience and divide function and meaning into pieces that presume the dominant locus. In effect, then, Southeast Asia's pieces presume a ruling centre. The city is built into culture and society. Elaborating these symbolic distinctions thus constitutes urbanization in its widest sense.

Indigenous Urbanization: Narrowly defined, urbanization is the rising percentage of a nation's population who live in urban areas. Useful as it is to know how many people are drawn physically into the city, this number does not reveal how deeply they are drawn into urban forms or how significant these forms are. As a physical place the city has a varied and limited impact but it is as social distinctions that urbanism imposes itself strictly and deeply on how people live.

In urbanization new and finer status distinctions appear within older and broader ones in a process of symbolic differentiation? Starting with localism, the first centre-creating step distinguishes lord from commoner as it makes the ruler's settlement into a "city" above what become "villages". Once accepted, this distinction settles if a centre will rule and starts a struggle over which centre will rule. Out of this struggle come further social distinctions that establish one city as the capital and its line as "royal" while the rest become provincial towns ruled by nobles. And so it goes. As one hierarchical distinction arises within another, the capital's elite and urban life get set above the larger society these distinctions create. Each step presumes prior ones and creates categories of people or place that then perpetuate themselves as the conditions out of which new distinctions arise.

How do distinctions arise? Urbanism's always foreign idiom creates a scarcity that inevitably breeds social distinctions. When only a few possess the outside's emblems, their value is high; as more people get these symbols their value falls; and finally some new distinctions come in at the top to start the cycle again. All who play politics manipulate this flow. In the traditional Balinese state rulers conferred status down from the top while lesser folk ceded power up from the bottom.[42] In this interplay we see how the region urbanizes, how the countryside comes under its urban courts. In nineteenth-century Siam, for example, archival records show the monarchy carefully awarding distinctions to align a royal temple hierarchy with the shifting politics of popular monks and powerful nobles.[43] Across the region sovereignty empowered a ruling centre to manufacture status distinctions—titles, honours, privileges, rights to reward allies and co-opt rivals, giving lesser leaders and local groups a stake in the centre. This century's bureaucratization hardly differs.[44] In effect, ruling groups create the nations they rule. Where the Western economy elaborates the product distinctions that create its culture,[45] Southeast Asian cities elaborate the status distinctions that urbanize society.

Overall, then, indigenous urbanization is the elaboration of status distinctions that presume a centre and organize society hierarchically.[46] It is these distinctions that explain urban dominance and build the city into society. They establish an urban autocracy—meaning not "absolute power" but rather more literally "self empowered" wherein urban life generates the status distinctions that govern the city and the larger society. Once this closure comes, the city rules a countryside it need never know. Urbane yet insular, elites can imagine peasantries and nations to suit themselves.

URBANISM TODAY: NATION, STATE AND CLASS

While urbanism shows great continuity, it is also true that Indianization, world religions and modernity have revolutionized the region in turn. Each epochal shift creates what Robert McKinley calls an era. Each era's socially constructed meanings constitute a "system of knowledge" that enters into a dialogue with still earlier systems.[47] As the new subordinates the old, later eras encapsulate earlier ones. In consequence, as McKinley shows for the Malay, an animist rite can exist within an Islamic explanation within a modern framework. Now if we go by dominance, then as the higher defines the lower's niche, modernity shapes the functions and meaning of all lesser systems. On the other hand, if we go by precedence, then as the lower comes earlier, Islam and still earlier systems restrict what modernity can be. I do not doubt modernity's dominance changes the rest, but my concern here is how precedence enforces continuity. History—merely what came before—explains urban behemoths better than present function or meaning ever will.

To study modernity's built in urban bias we shall focus on the inherited social forms whereby earlier institutions and ideologies condition the present. We touch on three contemporary complexes—the nation, the state and the middle class—to show how each embodies an earlier urbanism.

The Nation: A nation, Benedict Anderson suggests, is not only an imagined community but also an easily borrowed idea.[48] Once borrowed, this import adjusts to indigenous context and historical sequence. In Southeast Asia the result is nations that are new in principle but old in pattern. The egalitarianism of citizenship is a new and powerful ideology, but status distinctions and localism still decide which citizen gets what. To become a nation Thailand became a geopolitical body,[49] but this conspicuously modern construction is also an analog of emboxment, an indigenous construct.[50] Ideally the nation supersedes the city, but these new nations succumb readily to urban interests and remain heavily mortgaged to urban forms. Consider two major continuities.

First, the nation operates by the same self-conscious society-making process as urbanism and localism. All three readily impose rules lest chaos and corruption reign.[51] The fact that the region's new nations have seen chaos may indeed exert "a subtly addictive and a profoundly rigidifying force",[52] and yet a fascination with order and its collapse is too old and pervasive to attribute solely to recent politics. In imagining not just community but anarchy, the nation invests its rules with a moral authority that pits discipline against democracy, makes corruption a perennial issue, and stifles open debate.[53] If democracy presumes that a nation's rules come from its people, that they arise "within", then this clashes with the indigenous assumption that order comes from "without", that rules descend from elders, ancestors and kings.

While the nation, urbanism and localism are alike in their society-making rules, they differ in the arena where the rules are actually made. In localism it is the community with deference to the elders; in urbanism it was the court with deference to the king; and in the nation it is the city with deference to the people. Who are "the people"? A rich politics arises on this issue. While prebendal bureaucrats argue with foreign-funded Non-Governmental Organizations and the media swing from social science to sob stories, the one constant is that these are all urban voices articulating modern values on behalf of others or indeed an "other". In the end this cacophony is an acephelous urban autocracy that imagines a "people" to suit itself.

The second continuity is how the new subsumes the old. Just as urbanism is an order above localism and ethnicity, the nation now constitutes itself as a community above all lesser communities. Here social theorists once wrongly assumed that civil society itself was new and that its modern identity could succeed only at the expense of earlier traditional ones and their primordial sentiments? What actually happened is that a new civil society subsumed an older one. A crucial step, and the epitome of the process, was the formation of new national languages. In Thailand, for example, Standard Thai is now spoken almost everywhere but most local languages continue to prosper.[55] Similarly, in Indonesia a lingua franca used by the Dutch and spoken in Jakarta became the new language for the new reality of the nation.[56] For most it remains the language of citizenship and education whose formality sets it apart from mother tongues that mark home and neighbors by their intimacy.[57]

Adding a new national identity at the top institutes a hierarchy that subordinates other identities. No nation shows this better than Indonesia where local groups invent religions, edit customs and discover dances that accommodate national categories and tourist sensibilities.[58] In Indonesia fundamentalists and recent history raise the stakes, but this interplay pervades the region. On one side is the nation whose agents are urban in attitude, training and often background. On the other side are local groups who may resist or accommodate but can hardly deny the national order. In early modernizing, governments insisted on changing these supposedly backward folks for everyone's good, but elites have yet to decide if the nation is a cultural or political community[59] and lately sentimentalizing urbanites have targeted folk traditions for preservation. In Malay novels the once obstructionist village is now a reservoir of national virtue[60] while Bangkok's middle classes find the "true Thai" off in the countryside,[61] never mind that many peasants have Lao or even Mon ancestry. Indonesia's policies not only imply that national citizenship can accommodate ethnic and religious diversity, but officials actively encourage minorities to mark their differences.[62]

Why do officials and other urbanites now insist on diversity? If our perspective is not decades but centuries, then society has reverted to type after a brief homogenizing interim. Yet this is not to say that the nation's self-conscious modernizing was a trend that did not take. To the contrary, these higher rules are now so well established that local diversity threatens little. But why do customs that once got sneers now get an official nod or even an indulgent smile? It is not local groups who decide this. What we are seeing is neither disdain[63] nor paternalism nor even the "managerial and tutorial air" of bureaucrats,[64] but rather urbanites and nationals eager to establish their identity by who they are not. A touristic encounter collapses intricate status distinctions into juxtaposed kinds, into "us" and "them". Who does this serve? As this urban trope domesticates difference for the nation, it reassures the middle class of their place in urban society. It declares the city one, saying top and bottom differ only by degree. Difference in kind is not in the city but off in the countryside. Where national tropes meet urban needs, the city still rules society.

The State: Although easily conflated, a nation and a state are not the same.[65] A state may serve a nation by implementing popular will or a nation may serve a state by supporting its administrators' particular interests. A nation is an entire country but the character of a state is often urban because of the facilities it inherits, the customs it carries and the status its personnel hold.

In Southeast Asia when the interests of the state and nation differ, the state usually wins because it is older and better institutionalized. While the nation began only with independence, states took over personnel, offices and procedures from colonial or royal administrations. Such continuity may explain why Indonesia's national government sometimes acts as the Dutch colonial state once did,[66] and why Singapore's government has a sense of superior virtue that oddly resembles a British colonial administration. It is Thailand, however, where the continuity seems greatest. Here the absolute monarchy's fall left its one-time servant, the civil and military bureaucracy, the master of the nation. As the best established strategic group, the bureaucracy's often independent institutions have set the national agenda ever since.[67] Even at the other extreme, where the state is weak, the nation is hardly strong. In the Philippines landed interests hold sway while in Malaysia and Indonesia the government party decides what is good for the nation as well as the state.

Whether it is a continuity or a change, the modern state has secured its dominance by expanding enormously and co-opting the educated into its ranks. From 1940 to 1968 Indonesia's administration grew perhaps ten fold while during the 1970s the number of government employees grew 50 per cent in Thailand, 90 per cent in

Malaysia and almost 400 per cent in Indonesia.[68] In this "runaway bureaucratization", Hans-Dieter Evers sees the offspring of the "historical marriage of a patrimonial and a modern bureaucracy under colonial auspices".[69] Just as courts once elaborated status distinctions, states now manufacture jobs to consolidate control; and as these positions accumulate, their distinctions elaborate a national culture and create a middle class.

The Middle Class: It is not easy to be middle class where the niche is new. Urbanites who are above the poor but beneath the powerful have only a merchant's heritage to claim. In fact some are merchants or their offspring, but this minority niche hardly suits the growing number who fill the middle positions created by government expansion and economic growth. Their new condition requires new social forms.

The middle falls between conflicting conditions. On the one hand, if class arises from parental background and present occupation, then the middle still splits into two groups: a petty bourgeoisie who prosper as a minority, and a professional middle class whose education, identity and prospects are all national.[70] On the other hand, if the schools and bureaucracies that fostered today's generation have had their way, then the nation is a single whole whose core is those with the requisite education and income. Here consumerism's many ephemeral distinctions erode the few enduring lines that mark class and ethnicity, but whether this ends as atomization, life style pluralism, or a single middle remains to be seen.

Caught in this flux, urbanites seek social forms to place themselves. While some fads may stick, the emerging middle appears to rely heavily on social forms inherited from earlier and especially founding groups.[71] The middle is already too large and dispersed to renegotiate these customs, and it may well be too diverse ever to agree again.

So this new group relies on social forms that replicate the ways of founding groups. Consider Indonesia and Thailand.

In the 1920s a "metropolitan superculture" emerged among modern educated Indonesians in the colony's cities.[72] Combining "a colonial-derived Western style" with the outlook of the traditional elite (priyayi), this new culture "dominated the independence movement" that created the nation.[73] By the mid-1960s this mestizo culture was already into its second native-born generation and assimilating newcomers as biculturals.[74] Under Suharto it claimed the state whose New Order policies favour a middle class that now dominates the nation.[75] In roughly a half century the social forms created by "an extremely small"[76] urban group have come to shape the way an extremely large nation imagines and constructs itself.

In Thailand a middle class is only now emerging out of the proclivities of petty merchants, modern-day "courtiers" and a handful of ascetic bureaucrats. While the first two groups delight in a status competition that has dominated the Thai capital since Ayutthaya, these bureaucrats are relative newcomers who disdain the conspicuous consumption that drives the other two. I call these officials "ascetic" to mark the austere and self-denying discipline that orders their lives, but their other distinctive traits are an assertively modern insistence on reason and a decidedly conservative faith in expertise and institutions. Perhaps only a few officials continue this line but the real legacy of these ascetic bureaucrats is a civil and military service built around their values.

Any bureaucracy dotes on rules but this particular ascetic style has affinities with Buddhist monasticism and testifies to the social position of its founders. The closest Buddhist link is with the royally favoured Thammayut Order. Founded in the nineteenth century, this sect put reason above custom and discipline above all. It sought to reform Buddhism as the modern bureaucracy would later seek to reform government. Early in this century Thammayut reformers were at the height of their influence just when an impressionable first generation of modern educated commoners were beginning careers in the then emerging bureaucracy. As newcomers their vulnerable social position made asceticism an attractive stance. Coming into a court society of the well born and wealthy, these new civil servants were mostly commoners from farming or merchant families.[77] Their willing subordination to discipline is a stance we might expect from newcomers among the well connected. Whether they presented themselves humbly as dutiful servants of the king or claimed the high ground by refusing to play an old-boy game they could not win, adherence to discipline was their natural refuge. Their subordination to modernity—reason, efficiency, progress—was all the greater because it was all they had. Later, once these officials were well established, modernity and discipline would come to justify bureaucratic rule. As the best educated found government positions, Thailand failed to develop the kind of strong independent professional class that elsewhere in the region casts informed doubt on the bureaucracy's right to rule or the neutrality of its reason.[78] Today, secure in a discipline all revere and some follow, the civil and military service has values that are best explained by the bureaucracy's beginnings.

Turning from the bureaucracy to the middle class more generally, Nithi Aewsriwong notes their dependence on borrowed royal forms and attitudes.[79] Religion illustrates this nicely. Overall the middle class has largely copied a style of Buddhism whose gift-giving is better suited to court politics than bourgeois practicality.[80] While such ceremonies are still popular, their very success at enriching the Sangha has now encouraged new religious movements that decry corruption and insist on a conspicuously strict discipline. These movements are controversial but their admiration for discipline is as old as the Thammayut sect and as conservative as the bureaucracy. On one religious extreme the Santi Asok group has an austere asceticism that upholds the early bureaucrats' values, while on the other extreme the Thammakai movement's delight in wealth and authority updates the conspicuous displays that merchants and courtiers have always favoured.[81] In doctrine these two contemporary movements clash just as deeply as modernizing and traditional elites ever did, but their implicit agreement on discipline suggests the inherited trait that may come to distinguish bourgeois religion.

These politics are Thai but the dilemma is regional. Nowhere does income or education make people "middle class" spontaneously, but in Southeast Asia competing forms make the transition especially uncertain. As the middle expands rapidly, newcomers eager to validate their standing seem to prefer either to copy elite practices or adopt their predecessors' customs.

CONCLUSION

Southeast Asia's cities are indigenous in origin, function and meaning and yet research treats them as alien impositions. Cities are ancient to the region and home to almost a third of its people[82] but somehow scholars assume the "real" Southeast Asia is off in the countryside and back in the past. This myth misrepresents the region, all of its nations, and most of its cultures, and yet is the bedrock where research begins.

Our era romanticizes the countryside, but the deeper bias against the city is in how disciplines constitute themselves. It is not just that academic lines divide urban life arbitrarily, but that studying a city holistically upsets the accepted methods—the procedural rules and shortcuts—that define disciplines. It is these methods that reduce or deny the city. To make their subjects easier to study, it is commonplace for anthropology to isolate the countryside from the city, wrongly making "part societies" into autonomous wholes;[83] for geography to factor out indigenous meanings, naively making the city into an alien economic absolute; and for political science to focus on competing interests, forgetting how urbanism constructs the competition and biases the outcome. In these fields and others, as disciplines define reality, the city disappears.

Today's hot topic, the region's booming economies, shows how little scholars appreciate the city's significance. Research focuses on the drama's stars only to forget the urban stage. Chinese entrepreneurs and state officials are well worth studying in themselves, but these two groups did not arise independently or recently.[84] The activities and identity of each party are sensible not in themselves but only in relation to the symbolic differentiation that constructs urban life and relates these two groups to each other. Whether or not entrepreneurs and officials coalesce into a middle class, physically and culturally they already form part of an urban class that shares insider understandings and social advantages. It is not just that business alliances and bureaucratic careers benefit from urban social connections, but that these groups and their socializing rely on cultural forms and social conditions that require urban explanations.[85] To imagine that Thai bureaucrats and Sino-Thai merchants suddenly get along because it now suits their interests misunderstands how interests are culturally constructed.[86] Their solidarity arises from the way urban society has adapted traditional social forms (cremations, end-of-lent [kathin] and forest robes [phapa] gifts) to modern uses and authenticated modern forms (old school ties, a king above politics, birthday parties) as traditional. This city-made "social infrastructure" supports the booming Thai economy. To credit this economic success to foreign investment forgets that capital flows to whatever works. As the Thai economy flourishes, that of the Philippines languishes and Ferdinand Marcos takes the blame. Yet is this the work of one man or were Filipino social forms especially vulnerable to his style of domination?[87] All across the region distinctive social forms decide what groups win and lose, where resources flow, and how economies actually work.

To understand Southeast Asia we must study its cities holistically. Urbanism is a start but to get far we must shed a myth and avoid two earlier errors. The myth is that the city is just what practicality demands and not what a culture constructs. The errors arise from studying a social entity as if it were like a language that could be understood in itself and apart from time. The first mistakes heuristic fictions for literal truths. Easily made, this error is easily corrected now that we all know the "village" is neither self-contained nor timeless nor sometimes even a village. The second error accepts a single synchronic case as completed scholarship. Studying a culture or any whole "in itself" is vital as a rule of method but self-defeating as a principle for scholarship. Rigour requires regional comparison. If rescuing the city from reductive oblivion only reifies it into an all-or-none cultural whole, then perhaps it was best forgotten in the first place. My hope is that seeing the city regionally will allow historical generalizations that combine context and rigour.

NOTES

1. Louis Wirth, "Urbanism as a Way of Life", *The American Journal of Sociology* 44, 1 (1938): 1-24.
2. Louis Dumont, *Essays on Individualism: Modern Ideology in Anthropological Perspective* (Chicago: University of Chicago Press, 1986), pp. 223-33.
3. For example, the Tai city (muang) is culturally distinct from and superior to the village (muang vs. ban) in a larger whole (muang as both city and village) that the city epitomizes.

4. For example, R.M. Koentjarangrat, *Introduction to the Peoples and Cultures of Indonesia and Malaysia* (Menlo Park: Cummings Publishing Company, 1975), p. 53.

5. R.B. Smith and W. Watson, "Introduction", in *Early South East Asia*, ed. R.B. Smith and W. Watson (New York: Oxford University Press, 1979), pp. 3-14; Joyce C. White, "Prehistoric Roots for Hierarchy in Early Southeast Asian States" (Paper presented at the 57th Annual Meeting of the Society for American Archaeology, Pittsburgh, 1992).

6. O.W. Wolters, *History, Culture, and Region in Southeast Asian Perspectives* (Singapore: Institute of Southeast Asian Studies, 1982), p. 53.

7. Frank L. Lebar, Gerald C. Hickey and John K. Musgrave, *Ethnic Groups of Mainland Southeast Asia* (New Haven: HRAF, 1964), p. 3; F.M. and M. Keesing, *Taming Philippine Headhunters: A Study of Government and of Culture Change in North Luzon* (London: George Allen and Unwin, 1934), pp. 38-39.

8. Louis Golomb, *Brokers of Morality: Thai Ethnic Adaptation in a Rural Malaysian Setting* (Hawaii: University Press of Hawaii, 1978), p. 6; Lucien M. Hanks, "Comment", in *The Study of Thailand*, ed. E.B. Ayal (Athens, Ohio: Ohio University Center for International Studies, 1978), p. 62; Alexander Woodside, "Conceptions of Change and of Human Responsibility for Change in Late Traditional Vietnam", in *Moral Order and the Question of Change: Essays on Southeast Asian Thought*, ed. David K. Wyatt and A. Woodside (New Haven: Yale Southeast Asia Studies, 1982), pp. 136-37.

9. Neil L. Jamieson, "Multiple Models of Economics and Morality in Vietnam" (Paper presented at the Annual Meeting of the Association for Asian Studies, Boston, 1987), p. 17.

10. Golomb, *Brokers of Morality*, p. 6

11. Clifford Geertz, *Local Knowledge: Further Essays in Interpretive Anthropology* (New York: Basic Books), p. 176.

12. Charles Higham, *The Archaeology of Mainland Southeast Asia* (Cambridge: Cambridge University Press, 1989), p. 209; White, "Prehistoric Roots".

13. Its Southeast Asian twist is that solidarity arises not just within a society as it specializes but between societies as they adapt to each other. See Emile Durkheim, *The Division of Labor in Society* (New York: Free Press, 1964).

14. Michael Moerman, "Ethnic Identification in a Complex Civilization: Who are the Lue?", *American Anthropologist* 67 (1965): 1215-30.

15. James J. Fox, "Southeast Asian Religions: Insular Culture", in *Encyclopedia of Religion*, ed. M. Eliade (New York: Macmillian, 1987), vol. 13, p. 524.

16. P.B. Lafont, Genies, *anges et demons en Asie du Sud-est* (Paris: Editions du Seuil, 1971), pp. 345-32; A.W. Macdonald, "Notes sur la Claustration Villageoise dans L'Asie du Sud-Est", *Journal Asiatique* 245 (1957): 185-210.

17. Susan D. Russell and Clark E. Cunningham, "Introduction: Social Change, Cultural Identity, and Ritual Response", in *Changing Lives, Changing Rites: Ritual and Social Dynamics in Philippine and Indonesian Uplands*, ed. S.D. Russell and C.E. Cunningham (Ann Arbor: University of Michigan Center for South and Southeast Asian Studies, 1989), p. 3; G. Condominas, "Ritual Technology in Mnong Gar Swidden Agriculture", in *Rice Societies: Asian Problems and Prospects*, ed. I. Norlund, S. Cederroth and I. Gerdin (Riverdale, MD: The Riverdale Company, 1986), pp. 28-46.

18. On chaos see Michael Aung-Thwin, "Divinity, Spirit, and Human: Conceptions of Classical Burmese Kingship", in *Centers, Symbols, and Hierarchies' Essays on the Classical States of Southeast Asia Studies*, ed. L. Gesick (New Haven: Yale University Southeast Asia Studies, 1983), p. 74; J. Drakard, *A Malay Frontier: Unity and Duality in a Sumatran Kingdom* (Ithaca: Cornell University Southeast Asia Program, 1990), pp. 16-18; Karl G. Heider, *Indonesian Cinema: National Culture on Screen* (Honolulu: University of Hawaii Press, 1991), pp. 28-30.

19. Overt enthusiasm for such rules—how "good" they are to have—varies culturally. See Hildred Geertz, "The Balinese Village", in *Local, Ethnic, and National Loyalties in Village Indonesia: A Symposium*, ed. G. William Skinner (New Haven: Yale University Southeast Asia Studies, 1959), pp. 24-33, for a distinction between how custom attracts Balinese and repels Minangkabau. On the mainland this would distinguish Akha from Lisu, and Lawa from Karen.

20. Even in Bali, where everything seems prescribed, Boon observes that the fixity of temples allows flexibility to social groups. See James A. Boon, *The Anthropological Romance of Bali 1597-1972* (Cambridge: Cambridge University Press, 1977), p. 113.

21. A. Thomas Kirsch, "Loose Structure: Theory or Description?", *Loosely Structured Social Systems: Thailand in Comparative Perspective*, ed. Hans-Dieter Evers (New Haven: Yale University Southeast Asia Studies, 1969), p. 59.

22. Macdonald, "Notes sur la Claustration", p. 206.

23. In effect, as "society" stands above time, "custom" becomes how groups unfold. In contrast, modern thought treats "custom" as a past that is kept or lost and "society" as a present equilibrium of acts.

24. On adat see Geertz, *Local Knowledge*, pp. 207-214; on chthonic cults see Paul Mus, *India Seen from the East: Indian and Indigenous Cults in Champa*, trans. I.W. Mabbett (Monash University Centre of Southeast Asian Studies, 1975).

25. Marshall Sahlins, *Islands of History* (Chicago: University of Chicago Press, 1985), pp. 26-28. As Gibson puts it, "in many parts of Southeast Asia social action is thought of as being continuously constructed on the basis of certain shared rules, and not as being defined in advance by a rigid code of conduct prescribing correct behavior . . ." Thomas Gibson, *Sacrifice and Sharing in the Philippine Highlands: Religion and Society Among the Buid in Mindoro* (London: Athlone Press, 1986), p. 65.

26. Charles Archaimbault, "Religious Structures in Laos", *Journal of the Siam Society* 52, 1 (1964): 57-74.

27. Geoffrey Benjamin, "In the Long Term: Three Themes in Malayan Cultural Ecology", in *Cultural Values and Human Ecology in Southeast Asia*, ed. K.L. Hutterer, A.T. Rambo and G. Lovelace (Ann Arbor: University of Michigan Center for South and Southeast Asian Studies, 1985), pp. 219-78.

28. H.L. Shorto, "The Dewatau Sotapan: A Mort Prototype of the 37 Nats", *Bulletin of the School of Oriental and African Studies* 30 (1967): 127-41.

29. Claude Levi-Strauss, *The Elementary Structures of Kinship* (Boston: Beacon Press, 1969).

30. A. Thomas Kirsch, *Feasting and Social Oscillation: Religion and Society in Upland Southeast Asia* (Ithaca: Cornell Southeast Asia Program, 1973).

31. See for example G.C. Hickey, *Sons of the Mountains: Ethnohistory of the Vietnamese Central Highlands to 1954* (New Haven: Yale University Press, 1982); Gibson, Sacrifice and Sharing; V. Wee, "Material Dependence and Symbolic Independence: Constructions of Melayu Ethnicity in Island Riau, Indonesia", in *Ethnic Diversity and the Control of Natural Resources in Southeast Asia*, ed. A.T. Rambo, K. Gillogly and K.L. Hutterer (Ann Arbor: University of Michigan Center for South and Southeast Asian Studies, 1988), pp. 197-226.

32. Shorto, "The Dewatau Sotapan", p. 127.

33. James A. Boon, "Incest Recaptured: Some Contraries of Karma in Balinese Symbology", in *Karma: An Anthropological Inquiry*, ed. C.F. Keyes and E.V. Daniel (Berkeley: University of California Press, 1983), pp. 185-222.

34. John U. Wolff, "The Character of Borrowings from Spanish and English in Languages of the Philippines", *Philippine Journal of Linguistics* 4, 5 (1973-74): 72-81; and "Malay Borrowings in Tagalog", in *Southeast Asian History and Historiography: Essays Presented to D.G.E. Hall,* ed. C.D.

Cowan and O.W. Wolters (Ithaca: Cornell University Press, 1976), pp. 345-67.

35. If localism divided early Southeast Asia, it would be like Melanesia where big-men use outside borrowings to outdo rivals. If higher polities first arose by alien idioms, borrowing from the outside might become a built-in need. See Michael Allen, "Elders, Chiefs, and Big Men: Authority Legitimation and Political Evolution in Melanesia", *American Ethnologist* 11, 1 (1984): 20-41; and Richard A. O'Connor, *A Theory of Indigenous Southeast Asian Urbanism* (Singapore: Institute of Southeast Asian Studies, 1983), p. 29.

36. Jonathan Rigg, *Southeast Asia: A Region in Transition—A Thematic Human Geography of the ASEAN Region* (London: Unwin Hyman, 1991), pp. 133-35.

37. Stephen Jay Gould, "Evolution and the Triumph of Homology, or Why History Matters", *American Scientist* 74 (1986): 60-69.

38. On the Tai see Richard A. O'Connor, "Cultural Notes on Trade and the Tai", in *Ritual, Power and Economy: Upland-Lowland Contrasts in Mainland Southeast Asia*, ed. Susan D. Russell (DeKalb: Northern Illinois University Center for Southeast Asian Studies, 1989), pp. 27-65; and "From 'Fertility' to 'Order', Paternalism to Profits: The Thai City's Impact on the Culture-Environment Interface", in *Culture and the Environment in Thailand: A Symposium of the Siam Society* (Bangkok: The Siam Society, 1989), pp. 393-414; on the region see O'Connor, Indigenous Urbanism.

39. Marshall Sahlins, *Culture and Practical Reason* (Chicago: University of Chicago Press, 1976), p. 211.

40. Insofar as other regions have loci, likely candidates are the state in China, religious purity in India, exchange in Melanesia, and kinship in Africa.

41. O'Connor, *Indigenous Urbanism.*

42. Clifford Geertz, *Negara: The Theatre State in Nineteenth-Century Bali* (Princeton: Princeton University Press, 1980), pp. 62-63.

43. Richard A. O'Connor, "Urbanism and Religion: Community, Hierarchy and Sanctity in Urban Thai Buddhist Temples" (Ph.D. diss., Cornell University, 1978).

44. Hans-Dieter Evers, "The Bureaucratization of Southeast Asia", *Comparative Studies in Society and History* 29, 4 (1987): 666-85.

45. Sahlins, *Culture and Practical Reason.*

46. O'Connor, *Indigenous Urbanism.*

47. Robert McKinley, "Zaman dan Masa, Eras and Periods: Religious Evolution and the Permanence of Epistemological Ages in Malay Culture", in *The Imagination of Reality: Essays in Southeast Asian Coherence Systems*, ed. A. Becker and A. Yengoyan (Norwood, N J: Ablex, 1979), p. 306.

48. Benedict Anderson, *Imagined Communities: Reflections on the Origin and Spread of Nationalism* (Rev. ed.; London: Verso, 1991).

49. Thongchai Winichakul, *Siam Mapped: A History of the Geo-Body of a Nation* (Honolulu: University of Hawaii Press, 1994).

50. Georges Condominas, *L'espace social a propos de l'Asie de Sud-Est* (Paris: Flammarion, 1980); Macdonald, "Notes sur la Claustration".

51. For an ethnographic illustration see J. Joseph Errington, "Self and Self-conduct among the Javanese Priyayi Elite", *American Ethnologist* 11, 2 (1984): 275-90.

52. Clifford Geertz, *The Interpretation of Cultures* (New York: Basic Books, 1973), p. 324.

53. On exploiting the threat of ethnic chaos, see David Brown, *The State and Ethnic Politics in Southeast Asia* (London: Routledge, 1994). On the continuity, see James Cotton, "The Limits to Liberalization in Industrializing Asia: Three Views of the State", *Pacific Affairs* 64, 3 (1991): 311-27. On the "emphasis on rules" in Indonesia's New Order, see Ruth T. McVey, "The Beamtenstaat in Indonesia", in *Interpreting Indonesian Politics: Thirteen Contributions to the Debate*, ed. B. Anderson and A. Kahin (Ithaca: Cornell

University Southeast Asia Program, 1982), p. 87. McVey attributes this pattern to a legacy of the colonial state reinforced by the "rule-mindedness of the military" but in uncolonized Thailand even civilian officials pride themselves on their rule-determined "discipline" (rabiap). The larger issue is that the imagined alternative to such rule-mindedness is first corruption and finally chaos. Here corruption, as violating a specifically national trust, is clearly new.

54. Clifford Geertz, "The Integrative Revolution: Primordial Sentiments and Civil Politics in the New States", in *Old Societies and New Societies: The Quest for Modernity in Asia and Africa,* ed. C. Geertz (New York: The Free Press, 1963), pp. 105-157.

55. William A. Smalley, *Linguistic Diversity and National Unity: Language Ecology in Thailand* (Chicago: University of Chicago Press, 1994).

56. John Hoffman, "A Foreign Investment: Indies Malay to 1901", *Indonesia* 27 (1979): 65-92; Ben Anderson, "The Languages of Indonesian Politics", *Indonesia* 1 (1966): 89-116.

57. John U. Wolff, "The Functions of Indonesian in Central Java", in *South-East Asian Linguistic Studies*, ed. Nguyen Dang Liem (Pacific Linguistics, Series C, no. 42, 1976), pp. 219-35.

58. Greg Acciaioli, "Culture as Art: From Practice to Spectacle in Indonesia", *Canberra Anthropology* 8, 1-2 (1985): 148-72; Janet Hoskins, "Entering the Bitter House: Spirit Worship and Conversion in West Sumba", in *Indonesian Religions in Transition*, ed. Rita Smith Kipp and Susan Rodgers (Tucson: University of Arizona Press, 1987), pp. 136-60; Susan Rodgers, "Batak Tape Cassette Kinship: Constructive Kinship Through the Indonesian National Mass Media", *American Ethnologist* 13, 1 (1986): 23-42.

59. Brown, *The State*, p. 261.

60. David J. Banks, *From Class to Culture: Social Conscience in Malay Novels Since Independence* (New Haven: Yale University Southeast Asia Studies, 1987).

61. O'Connor, "From Fertility to Profits".

62. Acciaioli, "Culture as Art"; John R. Bowen, "Communications to the Editor", *Journal of Asian Studies* 49, 3 (1990): 609-611; Rita Smith Kipp, "The Secularization of an Ethnic Identity" (Paper presented at the Annual Meeting of the Association for Asian Studies, New Orleans, 1991).

63. Heather Sutherland, *The Making of a Bureaucratic Elite: The Colonial Transformation of the Javanese Priyayi* (Singapore: Heinemann, 1979), p. 30.

64. McVey, "The Beamtenstaat", p. 85.

65. Benedict Anderson, "Old State, New Society: Indonesia's New Order in Comparative Historical Perspective", *Journal of Asian Studies* 42, 3 (1983): 477-96; and Imagined Communities.

66. Anderson, "Old State"; Ruth McVey, "Faith as Outsider: Islam in Indonesian Politics", in *Islam in the Political Process*, ed. J. Piscatori (Cambridge: Cambridge University Press, 1983), pp. 199-225.

67. On strategic groups, see Hans-Dieter Evers, "Sequential Patterns of Strategic Group Formation and Political Change in Southeast Asia" (University of Bielefeld, Sociology of Development Research Centre, 1982); on institutions, see William H. Overhold, "Thailand: A Moving Equilibrium", *Pacific Review* 1, 1 (1988): 7-23.

68. Anderson, "Old State", p. 483; Evers, "Bureaucratization".

69. Evers, "Bureaucratization", pp. 666, 678.

70. Richard Robinson and David S.G. Goodman, "The New Rich in Asia: Affluence, Mobility, and Power", *Pacific Review* 5, 4 (1992): 321-27.

71. Our theory combines Evers' strategic groups with Foster's cultural crystallization to argue that the first group to dominate a niche generates the social forms that constrain all who come later. See Evers, "Sequential Patterns", and George M. Foster, *Culture and Conquest: America's Spanish Heritage* (Chicago: Quadrangle Books, 1960).

72. Hildred Geertz, "Indonesian Cultures and Communities", in *Indonesia*, ed. Ruth McVey (New Haven: HRAF, 1967), pp. 35-37; McVey, "Faith as Outsider"; Sutherland, *Bureaucratic Elite*, p. 43.

73. McVey, "Faith as Outsider", pp. 203-205.

74. Benedict Anderson, "Cartoons and Monuments: The Evolution of Political Communication Under the New Order", in *Political Power and Communications in Indonesia*, ed. K.D. Jackson and L.W. Pye (Berkeley: University of California Press, 1978), p. 319; Geertz, "Indonesian Cultures", pp. 35-36.

75. McVey, "Faith as Outsider", p. 219.

76. *Ibid.*, p. 204.

77. Surveying the most successful early civil servants, Evers found a remarkable 43 per cent were the children of farmers and 33 per cent were from merchant families. Only 19 per cent had a father in government service, the bastion of the traditional elite. See Hans-Dieter Evers, "The Formation of a Social Class Structure: Urbanization, Bureaucratization and Social Mobility in Thailand", *American Sociological Review* 31,4 (1966): 480-88.

78. A crucial juncture came early in this century when the rapidly expanding royal service coopted the newly educated into the monarchy's competition against traditional elites. In Indonesia, on the other hand, the colonial administration's failure to absorb many modern education Indonesians created an independent professional class that would later trouble the Dutch. On Indonesia see Sutherland, *Bureaucratic Elite*, p. 54.

79. Nithi Aewsriwong, "Watthanatham khong khonchanklang thai" [Culture of the Thai Middle Class], in *The Middle Class and Thai Democracy*, ed. Sungsidh Piriyarangsan and Pasuk Phongpaichit (Bangkok: Chulalongkorn University, 1993), pp. 49-65.

80. The Siamese elite's Buddhism has long served their status competition. See O'Connor, "Cultural Notes", p. 46. Continuing these customs, the middle class emphasizes

temple construction, end-of-lent offerings (kathin) and other conspicuous gift-giving ceremonies (e.g. "forest robes" or phapa).

81. Apinya Fuengfusakul, "Empire of Crystal and Utopian Commune: Two Types of Contemporary Theravada Reform in Thailand", *Sojourn* 8, 1 (1993): 153-83.

82. Jonathan Rigg, *Southeast Asia*, p. 133.

83. Robert Redfield, "The Social Organization of Tradition", *The Far Eastern Quarterly* 15, 1 (1955).

84. Ruth McVey, "The Materialization of the Southeast Asian Entrepreneur", in *Southeast Asian Capitalists*, ed. Ruth McVey (Ithaca: Cornell University Southeast Asia Program, 1992), pp. 7-33.

85. On connections see Kevin Hewison, *Bankers and Bureaucrats: Capital and the Role of the State in Thailand* (New Haven: Yale University Southeast Asia Studies, 1989).

86. Richard A. O'Connor, "Merit and the Market: Thai Symbolizations of Self-interest", *Journal of the Siam Society*, 74 (1986): 62-82.

87. Turner analyzes how Marcos gained legitimacy by tapping middle class discontent over corruption and exploiting a legalism established in Spanish and American eras. See Mark M. Turner, "Authoritarian Rule and the Dilemma of Legitimacy: The Case of President Marcos of the Philippines", I3,4 (1990): 349-62. Overhold observes that the relative autonomy of Thai institutions has impeded the centralizing control exercised by Marcos and evident in Indonesia's Golkar. See Overhold, "Thailand".

INDEX

A

B

C

X

Y